Conservative in Theology,
Liberal in Spirit

American Society of Missiology
Monograph Series

Chair of Series Editorial Committee, James R. Krabill

The ASM Monograph Series provides a forum for publishing quality dissertations and studies in the field of missiology. Collaborating with Pickwick Publications—a division of Wipf and Stock Publishers of Eugene, Oregon—the American Society of Missiology selects high quality dissertations and other monographic studies that offer research materials in mission studies for scholars, mission and church leaders, and the academic community at large. The ASM seeks scholarly work for publication in the series that throws light on issues confronting Christian world mission in its cultural, social, historical, biblical, and theological dimensions.

Missiology is an academic field that brings together scholars whose professional training ranges from doctoral-level preparation in areas such as Scripture, history and sociology of religions, anthropology, theology, international relations, interreligious interchange, mission history, inculturation, and church law. The American Society of Missiology, which sponsors this series, is an ecumenical body drawing members from Independent and Ecumenical Protestant, Catholic, Orthodox, and other traditions. Members of the ASM are united by their commitment to reflect on and do scholarly work relating to both mission history and the present-day mission of the church. The ASM Monograph Series aims to publish works of exceptional merit on specialized topics, with particular attention given to work by younger scholars, the dissemination and publication of which is difficult under the economic pressures of standard publishing models.

Persons seeking information about the ASM or the guidelines for having their dissertations considered for publication in the ASM Monograph Series should consult the Society's website—www.asmweb.org.

Members of the ASM Monograph Committee who approved this book are:

Susan Maros, Affiliate Assistant Professor of Christian Leadership
Fuller Theological Seminary

Sue Russell, Professor of Mission and Contextual Studies
Asbury Theological Seminary

RECENTLY PUBLISHED IN THE ASM MONOGRAPH SERIES

George Shakwelele, *Explaining the Practice of Elevating an Ancestor for Veneration*

Peter T. Lee, *Hybridizing Mission: Intercultural Social Dynamics among Christian Workers on Multicultural Teams in North Africa*

Conservative in Theology, Liberal in Spirit

Modernism and the American Presbyterian Mission in Thailand, 1891–1941

KARL DAHLFRED

Foreword by Brian Stanley

American Society of Missiology Monograph Series 69

☙PICKWICK *Publications* · Eugene, Oregon

CONSERVATIVE IN THEOLOGY, LIBERAL IN SPIRIT
Modernism and the American Presbyterian Mission in Thailand, 1891–1941

American Society of Missiology Monograph Series 69

Copyright © 2024 Karl Dahlfred. All rights reserved. Except for brief quotations in critical publications or reviews, no part of this book may be reproduced in any manner without prior written permission from the publisher. Write: Permissions, Wipf and Stock Publishers, 199 W. 8th Ave., Suite 3, Eugene, OR 97401.

Pickwick Publications
An Imprint of Wipf and Stock Publishers
199 W. 8th Ave., Suite 3
Eugene, OR 97401

www.wipfandstock.com

PAPERBACK ISBN: 978-1-6667-5556-5
HARDCOVER ISBN: 978-1-6667-5557-2
EBOOK ISBN: 978-1-6667-5558-9

Cataloguing-in-Publication data:

Names: Dahlfred, Karl, author. | Stanley, Brian, 1953–, foreword.

Title: Conservative in theology, liberal in spirit : modernism and the American Presbyterian mission in Thailand, 1891–1941 / by Karl Dahlfred ; foreword by Brian Stanley.

Description: Eugene, OR : Pickwick Publications, 2024 | American Society of Missiology Monograph Series 69 | Includes bibliographical references and index.

Identifiers: ISBN 978-1-6667-5556-5 (paperback) | ISBN 978-1-6667-5557-2 (hardcover) | ISBN 978-1-6667-5558-9 (ebook)

Subjects: LCSH: Missions. | Presbyterian Church in the U.S.A—Missions. | Presbyterian Church in the U.S. (General)—Missions. | Protestant churches—Thailand. | Missions—Thailand. | Thailand—Church history.

Classification: BV3315 .D34 2024 (paperback) | BV3315 .D34 (ebook)

VERSION NUMBER 01/15/25

Contents

List of Illustrations | vii
Foreword by Brian Stanley | ix
Preface | xiii
Acknowledgments | xvii
List of Abbreviations | xx

Introduction | xxi

1. What It Means to Be "Modern" | 1
2. Modernizing Trends in Theology and Ministry | 8
3. Modernism and Fundamentalism in the Presbyterian Church in the U.S.A. and its Board of Foreign Missions | 29
4. Modernization in Buddhist Thailand, 1820 to 1941 | 45
5. Missionary Work in Thailand Prior to World War II | 73
6. Dimensions of Modernism in the American Presbyterian Mission in Thailand | 99
7. Outsider Interactions with Modernism and Fundamentalism in Thailand | 146
8. Changing Perceptions and Approaches to Non-Christian Religions and Evangelism | 186
9. Contested Approaches to Evangelism in Mission Schools | 212

Conclusion: Six Reasons the American Presbyterian Mission in Thailand Experienced Little Modernist-Fundamentalist Controversy | 234

Appendix A: List of Thai Names in Romanized and Thai Script | 251
Appendix B: Photograph of American Presbyterian Mission in Siam, 1935 | 253
Bibliography | 255
Subject Index | 269

List of Illustrations

Map of "Siam and Laos," 1884 | 46
Map of Modern Thailand, 2013 | 50
Map of Siam—Unoccupied Fields, 1928 | 91
Annual Meeting of the Laos Mission, 1906 | 92
APM Mission Schools in Thailand, 1899–1938 | 94
Rev. Pluang Sudhikam, 1934 | 97
Rev. Paul Eakin, 1912 | 111
Dr. William Perkins, 1919 | 117
Rev. Carl Elder, 1922 | 136
Kenneth Landon and a Chinese Christian group in Satun | 137
Presbyterian Church in Trang, 1938 | 138
Rev. Paul Fuller, 1923 | 153
Allen Bassett, 1915 | 165
Accessions to the Church of Christ in Thailand, 1934 | 166
Rev. Loren Hanna, 1917 | 168
John Sung and witness bands in Thailand, 1938 | 176
Chapel built as a result of witness band work near Trang, 1940 | 176
Dr. John Horst, 1927 | 200
Boon Mark Gittisarn with wife Muan and child, 1938 | 210
Growth of APM Thailand Mission Schools, 1911–1938 | 215
Distribution of APM Thailand Missionaries, 1932 | 217
Dr. Lucius C. Bulkley and Trang Hospital Staff, 1940 | 242
Meeting of the American Presbyterian Mission in Siam, 1935 | 253

Foreword

KARL DAHLFRED HAS GIVEN us a truly original contribution to scholarship on the modern history of Christian missions in a transnational setting that spans the United States, Thailand, and China. There are at least three respects in which this book is of pioneering significance.

First, by focusing on Thailand (formerly Siam), the author has directed attention to a country whose Christian—and particularly Protestant—history has been largely neglected. Southeast Asia as a whole has not figured prominently in recent academic work on the history of Asian Christianity or the Western missions that have worked there. The volume of Anglophone scholarly writing devoted to Southeast Asian Christian history is tiny compared to that devoted to missions and the church in the Indian subcontinent or in China. In part such neglect can be explained simply in terms of the much smaller geographical scale of the country and the modest size of its Protestant community, but that is not a full explanation. A further significant factor may be the relative lack of scholarly interest in the degree of tolerance displayed by Theravada Buddhists to the Christian presence when compared to the numerous studies of Hindu-Christian polemic or the sometimes violent response of Chinese antiforeignism to the missionary impact. There is, however, particular value in studying the smaller and often forgotten theaters of Western missionary activity in addition to the obvious mega-theaters of India and China. As Dahlfred shows, American Presbyterian missionaries to Thailand often felt woefully underresourced in comparison to the vastly greater financial and human resources that their mission board devoted to China. Moreover, their comparative marginality in the eyes of the American mission board and its supporting religious public helped to contain the explosive potential of the theological arguments that surfaced in early twentieth-century Thailand, as in China and elsewhere. Whereas controversies between modernists and fundamentalists in China provoked schism, the parallel arguments in Thailand merely rocked the missionary boat a little as missionaries debated the relative priorities of evangelistic preaching, educational and medical work. Dahlfred's narrative suggests that the outcome of theological controversies may depend on the social and political context as much as—or even more than—the comparative theological competence or debating skills of the protagonists.

The second major contribution of Dahlfred's study is the unusual breadth of its analysis of the modernizing impetus, whether that was located in American Protestantism and its foreign missionary agencies, or equally evident in the aspirations of the Thai monarchy and governing elite. There are some excellent analyses of theological modernism in the United States and in China, many of which are cited in the footnotes, but none of these attempt to situate theological modernism among the diverse impulses towards political, economic, and technological modernization that animated much of the American Protestant constituency, especially when it came into face-to-face contact with supposedly "primitive" or "underdeveloped" societies. Conservatives as well as liberals were attracted by the lure of modernity. However, the former were more anxious than the latter to establish clear boundaries between the imperative to maintain the integrity of the faith once and for all delivered to the saints and the conviction, shared by almost all Western Protestants, that Christianity was the great divinely appointed engine of modernization that would propel traditional cultures along the golden pathway to "civilization" and prosperity. Furthermore, it was not Westerners alone who were determined to propel the Thai kingdom towards the "modern" age: successive Thai kings, from the reign of King Mongkut (or "Rama IV", 1851-1868) onwards, were keen to adopt those Western ways that they believed to be advantageous to the well-being of the kingdom. However, just as American conservative Protestants were in favor of some aspects of the modern and decidedly against others, so the Thai elite took pains to discriminate between the good, the bad, and the downright ugly in the varied menu offered by Western diplomats, merchants, and missionaries. Scientific progress was an unambiguous good, and even selective modernization of Buddhist traditions and beliefs in accord with modern rational principles was to be welcomed, but acceptance of the Christian religion of the West was another matter altogether. Both conservative missionaries and indigenous authorities, therefore, wished to deconstruct the "modern" and to pick and choose from what they found.

The third aspect of this book that deserves to be highlighted is the illuminating way it brings the distinct contexts of the United States, Thailand, and—in chapter 7—China into mutual connection. Policy making in every theater of mission operations was, and still remains, the product of multiple interactions between the respective and potentially divergent priorities of mission board members, their domestic supporters, missionaries on the ground, and (by no means least) national Christians. A further strand in this intricate transnational web of Christian connections began to be apparent in the Protestant missionary landscape from about the 1930s—namely visits made by national Christian leaders from one mission field to another. One of the most fascinating dimensions of this book is the description and analysis in chapter 7 of three trips made to Thailand by three very different overseas visitors. Charles Selden, an American Unitarian journalist, visited Thailand in 1927. Selden observed, not only that the fundamentalist-modernist controversy had spilled over from the USA to Thailand, which was a truism, but also that the theological divisions were seeding "bitterness and bigotry" in the mission, which was largely untrue. Then in 1935, came the renowned Presbyterian preacher from Philadelphia, Donald Grey Barnhouse. Barnhouse, who had pronounced fundamentalist sympathies, arrived in Thailand expecting to find alarming evidence of the spread of modernist error. Though he certainly found some such evidence, his overall conclusion was more favorable—theological differences among missionaries were largely confined to the private sphere and were not diverting the mission as a whole from its evangelistic objectives. Finally, in 1938-9, Thailand was the scene of two preaching tours by the highly gifted but controversial Chinese evangelist, John Sung (known in China as Dr Song Shangjie). Whilst Sung's passionate revivalist preaching produced some remarkable results in terms of conversions and re-commitments to Christ, his outspoken condemnations of theological modernism and his controversial pentecostal tendencies served to bring to the surface the divisions in the Presbyterian mission on whose apparent absence Barnhouse had commented in 1935.

I have picked out just three of the dimensions of Karl Dahlfred's book that strike me as particularly interesting and commendable. I could have selected others. Dr Dahlfred knows Thailand well on the basis of many years of Christian work there with the Overseas Missionary Fellowship. The appearance of this book, based on his PhD dissertation at the University of Edinburgh, is to be warmly welcomed. It deserves to be read and studied very widely, and not simply by the rather select company of those with a scholarly interest in the religious history of Thailand.

Brian Stanley,
Professor of World Christianity, University of Edinburgh

Preface

WHY WRITE ABOUT THE impact of modernism on missionaries in Thailand? For nearly five years, I annually taught a course on "Thai and Asian Church History" at Bangkok Bible Seminary and among all the books and articles that I read in order to prepare my lectures, the question of modernism and fundamentalism never came up. But I always thought that it should have.

From the mid-1800s through the mid-1900s, the vast majority of missionaries in Thailand came from a denomination currently known as the Presbyterian Church in the USA (PCUSA). During the 1920s and 1930s, the PCUSA was wracked by intense debate over theology, commonly known as the fundamentalist-modernist conflict. If the home denomination of these Thailand-based missionaries was being rent asunder by divergent theological understandings about nature and purpose of Christianity, how could these Thailand missionaries remain unaffected? Surely, as missionaries went back and forth between the United States and Thailand, and new missionaries came to the field, these different understandings of the faith would cause conflict among them in Thailand just as they had among their colleagues in the United States, right? But everything I read was silent on the topic.

Writers on Christianity in Thailand have spilled much ink on church growth, evangelistic strategy, contextualization, Buddhism, Thai cultural values, and leadership. However, there has been little work done on the impact of changing theology among the missionaries. None of the handful of books on the history of Protestant Christianity in Thailand are primarily concerned with theology. George McFarland's edited volume, *Historical Sketch of Protestant Missions in Siam 1828-1928*, was written by a variety of American Presbyterian missionaries to celebrate the centennial of Protestant missions in Thailand in 1928. This book was later abridged and updated by American Presbyterian missionary Kenneth Wells and published as *History of Protestant Work in Thailand*. Wells brought the narrative up to 1958 but like its predecessor, the goal of this newer book was to chronicle and celebrate rather than examine or critique mission work. The most recent English-language book length survey of Christianity in Thailand is Alex Smith's *Siamese Gold: the Church in Thailand 1816-1982*. A student of Donald McGavran, Smith gave much attention to analyzing church growth and conversion statistics. From time to time, Smith touched on issues of theology but mainly for the purpose of analyzing church growth. As such, in a section reflecting on possible reasons for a slow-down in church growth after 1914, Smith wonders if theological liberalism played a part. However, this question is not explored further. Smith's book has been reprinted twice and still stands as the most recent in-depth survey of Thai church history in the English language despite being forty years old. Aside from these book length surveys, there have been multiple dissertations, articles, and other writings, in both English and Thai, that concern themselves with Christianity in Thailand, touching on issues of theology and history. But none have specifically focused on the impact of modernism, on either the American Presbyterian missionaries or Thai Christians. What practical impact did those with modernist and fundamentalist leanings have on the work of the missionaries themselves, on their Thai Christian colleagues, and the growth and development of Thai churches?

I wanted to find out. I am convinced that what a person believes has a profound impact on what they do. In short, theology drives methodology. Modernism and fundamentalism surely had an impact on the missionaries in Thailand. What was it?

My search for answers led me to read many books, articles, blogs, and eventually to doctoral studies in World Christianity at the University of Edinburgh. Under the astute guidance of Professor Brian Stanley, I gained a better grasp of the broader context of the questions I was asking and realized the scope of the work set before me.

The research for this book, which is an adaptation of my PhD thesis written in Edinburgh, Scotland, has relied primarily on archival sources in the United States and Thailand, specifically the Presbyterian Historical Society in Philadelphia, Pennsylvania, Wheaton College

Special Collections in Wheaton, Illinois, and Payap University Archives in Chiang Mai, Thailand. Records examined included intra-mission correspondence and reports, published articles and books, and personal correspondence. These sources included a limited number of letters and reports written by Thai Christians, in either English or Thai, but it was difficult to gain a broad understanding of Thai perspectives because Thai Christians left far fewer written records when compared to the voluminous records produced by American Presbyterian missionaries and the PCUSA Board of Foreign Missions secretaries. As a result, this book is largely a narrative of the American Presbyterian missionaries in Thailand and the paucity of Thai voices is regrettable but unavoidable. Perhaps someday a Thai Christian will discover long-forgotten boxes of Thai-language letters and reports hidden away in the back of a cabinet in an old church building. Until then, researchers of the history of Christianity in Thailand before World War II must rely primarily on missionary sources.

Aside from the lack of Thai voices, another challenge in writing this book has been discerning theological positions among missionaries who rarely wrote about their own doctrinal positions, and even less frequently left written records explaining how their activities and priorities related to their theological positions. Occasionally the veil was lifted and explicit connections could be made, but in many instances I had to try to connect the dots and assemble a composite picture of probable reasons behind the actions and decisions of the people involved. Closely related to this challenge was that of accurately defining and using fluid and contested terms such as "modern", "modernism", and "fundamentalism". In the early chapters of this book, each of these terms will be examined historically in order to come to a working definition for understanding the narrative and analysis in later chapters. However, it must be acknowledged at the outset that the use of these terms, both historically and currently, is often imprecise and contested. When these theological labels appear in the historical record, they are rarely defined and often filled with various meanings or connotations depending on who is using them. Evidence will suggest that in the Thailand mission context, it may be more accurate to say that particular missionaries had modernist or fundamentalist tendencies, sympathies, or leanings rather than attempting to firmly assign them to a demarcated theological camp.

Acknowledgments

FOR MANY YEARS, I always skipped the Acknowledgments page in books. I had no interest in plodding through a collection of names unknown to me and simply wanted to get to the book itself. But in recent years, I have begun to read the Acknowledgements section with greater interest. It is the place where the author lifts the veil on the impression that the work that I have before me is the single-handed work of an industrious and brilliant person in whose footsteps I could barely be expected to follow. Truth be told, although the author of any book has worked hard, it has rarely been a purely solo effort. My own experience of researching and writing a PhD thesis (from which this book emerged) has provided ample anecdotal evidence that, as the Beatles once sang, we all get by with a little help from our friends.

I am thankful for a great multitude of people who have provided immeasurable assistance to me along the way and I write this acknowledgements section with a bit of fear and trepidation because I will surely forget to include some who should not be forgotten. If that is you, please forgive my oversight of your valuable contribution.

Some have asked why I moved to Scotland to write a PhD thesis about Thailand. The answer is Brian Stanley. I am forever grateful for the prompt feedback, helpful suggestions, and broad insight borne from years of experience as an historian of mission that Professor Stanley provided as my doctoral supervisor at the University of Edinburgh. Without his help and guidance, the book before you would be a far inferior piece of writing. I am also grateful for my secondary supervisor, Dr. Alexander

Chow, whose feedback and suggestions as a scholar of Chinese Christianity have brought numerous helpful improvements to my work.

The history of Christianity in Thailand is a niche subject and there are few who have studied it in-depth. For that reason, I am thankful for Herbert Swanson, Austin House, and Edwin Zehner who have graciously pointed me to sources, suggested lines of inquiry, and been invaluable conversation partners as my research and writing progressed.

Without archival sources, historical research is virtually impossible and I am grateful for all the library and archives staff who so helpfully fetched box after box of documents for me at the Presbyterian Historical Society (Philadelphia, Pennsylvania), Payap University Archives (Chiang Mai, Thailand), and the Wheaton College Special Collections (Wheaton, Ill.). Without your tireless assistance, this book would never have been written.

Aside from a handful of overseas trips, the majority of research for this book was done from my desk in the Hewat postgraduate study room at New College, University of Edinburgh. Before COVID-19 scuttled it all, the postgraduate study rooms at New College were a fantastic place to not only pour over documents and write up my results but also trade thoughts, exchange opinions, get help, and make friends with other PhD students from a variety of fields in divinity and religion. The atmosphere was collegial and friendly, and I enjoyed a plethora of serious conversations and hearty laughs. I am thankful for my interactions with too many fellow researchers at New College to name them all, both fellow students and faculty, yet I am thankful for all of you who have made my doctoral research experience in Edinburgh so much richer.

Speaking of being richer, I am grateful for generous partial tuition scholarships from the School of Divinity, University of Edinburgh and the Aldis Trust Fund administered by OMF International, U.S. Both of these helped take the bite out of expensive international tuition fees. Yet even with substantial tuition assistance, it would have been challenging to put food on the table or keep a roof over our heads without the on-going generous support of the churches, families, and individuals who have stood behind us for many years during our work with OMF International in Thailand. You did not need to support us while I took a few years away from full-time ministry to pursue a PhD but you believed this was important and have made these studies possible. Thank you. I also wish to thank OMF Thailand for their kind permission to temporarily set aside my regular responsibilities to pursue further studies in hope for greater usefulness in the future.

The time that my family and I have spent in Scotland to research this book has been a joy, and not nearly as rainy as we expected or feared. Edinburgh is a great place to live, and our family has enjoyed the many wonderful people we have met, both Scottish and international, during our sojourn here. We are especially thankful for our friends and fellow pilgrims at Buccleuch Free Church where we have enjoyed fellowship and community as we worshipped together.

Doctoral studies are a long journey, and I would not have made it to the end without the indefatigable encouragement of my wife, Sun. When I was discouraged and doubting whether this thesis would really come together, she was always there telling me she was sure I could do it. Though my three children have not always understood what I have been doing, other than reading dead people's mail, they have cheerfully gone with the flow and embraced their own Scottish adventures. I am thankful that they have not minded the massive amount of time that I have spent in front of the computer for research or away visiting archives.

Last but certainly not least, I wish to thank the Lord Jesus Christ without whom nothing is possible. He has been a faithful sustainer and provider in all things. Soli Deo Gloria.

List of Abbreviations

ABCFM	American Board of Commissioners of Foreign Missions
APM	American Presbyterian Mission
BFM	Board of Foreign Missions
CCT	Church of Christ in Thailand
COEMAR	Commission on Ecumenical Mission and Relations
HRS	Herbert R. Swanson Research Papers
IBMR	International Bulletin of Mission/ary Research
MO	Mission Opinion
MRW	Missionary Review of the World
MVF	Missionary Vertical Files
OHE	Oral History English
OHT	Oral History Thai
PCUSA	Presbyterian Church in the United States of America
PHS	Presbyterian Historical Society
PUA	Payap University Archives
RG	Record Group
SO	Siam Outlook
SWC	Studies in World Christianity
TO	Thailand Outlook
UPCUSA	United Presbyterian Church in the United States of America
WCSC	Wheaton College Special Collections

Introduction

IN 1927, THE EXECUTIVE secretary of the American Presbyterian mission (APM) in Thailand was asked a loaded question. Visiting American journalist Charles Selden, having heard the day before a missionary sermon on the verbal inspiration of the Bible, asked Paul Eakin whether or not the Presbyterian missionaries in Thailand were fundamentalists. Realizing his answer might appear in print and be read by those in his home denomination, the Presbyterian Church USA (PCUSA), Eakin chose his words carefully. In the late nineteenth and early twentieth centuries, theological liberalism, from which modernism developed, was spreading and receiving a strong conservative reaction in some quarters, most notably from so-called fundamentalists. Wanting to reassure an increasingly divided home constituency and avoid any unwanted scrutiny of the APM Thailand mission, Eakin diplomatically answered, "Mr. Selden, I should say that almost all of our Mission, both old and young, are conservative in their Theology, and liberal in their spirit."[1] Eakin's answer, which will be discussed in chapter 7, conceals as much as it reveals about American Presbyterian missionaries in Thailand prior to the outbreak of World War II. Did Eakin believe his answer reflected the true state of the APM Thailand mission, or was it merely what he wanted to be true? When Eakin said "almost all" of the missionaries were conservative in theology and liberal in spirit, he obviously had exceptions in mind. Who were they and what impact did they have upon their fellow missionaries? In order to test and interrogate Eakin's generalization, this book will examine the ways and

1. Eakin to Brown, September 6, 1927, PHS.

extent to which modernism impacted the relationships and work of the APM Thailand mission, and how the missionaries themselves navigated shifting theological currents in a modernizing world.

Protestant missionaries have worked in Thailand since the second quarter of the nineteenth century and multiple studies have been written on factors affecting Christianity in Thailand and the growth of Thai Protestant churches. Factors frequently discussed have included church growth, evangelistic strategy, contextualization, Buddhism, Thai cultural values, and leadership. However, there has been little work done on the impact of changing theology among the missionaries, in particular the rise of modernism during the late nineteenth and early twentieth centuries. This is a notable gap in the study of the history of Christianity in Thailand because the vast majority of missionaries in Thailand, from the mid-nineteenth century through the start of World War II, were sent out from the PCUSA, a denomination seriously impacted by modernist-fundamentalist controversies during the interwar years. Even in an era before rapid global communication, it is unthinkable that APM Thailand missionaries would have been unaffected by the changes and controversies happening in their home denomination. However, no one has conducted a focused examination of how these changing theological currents affected the missionaries in Thailand and their work. As such, this book aims to fill that gap by examining how theological modernism and modernizing changes in American and Thai society affected the American Presbyterian mission in Thailand between 1891 and 1941. Ideally, identifying the impact of modernism upon Thai Christians would have been another major goal of this book but substantial investigation has been impossible due to a paucity of sources providing Thai perspectives.

Over the course of this book, there are three main questions that will be addressed. First, how far and in what ways were APM missionaries in Thailand in this period affected by theological modernism and the associated fundamentalist-modernist controversies happening in the PCUSA? Secondly, did the influence of modernism lead to controversies and theological polarization between modernists and fundamentalists of the kind witnessed in the USA and, to a large extent, also in China? Thirdly, to what extent, and in what ways, did modernist influence lead to a change in mission strategic priorities and field practice in evangelism and education between 1891 and 1941? The answers to these questions will provide insight into studies of modernism and fundamentalism by illustrating how a non-Western mission context impacted and intersected

Introduction xxiii

with the reception of these theological perspectives. Furthermore, this book may be read as a case study of how theological differences were negotiated in a mission organization and how theological diversity, as one of multiple contributing factors, impacted missionary relationships and priorities. For those with a personal connection or interest in Christianity in Thailand, both Thai and foreign, this book will pull the veil back on an understudied era of Thai church history by describing some of the people, trends, and events that have impacted the long-term development of Thai churches and mission work in Thailand.

To properly examine the question of how modernism impacted the American Presbyterian mission in Thailand, this book is divided into two parts. Part I provides necessary background for understanding modernism and modernization in the Presbyterian Church USA and Thailand. Chapters 1 to 3 explore the range of meanings of the terms modern, modernism / liberalism, and fundamentalism, and present a narrative account of the contested reception of modernism in the PCUSA and its Board of Foreign Missions. Chapter 4 then moves across the Pacific to orient the reader to the political, cultural, and religious development of Thailand. Chapter 5 surveys the introduction and development of Protestant Christianity in Thailand to the start of wartime Japanese occupation. Having established in Part I the necessary background context for the following chapters, Part II presents the primary findings of my research on the impact of modernism on the American Presbyterian Mission in Thailand. Chapter 6 examines four dimensions of modernism as experienced by American Presbyterian missionaries in Thailand. These dimensions included responses to modern biblical criticism, the influence of theological revisionism in the west, missionary encounters with Thai Buddhism and their implications for an understanding of Christian uniqueness, and the desire to modernize Christianity in order to appeal to an educated Thai Buddhist elite. These four aspects of modernist intersection with the American Presbyterian mission in Thailand are set against the backdrop of a mission that sought to maintain both internal harmony and the former American Protestant missionary consensus that valued both evangelism and social service. The existence and ramifications of the presence of modernist sympathies and conservative reactions are then further explored in chapter 7 by examining the findings of three foreign visitors who interpreted what they found in Thailand through the lens of their experience with modernism and fundamentalism in the United States and China.

Firstly, Unitarian journalist Charles Selden's experiences in Bangkok led him to wonder if the modernist-fundamentalist controversy had come to Thailand. Secondly, fundamentalist Donald Grey Barnhouse came to Thailand as one leg of a fact-finding world tour to discover if modernism was negatively impacting American Presbyterian foreign missions as rumored. Lastly, Chinese evangelist John Sung, who associated himself with fundamentalists in China, came to conduct revival campaigns, and catalyzed existing tensions, theological and otherwise, among both APM missionaries and Thai Christians. Chapter 8 will then examine the ways in which modernist sympathies likely contributed to Protestant perceptions of non-Christian religions, changing missionary thinking about the eternal destiny of Thai Buddhists, and appropriate modes of evangelism. Chapter 9 is devoted to examining competing conceptions of evangelism in APM Thailand mission schools, institutions which consumed an increasing amount of mission funds and personnel during the course of the early twentieth century. Key points from chapters 1 to 9 are then summarized and analyzed in a Conclusion that identifies six reasons why the American Presbyterian mission in Thailand experienced little modernist-fundamentalist controversy when compared to the United States and China. Modernist influence was not absent in Thailand but its impact and the reactions it prompted were shaped by distinctive factors within the Thailand context that distinguished it from nations where modernism directly contributed to public and protracted theological controversy.

1

What It Means to Be "Modern"

"Modern" is one of those words everyone understands until they try to define it. Finding commonly agreed upon definitions for "modern" and its associated terms, "modernity," "modernization," and "modernism," is a perennial difficulty, a fact commonly acknowledged in scholarship.[1] Different scholars locate the beginning of the modern period at different times and attribute to modernity a variety of characteristics. There is, however, a certain commonality among the various characteristics of modernity routinely cited such that a composite sketch of what it means to be modern can be assembled. To that end, this chapter will explore the meaning of "modern" and its associated concepts in order to set subsequent discussion of theological modernism among missionaries in Thailand in proper context.

CHARACTERISTICS OF A MODERN WORLDVIEW

At the most basic level, "modern" simply means "new," as contrasted with something older. "Modern" is thus a temporal marker, declaring a break between what has gone before and what is recent. This differentiation between modern and ancient, however, indicates not only chronological age but also trajectory. To embrace modernity is to embrace a certain teleology and moral judgements about the past and the present. Embedded in modernity is a view of history that the world is progressing from the primitive and the inferior to the mature and the superior. The "new," or

---

1. See Lauzon, "Modernity," 1; Saler, "Modernity and Enchantment," 694; Gay, *Modernism*, 1–2.

"modern" is assumed to be better than the "old" merely because it is new. History has a forward direction and is progressing towards perfection, even if perfection may never be fully realized.

Though a modern view of history is progressive, the development of history is not to be passively observed. It is to be pursued. As Michael Lauzon has noted, modernity is not just "the latest form of historical discontinuity," but rather something to be accomplished by applying rational principles and scientific laws. As such, modernity is a project modern people actively attempt to achieve.[2] This pursuit of modernity is made possible by a "reflexive awareness" of oneself and the world, greater value being assigned to attainment of what is deemed "modern," and lesser value assigned to that which is not modern. Thus, it is possible to "stand in the way of progress" by questioning the assumption that newer is better. This pursuit of modernity is driven by self-conscious reflection upon one's location in history and where history should be going.[3] This awareness of the need to pursue modernity sets the modern person apart from those of other eras. In the history of the world, many people have observed colossal changes within their lifetimes, but before the modern period these changes have not necessarily been viewed as progress. In *The Birth of the Modern World*, C.A. Bayly noted that prior to the nineteenth century people perceived major changes in society as either "renovations" of the past or as a millenarian in-breaking.[4] A modern view of history asserts human agents are at the forefront of creating a new world that is different and superior to previous eras.

In addition to a self-reflective awareness of the progress of history, a mechanistic view of the universe is another factor that has enabled modernity to be pursued as a project. The divine is not necessarily excluded but modernity emphasizes the ability of people to change the world as they choose. Lauzon notes that this view is based on two ideas that arose from the Scientific Revolution. "First, nature came to be thought of as something like a machine that operates according to discrete, regular, and consistent laws and, second, that these laws of nature can be grasped, expressed, and potentially and self-consciously manipulated by individual rational human beings."[5] In pursing forward progress, modern people are characterized by a willingness to break

---

2. See Lauzon, "Modernity," 5.
3. See Lauzon, "Modernity," 2.
4. Bayly, *Birth*, 11.
5. See Lauzon, "Modernity," 3.

with tradition and social conventions in the pursuit of something better, a characteristic of modernity noted by Peter Gay in *Modernism: The Lure of Heresy*.[6] Though his primary reference point is the arts, Gay's observation that non-conformity and a bias against the "traditional" are characteristic of modernity also bears relevance for discussions of modernity in other areas. The willingness to break with traditional beliefs, for example, is an important characteristic of theological modernism, as we shall see in chapters 2 and 3.

MARKERS OF MODERNIZATION

Social theorists from the late nineteenth century onward have often explained modernity in reference to the development of various social and economic institutions, and the rise of capitalism.[7] These developments include industrialization, urbanization, bureaucratization, routinization, scientific and technological knowledge, education, democracy, movements of protest, mass media, public intellectuals, professionalization, the nuclear family, individual political rights, the nation-state, and secularization.[8] Though the ideological foundations for modernity were laid much earlier, starting in the mid-nineteenth century developments in many of these areas began to accelerate, contributing to the perception the world was entering a new era. Bayly notes that after 1840 industrialization started "to kick in at a global level" and by 1870 the age of capital had arrived. By the turn of the century, "icons of technological modernization—the car, the airplane, the telephone—were all around to dramatize this sensibility" of being in a new era. Bayly rightly observes that an essential part of being modern is the sense of being in a new era. People become modern because they think they are modern.[9] This criterion of modernity is obviously subjective. However, self-identification and self-perception are not insignificant in assessing societal changes. Given that modernity was a project to be pursued, not merely a phenomenon to be observed, a person's self-identification as modern is an indicator of their aspirations and values, which in turn influences their activities and interactions with others. By the turn of the century,

---

6. Gay, *Modernism*, 2–8.

7. See Lauzon, "Modernity," 7; Van Der Veer, "Global History," 286.

8. See Lauzon, "Modernity," 7; Bayly, *Birth*, 9–11; Saler, "Modernity," 695; Van Der Veer, "Global History," 285; Eisenstadt, *Multiple*, 3–11; Treloar, *Disruption*, 11–13.

9. Bayly, *Birth*, 7–11.

leaders of society from Western nations felt the world was entering a modern era, and elite Africans and Asians were likewise beginning to pursue the markers of modernity in hopes of improving the status and well-being of themselves and their cultures. As we will see in chapter 4, Thailand's elite were both conscious of changes in the modern world and eager to be respected as modern, civilized people.[10]

MULTIPLE AND ALTERNATIVE MODERNITIES

Until recent decades, scholarship has largely assumed the West as both the originator and benchmark of modernity against which modernity in other parts of the world is to be measured.[11] However, multiple scholars have called into question the normative value of Western modernity, noting non-Western cultures have not grown increasingly Western as was expected. The actual development of non-Western societies has, in fact, refuted the "homogenizing and hegemonic assumptions" of the Western program of modernity and given rise to the theory of multiple modernities.[12] This theory posits that modernity has developed differently in various societies and a society can be authentically modern without being identical to the West. This theory acknowledges the legitimacy of alternative versions of modernity, reflecting "multiple institutional and ideological patterns" that are "distinctively modern, though distinctively influenced by specific cultural premises, traditions, and historical experiences."[13] Shmuel N. Eisenstadt, whose edited volume *Multiple Modernities* is a common point of scholarly reference on this topic, asserts "the best way to understand the contemporary world— indeed to explain the history of modernity—is to see it as a continual constitution and reconstitution of a multiplicity of cultural programs."[14] Ideas and institutions associated with modernity may have originated in a culturally Western context but "modernity and Westernization are not identical; [and] Western patterns of modernity are not the only 'authentic' modernities, though they enjoy historical precedence and continue

---

10. A key source summarizing Thai elite aspirations is Winichakul, "Quest for 'Siwilai,'" 528–49.
11. Bayly, *Birth*, 10; Eisenstadt, *Multiple*, viii, 1–2.
12. Eisenstadt, *Multiple*, 1.
13. See Lauzon, "Modernity," 12; Eisenstadt, *Multiple*, 2.
14. Eisenstadt, *Multiple*, 2.

to be a basic reference point for the others."[15] Their use as reference points, however, does not imply uncritical acceptance. Lauzon notes that non-Europeans have "long criticized the conventional conceptions and instantiations of modernity and their implication that traditional cultures and values are at best quaintly irrational signs of an unchanging immature society that should be radically transformed."[16] As will be seen in chapter 4, Western modernity served as a reference point for the Thai elite who sought to form a uniquely Thai modernity, selectively embracing or rejecting those elements of Western civilization as seemed best to them. As the Buddhist leaders of a developing nation, their vision both merged with and diverged from American Presbyterian missionary aspirations for a modernized Thailand. One commonality between them was the desire for modern Thailand to also be religious. Though secularization has been commonly cited as a hallmark of modernity, the correlation between modernization and religious decline that has been commonly assumed for the West has become more tenuous for non-Western contexts since secularization has not occurred as rapidly, nor in the same manner, as it has in the West.[17] The idea of multiple modernities presses one to ask whether a society may be authentically modern and genuinely religious at the same time. Such "enchanted modernity" must be entertained as a valid option unless one wishes to persist in Western-centric models of the past.[18]

MODERNIZATION AS A GLOBAL PHENOMENON

In thinking about the nature of modernity and the course of modernization in different contexts, it is necessary to remember modernity is not simply a cultural and civilizational program the West has exported to the rest of the world. Rather than a "West-to-the-rest" model, the spread of modernity is best viewed as a global phenomenon, consisting of interactions, appropriations, and adaptations between cultures.[19] Non-Western peoples have been neither passive beneficiaries nor unwitting victims of the West, but rather active agents in molding their own modernities

---

15. Eisenstadt, *Multiple*, 2–3.
16. See Lauzon, "Modernity," 11.
17. Paas, "Notoriously Religious," 26–50.
18. See Lauzon, "Modernity," 2; Paas, "Notoriously Religious," 40.
19. Lauzon, "Modernity," 9.

based on varying "civilizational religious cores."[20] Bayly contends that even as the rise of "nation-states and contending territorial empires" highlighted global differences, "similarities, connections, and linkages between them proliferated."[21] The agency of indigenous actors and the multi-directional nature of modernizing influences should be kept in mind as we consider the various dimensions of modernist influence in the American Presbyterian mission in Thailand.

MODERNIZATION AND CIVILIZATION

The term "civilization" has a long history in the English language but was previously considered to be a state rather than a process. However, during the time period covered by this book, the related concepts of civilization and civilizing became linked with modernity and modernization as not only a state to be attained but also a process. This is reflected in the 2019 online edition of the *Oxford English Dictionary*, which defined "civilization" as either a descriptor of "human cultural, social, and intellectual development when considered to be advanced and progressive in nature" or in its verbal form, meaning the "action or process of civilizing or becoming civilized; (also) the action or process of being made civilized by an external force." The inclusion of "progressive" in the definition of civilization is indicative of the influence of a modern mindset that assumes history to have a progressive teleology. As such, the term "civilization," when used as a descriptor, is largely synonymous with modernity. When used as a verbal noun, "civilizing" bears the marks of modernity viewed as a project, namely something to be achieved and accomplished, not merely observed. For the purposes of this book, modernizing and civilizing are interchangeable terms. When late nineteenth- and early twentieth-century Thai elite talked of being *siwilai* (civilized) and American missionaries talked of civilizing the Thai, the goals they had in mind were largely identical to those of modernization as discussed above.

In the nineteenth century, historians discussed the "civilizing mission" of the West, a mission powered by the instruments of modernity.[22] Influenced by evolutionary thought, Western historians ranked the peoples of the world on a scale from "savage" to "civilized" and it was the process of modernization that would move them up the ladder.[23]

---

20. Lauzon's language of "civilizational religious cores" is borrowed from Eisenstadt. Lauzon, "Modernity," 12.

21. Bayly, *Birth*, 2–3.

22. Bayly, *Birth*, 5–12.

23. See Lauzon, "Modernity," 4.

Both missionaries and other expatriate foreigners in non-Western lands agreed "the colonized had to be converted to modernity."[24] For the missionaries, however, the aim of civilizing the "natives" into a modernity on par with the West was complicated by their competing aim of evangelization. From the mid-eighteenth century onward the question of evangelizing versus civilizing was an ongoing debate for missionaries and mission supporters. While some thought one must civilize in order to evangelize, others believed civilization would follow on the heels of evangelization.[25] This question remained an unsolved tension well into the twentieth century and was part of the background for missionaries in Thailand, though there is little evidence they questioned the merits of "civilizing" alongside "Christianizing."

WHAT DOES IT MEAN TO BE MODERN?

Although the word eludes precise definition that commands universal recognition, "modern" and its associated terms, "modernity," "modernization," and "modernism," are meaningful reference points when understood within the parameters discussed above. The terms of modernity and their use were originally set by the West but have more recently been called into question by both non-Western peoples and self-critical Western scholars. These terms still have meaning, however, and are necessary reference points for discussion of the topic of modernity.

In sum, to be modern is to be committed to pursuing what is new because new is better. The world is progressing in a forward-looking direction, driven by rational thought and scientific inquiry. Modern people are willing to break with tradition and social convention in the name of progress and the betterment of humanity. Though modernity is sometimes dated to the beginning of the Enlightenment, the development of a modern worldview has occurred progressively with a significant leap forward occurring in the nineteenth century. During this period, changes in social organization, economic institutions, transportation, and communication began to advance at a more rapid pace than before, triggering a new self-conscious sense of modernity among many.[26]

---

24. Van Der Veer, "Global History," 290–91; Paas, "Notoriously Religious," 33–36.

25. See chapters 10–12 in Stanley, *Christian Missions*; Treloar, *Disruption*, 39–40; Speer, "Civilizing Influence," 412–42; and "Christianity and Civilization," 118.

26. Bayly, *Birth*, 9–11.

2

Modernizing Trends in Theology and Ministry

IN CHAPTER 1 WE looked at what is means to be "modern" and the present chapter will build upon that understanding by examining several modernizing trends that had a profound effect on the theology and work of Protestant churches and their foreign missions during the late nineteenth and early twentieth centuries.

The first part of this chapter will explore the ways in which the dissemination of scientific knowledge and methods, in particular the concept of evolution, was applied to religion and influenced thinking on a wide variety of issues far beyond the issue of human origins. The second part of the chapter will note modernizing trends in theology that would come to be associated with theological modernism. We will then briefly survey the historical development of theological liberalism and modernism, and conclude with some general observations on how theological modernism manifested itself in the domain of foreign missions.

MODERNIZING TREND 1: SCIENTIFIC KNOWLEDGE AND METHODS APPLIED TO RELIGION

Prior to Darwin, scientific inquiry was seen by many as an aspect of natural theology, or the study of what one could learn about God by empirical study of the created order.[1] As such, science and theology commonly functioned together harmoniously within a worldview that assumed

---

1. Livingstone, *Darwin*, 3.

divine creation and superintendence of the universe. Protestants of all theological varieties happily endorsed this empirical type of scientific inquiry. Science underwent a change, however, with the advent of Darwinian evolution.[2] The idea that things develop through gradual processes due to natural selection came to have a wide-ranging impact on all fields of human learning, a point to which we will return momentarily.

Evolutionary Thought and Human Origins

In the area of biology and human origins, Darwin's theory of evolution, as it came to be called, was seen by some as a challenge to the Genesis account of supernatural creation of the universe and humanity. Nevertheless, the theory of evolution was met with varied responses. While both conservatives and liberals were modern in their embrace of scientific inquiry, they differed with each other, and among themselves, on the degree to which the results of such inquiry be allowed to modify traditionally held understandings of biblical teaching. Some theological conservatives rejected theories of human origins that conflicted with traditional understandings of the Bible as unscientific speculation. Others, however, sought ways to reconcile the new learning with traditional doctrines.[3] Benjamin B. Warfield, the staunch Princetonian defender of biblical inerrancy, held to a form of theistic evolution and J. Gresham Machen may have been cautiously open to evolution as well.[4] Robert E. Speer, who directed the Presbyterian Church USA's Board of Foreign Mission, dismissed fears evolutionary thought threatened foreign missions because even if true, it did not affect humanity's need for God.[5] Theological liberals, on the other hand, more freely embraced evolutionary thought on human origins, unfettered by the authority of creeds, dogmas, or belief in an inerrant Bible.[6] In *The Faith of Modernism*, University of Chicago theology professor Shailer Mathews wrote, "Modernists are Christians who accept the results of scientific research as data with which to think religiously."[7] William Adams Brown, theology professor at Union Theological Seminary,

---

2. George Marsden discusses this development in terms of a first and second scientific revolution. Marsden, *Fundamentalism*, 20–21.

3. Numbers, *Creationists*, 65–68; Marsden, *Fundamentalism*, 7, 19–20.

4. Hart, *Defending*, 97–99.

5. See Hutchison, "Modernism and Missions," 129.

6. For a discussion of the spectrum of Protestant stances vis-à-vis science, see Treloar, *Disruption*, 12–17.

7. Mathews, *Faith*, 29.

defined himself in a similar way, writing, "I am a Modernist, and as such I am committed to follow the scientific method to its limit wherever it shall take me."[8] Modernists took evangelical faith as their starting point but the findings of modern science determined which elements of faith were no longer tenable.[9]

Evolutionary Thought and Biblical Criticism

As hinted at in the statements of Mathews and Brown just referenced, scientific learning and the evolutionary idea were applied to other areas of religious thought in addition to the question of human origins. As George Marsden noted, the new biblical (or higher) criticism developed at the end of the nineteenth century was based on virtually the same naturalistic assumptions of historical development as biological evolution.[10] Reflecting the evolutionary idea of gradual progress, Julius Wellhausen hypothesized in 1878 that the Pentateuch was written by multiple authors over a thousand years, challenging claims of Mosaic authorship. This development in thinking about the composition of the Bible was accompanied by the 1876 decipherment of Babylonian myths about creation and the flood, which taken together called into question the uniqueness and authority of the Bible as traditionally understood.[11]

On the one hand, the idea of the progressive evolution of the Bible allowed modern Christians to retain those elements of Scripture which they valued while simultaneously distancing themselves from its premodern elements, explaining miracles as merely the unsophisticated poetic memories of an unscientific primitive people.[12] On the other hand, some Christians reacted strongly against the new criticism, arguing that calling into question the accuracy of any part of the Bible constituted an attack on the authority and accuracy of the whole Bible. However, yet others sought a middle ground, seeking to incorporate the best insights of modern criticism into their study of the Bible while continuing to maintain its authority. As a consequence of these developments, there was a shift in modes of thinking about biblical authority and inspiration.

---

8. Dorrien, *Making of American Liberal Theology*, 60.

9. "Liberal" and "Modernist" are used largely interchangeably. The (slight) difference between them will be noted later in this chapter.

10. Marsden, *Fundamentalism*, 20.

11. See Enns, "Protestantism and Biblical Criticism," 135.

12. Treloar, *Disruption*, 74–78.

It became common for Christians to affirm the inspiration of the writers of the Bible rather than the words of the Bible themselves, and there was a subtle shift towards "experience, pre-eminently of the Bible's writers, but also of its readers, as the locus of religious authority."[13]

Evolutionary Thought and Other Religions

The evolutionary idea was applied to the study of not only the development of Christianity, but also other world religions, yielding new thought on the way in which religions developed naturally, from a more primitive to a more developed state. This idea of the evolution of religions underlies the presupposition of theological liberals that there exists "a universal religious sentiment" that is the "common source of particular religious forms."[14] This theory of the evolution of religions combined with the experience of other cultures led some to see greater value in the study of other religions than was previously thought, which caused a shadow to be cast over Christian claims of uniqueness.[15] In *Re-Thinking Missions*, William Hocking and his fellow appraisers of the missionary enterprise asserted that under every religion there is an "inalienable religious intuition of the human soul" that points to a "universal religion."[16] Therefore, they claimed, Christians should not oppose other religions, but rather co-operate with them for good of all humanity.[17] The assumption of the evolution of religion did not always lead away from the affirmation of Christian uniqueness, however, as evidenced in the reconciling position of John Nicol Farquhar's fulfilment theory. This theory posited religions developed from lower forms to higher forms, with non-Christian religions and beliefs located at lower rungs on the ladder and Christ at the top as the fulfilment of all non-Christian aspirations. This theory both accommodated the relative value of other religions while also maintaining Christianity as the superior religion and re-affirming the value of the missionary goal of converting other religious adherents to Christianity.[18]

---

13. Treloar, *Disruption*, 76.

14. See Hutchison, "Modernism and Missions," 111.

15. Frank Rawlinson and Pearl Buck are two notable examples of missionaries whose views of non-Christian religions were changed through practical experience and comparative study. See Xi, *Conversion*.

16. Hocking, *Re-Thinking Missions*, 37.

17. Hocking, *Re-Thinking Missions*, 29–33.

18. Treloar, *Disruption*, 39–40; Bosch, *Transforming Mission*, 490–92.

The Evolution of Language

Evolutionary thought also called into question the ability of language to relay lasting and abiding meaning. All statements of doctrine are expressed in words but if language evolves, do old forms of words still accurately convey the abiding truths of Christianity? Theological liberal Shailer Mathews, as well as centrist conservative Robert E. Speer, presupposed language is not entirely sufficient to accurately convey truth. Although Mathews claimed he did not object to those who wanted to use "old doctrinal patterns," he thought the essence of Christianity was in "deep and continuing attitudes and convictions which doctrines have expressed." One must, Mathews believed, look under the language in which doctrine is expressed in order to find the essence of Christianity. As such, doctrine and language used to express Christian truth is always contingent.[19] Robert Speer, who continued to affirm traditional doctrines in traditional language, believed no language was adequate to contain all Christian truth and even the best creedal statements become outdated and need new interpretations.[20]

An evolutionary view of the development of language led to various responses to the use of traditional Christian language. As noted by the authors of *Re-Thinking Missions*, some desired "to avoid the language of tradition, not as untrue, but perhaps as obscurely figurative or symbolical" and thus an obstacle to the recognition of God.[21] On the other hand, use of traditional language became a source of frustration to fundamentalists such as J. Gresham Machen and James Walter Lowrie who were convinced theological liberals disingenuously used traditional language as a cover for their unorthodox beliefs.[22] In *The Presbyterian Controversy*, Bradley Longfield argues Speer's belief in the malleability and insufficiency of language allowed him to view more liberal colleagues as within the Christian fold.[23] Belief in the evolving

---

19. Mathews, *Faith*, 169–71.
20. Longfield, *Presbyterian Controversy*, 193.
21. Hocking, *Re-Thinking Missions*, xiv–xv.
22. Longfield, *Presbyterian Controversy*, 182–83; Yao, *Fundamentalist Movement*, 70.
23. Longfield, *Presbyterian Controversy*, 194.

nature of language allowed for public affirmation of traditional doctrinal statements and private non-literal interpretation of that language such that one could appear simultaneously both to affirm and deny the virgin birth, miracles, the resurrection of Christ, and the Second Coming.[24] The resurrection, for example, might be affirmed in the sense that Jesus continues to live in the experience of his disciples. Paul Eakin of the Presbyterian Mission in Thailand, whose theological convictions will be discussed later, affirmed the resurrection of Christ but equivocated on what that meant, whether Jesus made his presence known "through a body or spirit or a new substance."[25]

The Evolution of Doctrine

Those who applied evolutionary principles to the development of doctrine viewed the history of Christianity as progressive. The religion of Jesus consisted of certain abiding principles which were subsequently given expression in the form of doctrines, dogmas, and symbols through succeeding generations. The history of Christianity, claimed Shailer Mathews, is that of Christians employing the permanent elements of faith in culturally specific ways to meet the needs of that time. As time and culture changed, forms and doctrines necessarily changed as well.[26] In religion, thought Mathews, there is development and evolution, the old giving way to the new in response to the needs and experiences of a new generation.[27] Arthur McGiffert, president of Union Theological Seminary from 1917 to 1926, asserted that certain traditional doctrines had been modified by the idea of evolution, breaking down "the sharp contrasts of the old theology" and contributing the "substitution of relativity for absoluteness in all departments of thought."[28]

Mathews claimed newer generations could not be expected to cling to older doctrines that were suited to different times and places since such doctrinal formulae do not belong to the essence of Christianity. "The Christianity to which the world has always appealed is more than a system of doctrines. *It is a moral and spiritual movement, born of*

---

24. Mathews, *Faith*, 176–77; Hocking, *Re-Thinking Missions*, 19.
25. Eakin, "My Reasonable Faith."
26. Mathews, *Faith*, 2.
27. The Laymen's Commission of Appraisal saw this evolutionary principle at work in non-Christian religions as well. Hocking, *Re-Thinking Missions*, 37–38.
28. McGiffert, *Rise*, 184–85.

the experience of God known through Jesus Christ as Savior. It is a community of life, not a system of philosophy or theology" (italics original).[29] As Mathews looked at the successive changes throughout the history of Christianity, he observed "[o]ne might go on indefinitely showing how doctrines are not repudiated, but cease to function in the life of earnest Christians whose attention has shifted from technical theology to practical religious interests."[30] In many instances, modernists such as Mathews did not directly repudiate traditional doctrines affirmed by their conservative counterparts but rather neglected them in favor of other priorities. Reiterating traditional doctrinal formulae or forging new ones were not useful tools in helping people gain religious experiences that would meet the demands of the modern world.

For modernists, Christianity consisted primarily of the experiences of God's people in relation to Jesus Christ rather than in adherence to any particular doctrinal formulae. The writers of *Re-Thinking Missions* agreed that "religion cannot be handed on as a finished doctrine" and Harry Emerson Fosdick similarly asserted that modern man's interpretation of the Bible concerns "abiding experiences" rather than "mental frameworks."[31] It is the experience of Jesus Christ that is important rather than particular statements about him. Albert Knudson believed salvation consisted in the ability to experience Jesus Christ, stating that "[t]he overwhelming sense of the reality, power, and supremacy of the spiritual life of men as a living, present experience is the insight which constitutes the saviourhood of Jesus Christ. His Gospel is an insight experimentally won by himself and offered by him for experimental verification of all men."[32] Doctrinal formulations vary and evolve over time, but Christianity, at its core, was primarily experiential and ethical.[33]

Evolutionary Thought and Missionary Methodology

The application of various methodologies to the practice of missions was nothing new at the turn of the century, but there was increasing self-consciousness in the application of the scientific method to modernizing

29. Mathews, *Faith*, 12.

30. Mathews, *Faith*, 27.

31. Hocking, *Re-Thinking Missions*, 45; Rall, "Some Modern Interpretations," 196–202; Dorrien, *American Liberal Theology*, 59.

32. Knudson, *Present Tendencies*, 8 in Rall, *Some Modern Interpretations*, 200.

33. Dorrien, *American Liberal Theology*, 51; Stanley, "Christianity, Modernism, and Modernization," 24; Mathews, *Faith*, 25–26; Hocking, *Re-Thinking Missions*, 50–51.

the missionary task with the aim of greater efficiency. The World Missionary Conference of 1910 in Edinburgh was intended to be "a Grand Council for the Advancement of Missionary Science" that would apply the "rigorous methods of modern social science to the challenges and problems which missionaries faced on the field." It was hoped that an analysis of "ascertained and sifted facts" would lay the "foundations for the emergence of a new 'science of missions' that would inform all future practice."[34] The scientific advancement of missionary methods begun at the 1910 Edinburgh conference was continued at subsequent meetings of the International Missionary Council in Jerusalem (1928) and Madras (1938). The Laymen's Foreign Missions Inquiry (1932) likewise represented an effort to modernize missionary methods and practice, albeit within a more liberal theological framework than that represented by the International Missionary Council.[35]

In considering the various areas of religious thought influenced by scientific thinking and the idea of evolution – namely human origins, biblical criticism, comparative religion, language, doctrine, and mission methodology – we may note the wide-ranging impact that these modes of thinking had upon Christian thought and practice, far beyond the question of biological evolution alone. By the second decade of the twentieth century, the influence of evolutionary thinking was so widely felt that Union Seminary professor Arthur McGiffert wrote that the "changed concept of human history as a process of evolution . . . took increasing possession of the nineteenth century, until it became dominant . . . The result is that all our thinking to-day [sic] proceeds largely along evolutionary lines."[36] McGiffert's assertion gives helpful perspective on the impact of evolutionary thought during the early twentieth century. However, as we shall shortly see, its dominance was not as total as he claimed. McGiffert himself narrowly avoided a heresy trial at the turn of the century by leaving the Presbyterian Church USA and joining a congregational church.[37]

---

34. Stanley, *World Missionary Conference*, 4–5.
35. Treloar, *Disruption*, 246–49.
36. McGiffert, *Rise*, 174–75.
37. Rockwell, "Arthur Cushman McGiffert," 105–6.

MODERNIZING TREND 2: BROADENING THEOLOGY

From the late nineteenth century through the middle of the twentieth century, modern thinking led to broadening theological boundaries to allow for more diverse understandings of the Christian faith. Evolutionary thought prompted belief in the evolution of doctrine, namely the conviction that doctrine must change in line with the times, a change that often led away from traditional formulations and favored more liberal interpretations. Broadening of theological horizons is not synonymous with theological liberalism though there is a large overlap between the two.[38] As previously noted, the early twentieth century was a period of theological transition and only some broadening changes came to be clearly identified with liberalism as theological positions became more polarized starting in the 1920s. On the one hand, non-literal interpretations of doctrines such as the virgin birth and the resurrection of Christ represented broadening theological interpretations that came to be associated with theological liberalism. However, other broadening theological changes such as emphases upon the kingdom of God, divine immanence, and the fatherhood of God were not necessarily incompatible with conservative theology but nonetheless received more prominence in liberal thinking and were sometimes interpreted in ways conservatives rejected. For example, liberals emphasized not only the fatherhood of God, but specifically the universality of the fatherhood of God with its accompanying implication that all humans are children of God by creation, an assertion rejected by conservatives. Broadening theology largely overlaps with liberalizing theology but the two are not completely identical and broadening changes were occurring among both liberals and conservatives, albeit in diverse ways.

Shifting Attitudes Towards Biblical Authority

One aspect of broadening of theology was voices calling for a re-evaluation of categories of biblical authority. European scholars suggested some Old Testament books were written later than traditionally thought, by multiple authors, and in some cases bore resemblance to other Ancient Near Eastern sources.[39] Application of historical-critical methods

---

38. For a history of the PCUSA through the lens of doctrinal broadening, see Loetscher, *Broadening Church*. For a narrower focus on conflicts related to theological broadening in the 1920s and 1930s, see Longfield, *Presbyterian Controversy*.

39. See Enns, "Protestantism and Biblical Criticism," 136.

to New Testament studies led other scholars to conclude there is little we can know about Jesus with accuracy and even if the Gospel accounts are an accurate record of Jesus's message, his self-identification as an eschatological prophet has been proven wrong by subsequent history.[40] As the findings of these modern scholars gained intellectual traction, some theologians and lay people adjusted their views on biblical authority and accuracy. Shailer Mathews expressed the thoughts of many when he affirmed the Bible as "a source of religious inspiration and guidance."[41] However, others resisted these challenges from modern scholarship, issuing calls to defend the Scripture, such as B.B. Warfield's well-known volume, *The Inspiration and Authority of the Bible*.

Scientific Naturalism and Anti-Supernaturalism

Underlying biblical criticism and challenges to biblical authority was a penchant to seek naturalistic rather than supernatural explanations for both the development of the biblical texts as well as the Biblical narrative itself. Modern people tended to see the world in terms of mechanized processes and evolutionary development rather than divine interventions in human affairs.[42] This modern understanding of the world led to the discounting of the miraculous aspects of Scripture, such as the parting of the Red Sea, the virgin birth, the healing miracles of Jesus, and the bodily resurrection of Christ. This trend towards the rejection of the supernatural solicited strong reactions in some quarters and not a few Christians became concerned about the erosion of traditional Christian belief. Such concerns prompted the 1910 General Assembly of the Presbyterian Church USA to require ministerial candidates to affirm the inerrancy of the Bible, the virgin birth, substitutionary atonement, the bodily resurrection of Christ, and the miracle-working power of Christ. These key concerns, corresponding to liberal denials of the same, also formed the basis of a widely distributed book series titled *The Fundamentals* which sought to rebut the claims of modern scholarship that undermined traditional doctrines.[43]

---

40. Livingston, *Modern Christian Thought*, 9–13; Braaten, *History and Hermeneutics*, 160.

41. Mathews, *Faith*, 170.

42. Hill, *History of Christian Thought*, 272–73.

43. Longfield, *Presbyterian Controversy*, 21, 25.

The Kingdom of God

Decreasing confidence in the reliability of the Bible in its particulars and increasing scientific anti-supernaturalism in modern thinking were favorable to changing perceptions of what constituted the "kingdom of God." In the nineteenth century, liberal theologians popularized conceptions of the kingdom of God as ethical and social rather than doctrinal or ecclesiastical in scope. The ethical visions of the kingdom of God of Albrecht Ritschl and Adolf Von Harnack blended well with postmillennialism, end-of-the-century optimistic views of the perfectibility of humanity, and the narrative of social progress.[44] Despite being undermined by Johannes Weiss and Albert Schweitzer's assertions that Jesus was primarily an eschatological prophet who was wrong about the future and thus alien to modern needs and sensibilities, this ethical and social vision of the kingdom proved incredibly resilient. Though both liberals and conservatives spoke of the "kingdom of God" in reference to advancing Christian influence in society at large, it was also utilized in liberal discourse to refer to Christian influence in society to the deprecation or exclusion of the goal of individual conversion. On the heels of the American Congregationalists' 1893 decision to allow the service of missionaries who declined to affirm eternal damnation, Lyman Abbott rejoiced that the new "missionary spirit" was helping the Church see its true function, which was to "establish the kingdom of God here and now on this earth, not to save men."[45]

Divine Immanence and the Fatherhood of God

As hinted at in the quotation from Lyman Abbott just referenced, modernization entailed re-evaluations of how God relates to people and the world, and how people are to respond to God. With increasing knowledge of the world's people, and acknowledgement of their value and contribution to humanity as a whole, "saving the heathen" from hell gave way in many instances to seeking God in unison with them.[46] As Shailer Mathews observed, salvation conceived as escape from hellfire was not in accord with modern sensibilities and, as the Laymen's Foreign Missions Inquiry noted, it seemed preferable to work with adherents of

---

44. Hill, *History of Christian Thought*, 245–46, 56; Braaten, *History and Hermeneutics*, 160; Mostert, *God and the Future*, 7.

45. Xi, *Conversion*, 211.

46. See Hutchison, "Modernism and Missions," 111.

other religions against the forces of secularism and materialism, rather than try to convert them.[47]

An increasing openness to the value of other religions and a bias towards viewing the natural world as working through gradual, mechanized processes meshed well with a rising emphasis upon divine immanence.[48] While conservatives did not have a problem affirming God is working in the world through the created order, the early twentieth-century emphasis on immanence reflected the liberal belief that God's work in history was through natural processes rather than through supernatural inbreaking into the natural order. This concept of immanence was front and center in Shailer Mathews's modernist credo which began, "I believe in God, immanent in the forces and processes of nature, revealed in Jesus Christ and human history as Love."[49]

Closely related to immanence was an emphasis on the Fatherhood of God toward all humanity. This idea was closely connected with the brotherhood of all men and together they were used to find common ground with non-Christians as either a basis for calling them to put their faith in Christ or to engage in interfaith dialogue and co-operation.[50] The fatherhood of God and universal brotherhood of man was given positive emphasis by modernist Shailer Mathews and moderate conservative Robert Speer yet attracted severe criticism from fundamentalists.[51] William Chisholm, a Presbyterian missionary doctor in Korea, objected that only those who have been given new spiritual life in Christ can truly be children of God and J. Gresham Machen thought liberal teaching on the fatherhood of God bordered on pantheism.[52]

DEFINING THEOLOGICAL MODERNISM: ORIGINS AND DEVELOPMENT

Broadening trends in theology that would bloom into modernism began to exert influence in American Protestantism during the late nineteenth and early twentieth centuries, yet it is difficult to pinpoint their entry

---

47. Mathews, *Faith*, 90; Hocking, *Re-Thinking Missions*, 32–33.

48. Arthur McGiffert saw the emphasis on immanence as a result of evolutionary thinking. McGiffert, *Rise*, 180–83.

49. Mathews, *Faith*, 180.

50. Treloar, *Disruption*, 45–46, 80–81; Irvine, "Inter-Religious Movement," 8.

51. Mathews, *Faith*, 118–22; Speer, *Report of Deputation 1915*, 43.

52. Chisholm, "Hospital Evangelism," 4; Hart, "When Is a Fundamentalist a Modernist?," 611.

points into American Protestant thinking. While liberal theological ideas found an early home among Unitarians in the United States, it was not until the late nineteenth century that they were beginning to appear, and stir conflict, in larger Protestant denominations, namely Congregational, Episcopal, Methodist, Baptist, Disciples of Christ, and Presbyterian churches.[53] Around the time of the American Civil War, Darwin's ideas on the origin of man began to be known in the United States, casting doubt over the Genesis account of special revelation.[54] Influenced by this new learning, Rev. David Swing of Fourth Presbyterian Church in Chicago was tried for heresy (and subsequently acquitted) in 1874 for arguing neither instructors or students of theology "could be expected to subscribe to belief in a six-thousand-year-old earth or a worldwide deluge."[55] In the early 1890s, Congregationalists debated the doctrine of eternal punishment and by 1895, the Congregationalist-associated American Board of Commissioners for Foreign Missions (ABCFM) overturned the policy of its executive secretary who consistently refused to send missionaries who could not affirm the doctrine. It was now up to individual congregations, not the board, to determine the theological soundness of candidates. Although this change was a return to the traditional Congregationalist position of locating final authority in the local congregation, the motive behind the policy change was to allow missionaries of broader theological views to serve with the ABCFM.[56] During the same time period, the Presbyterian Church USA was deciding how to respond to Charles Augustus Briggs, a Presbyterian clergyman and Union Theological Seminary instructor who denied the inerrancy of the Bible. Because of his views, the General Assembly vetoed his appointment to a chair at Union Seminary and specifically affirmed biblical inerrancy in a statement that came to be known as the Portland Deliverance of 1892. In 1893, the General Assembly convicted Briggs of heresy charges and disavowed any responsibility for Union Theological Seminary.[57]

Liberal strains of thought that prior to 1910 came under labels such "New Theology" or "liberalism" came increasingly to be associated with "modernism." In *The Modernist Impulse in American Protestantism*, a masterly survey of theological modernism from the 1870s to the 1930s,

53. Hutchison, *Modernist Impulse*, 3.
54. Winship, "Oren Root," 112.
55. Winship, "Oren Root," 113–14.
56. Hutchison, *Modernist Impulse*, 134; Xi, *Conversion*, 208–11.
57. Longfield, *Presbyterian Controversy*, 22–23.

William Hutchison helpfully framed modernism as an expression of theological liberalism with a self-conscious relation to the modern world. He notes that up until the later part of the nineteenth century, theological liberalism often proceeded without conscious reference to the modern world, basing its assertions upon Scripture, universal and timeless reason, or intuition. But theological modernism as an identifiable movement began when theological liberals started formulating their convictions in relation to the narrative of progress.[58] The term "modernist" itself came into common usage among Protestants by the 1920s, having been earlier employed among Roman Catholics in Europe.[59] Yet Hutchison's distinction notwithstanding, the difference between "liberalism" and "modernism" was far from clear to the general public in the early twentieth century, the two terms often being used interchangeably by proponents and opponents alike.[60] Some who self-identified as modernists sought to differentiate themselves from liberals but the two groups were lumped together as "modernists" by newspapers and the general public as fundamentalist-modernist controversies intensified in the 1920s.[61] Shailer Mathews, who worked as the dean of the School of Divinity at the University of Chicago from 1908-1933, was not entirely happy with the terms "modernism" and "modernist." Nevertheless, he decided to employ them in his 1924 book *The Faith of Modernism* because they were in common usage.[62] In 1932, the writers of *Re-Thinking Missions: A Laymen's Inquiry*, however, chose to avoid the term entirely, with the exception of a dismissive footnote which seemingly associated "modernism" with more secular ideas of cultural modernism or liberalism.[63]

Mathews sought to differentiate modernism from liberalism even while acknowledging that the former was indebted to the later. He held that modernism was merely a modern restatement of Christianity, and

---

58. Hutchison, *Modernist Impulse*, 4–5.

59. See Stanley, "Christianity, Modernism, and Modernization," 22–23; Hutchison, *Modernist Impulse*, 2.

60. See Hutchison, "Modernism and Missions," 110.

61. Marty, *Noise of Conflict*, 155; Mathews, *Faith*, 178; Dorrien, *American Liberal Theology*, 45–46.

62. Mathews, *Faith*, 14–16.

63. "[I]t is precisely the function of religion to bring man into the presence of the everlasting and real . . . It is the folly of "modernism," so-called, to overlook this, the most important aspect of religious truth." Hocking, *Re-Thinking Missions*, 18.

modernists were evangelical Christians who used modern methods.[64] In his book length apology, *The Faith of Modernism*, Mathews asserted,

> Modernists as a class are evangelical Christians. That is, they accept Jesus Christ as the revelation of a Savior God. The Modernist movement is, therefore, not identical with Liberalism. With all due respect for the influence of Liberalism in clarifying religious thought, its origin and interest tend toward the emphasis of intellectual belief and the criticism and repudiation of doctrines per se. The Modernist like any other investigator has a presumption in favor of the reality of that which he is studying. Both historically and by preference his religious starting point is the inherited orthodoxy of a continuing community of evangelical Christians.[65]

Mathews thus viewed modernism as an improvement on liberalism which, in contrast, tended to be deconstructive in its evaluation of traditional beliefs and failed to retain the vital spiritual elements and abiding principles of the Christian faith.[66] William Adams Brown of Union Theological Seminary, an influential modernist, likewise sought to retain the morality, values, and spiritual life of his Christian upbringing while wholeheartedly embracing modern scientific thought.[67] Modernists such as Brown and Mathews viewed themselves as standing in the evangelical tradition, building upon the abiding elements of the past and updating them for the needs of the modern world.[68] They sought to maintain a dual identity as both evangelical and modern, as seen in Mathews' succinct definition of modernism as, *"the use of scientific, historical, social method in understanding and applying evangelical Christianity to the needs of living persons"* (italics original).[69] Brown and Mathews did not want to completely equate modernism and liberalism but such distinction was regularly ignored by those on both sides of the theological spectrum.[70]

Modernism as a movement had distinctive tendencies but it cannot be summarized as a fixed set of beliefs. It was suspicious of creeds

---

64. Mathews, *Faith*, 17–20, 21, 23, 30.
65. Mathews, *Faith*, 34–35.
66. Dorrien, *American Liberal Theology*, 204–5.
67. Dorrien, *American Liberal Theology*, 41.
68. Dorrien, *American Liberal Theology*, 59–61.
69. Mathews, *Faith*, 35.
70. Machen, *Christianity and Liberalism*, 2; Dorrien, *American Liberal Theology*, 204; Hutchison, "Modernism and Missions," 110.

and was not embodied by any particular denomination or institution. Rather, modernism incorporated a range of associated convictions and attitudes towards faith and the world. In *The Modernist Impulse in American Protestantism*, William Hutchison summarized three broad tendencies present in modernist thinking, namely "conscious, intended adaptation of religious ideas to modern culture," the belief that "God is immanent in human cultural development and revealed through it," and the conviction that "human society is moving toward realization... of the Kingdom of God."[71] The broadening trends in theology surveyed earlier are discernable in Hutchison's summary of modernism yet it is significant that he summarized the movement in practical terms rather than theological formulae per se. While modernists certainly had theological beliefs, their primary concerns were the church's mission in the world and responsibility towards humanity.

MODERNIZING TREND 3: BROADENING MISSION

Like their more conservative contemporaries, modernists were driven by a desire to improve the world and to help humanity in practical terms. Where they differed from theological conservatives was in the nature and scope of their mission. The mission that modernists engaged in was broader than that of conservatives in the sense that their convictions allowed them to devote greater time and attention to social matters than they did to personal salvation or doctrine. Many, but not all, conservatives desired to maintain or prioritize evangelism and personal salvation while also engaging in educational, medical, and other social endeavors. The China Inland Mission (CIM) is a notable example of a conservative mission that focused almost exclusively on personal salvation. In contrast, on-going widespread interest in pursuing both personal and social salvation was evidenced in the range of topics covered in the meetings of the International Missionary Council (IMC) in 1928. The series of reports issued by the council included volumes on the Christian message, religious education, the relationship of younger and older churches, race conflict, industrialism, rural problems, and international missionary co-operation.[72] Modernists, meanwhile, found the capacity to broaden their engagement in social works because they

---

71. Hutchison, *Modernist Impulse*, 2.

72. Yao, *Fundamentalist Movement*, 32–33; International Missionary Council, *Report of the Jerusalem Meeting*.

were less encumbered with the need to preach for the conversion of individuals. Though modernists often wanted individuals to embrace Christ in some manner, the salvation of society was more important than that of individuals, who in any case were probably not in danger of going to hell. Without the need to evangelize, it was easier for modernists to devote time to other endeavors. Therefore, although the mission mandate of modernists narrowed in the sense that they dropped from their agenda evangelization as traditionally conceived, it also broadened when the range of works they pursued is considered.

The modernist conception of mission put little priority on doctrinal formulae but rather focused on the role of religion in meeting the needs of the modern world.[73] However, religion showed itself to be the "enemy of progress when it has fastened upon society the authority of the past."[74] Particular historical expressions of faith, it was thought, arose only because people were seeking to adapt Christianity to their own situation. Mathews summarized the history of doctrine with the affirmation "Christianity has been the attempt of men to rely upon Christian principles in meeting the needs of their actual life-situations."[75] Received doctrines should be evaluated for their usefulness "to nerve men and women for more courageous living."[76]

For modernists, ethics and improving humanity were at the core of Christianity. In their view, the premillennial pessimism and individualistic salvation preached by some conservatives would not save the world.[77] Love was the force that would change the world, not truths.[78] Modernists saw the world being civilized but saw forces opposed to religion rising up amidst that civilization as well. Marxism and materialism threatened the progressive development of peace and human progress but a modern form of Christianity, they claimed, had the power to save the world.[79] The assessment of *Re-Thinking Missions* was that secularism, materialism, and naturalism were the main opponents to faith. Therefore, Christians

---

73. Mathews, *Faith*, 1–2.
74. Mathews, *Faith*, 2.
75. Mathews, *Faith*, 17.
76. Mathews, *Faith*, 30.
77. Mathews, *Faith*, 10.
78. Mathews, *Faith*, 13; Yao, *Fundamentalist Movement*, 191.
79. Dorrien, *American Liberal Theology*, 199.

should stand with other religions against these common enemies rather than oppose non-Christian religions as in the past.[80]

Even while affirming the good in other religions, modernists did not give up their evangelistic mandate. However, evangelism for modernists was less about preaching and more about helping others experience Jesus Christ through social service ministries. On the surface, modernists and conservatives sometimes appeared to be saying the same things and to be in agreement. But modernists often filled traditional terms with new meaning. Fundamentalists often asserted that the use of traditional phrases without further clarification allowed modernists to hide their real views.[81] The modernist talked of salvation, but being "saved" may have implied no more than adopting the spirit of Christ and following his example of good will towards men.[82] The language of evangelization persisted but salvation was conceived as social development and moral improvement, a departure from the former Protestant consensus that encompassed both personal and social salvation. Modernists employed the language of "salvation" but it was the corruptions of the modern world, not eternal punishment, that people needed to be saved from. They wanted to "bring others into the very presence of God revealed in Jesus Christ" and to "find the way to spiritual reserves in order that they may get power to resist evil and endure success."[83] The writers of *Re-Thinking Missions* adopted and re-interpreted the older language of salvation to affirm the evangelistic mandate of missions, though they marked off the word "saving" with quotation marks to indicate that the traditional Christian idea of salvation from hell was obsolete. They wrote that the "motive of all religious missions is an ardent desire to communicate a spiritual value regarded as unique and of supreme importance. It is an integral part of the passion for 'saving' men and peoples, and implies a peculiar sense of tragedy and danger of the unsaved."[84] Modernists sought the establishment of the kingdom of God in this world, which consisted of bringing the spiritual, material, and educational resources of the West to the rest of the world.[85] While conservatives continued

---

80. Hocking, *Re-Thinking Missions*, 30–33.

81. "Laymen's Foreign Missions Inquiry," 18–22; Yao, *Fundamentalist Movement*, 70; See Machen, "Modernism and the Board," 10–11.

82. Baker, "Reactions," 391.

83. Mathews, *Faith*, 173.

84. Hocking, *Re-Thinking Missions*, 6.

85. As a consequence of the First World War, there was increasing doubt cast

to affirm the necessity of personal salvation alongside societal development, modernists were less certain of the necessity of personal salvation. They were more concerned with bringing spiritual and physical resources for the improvement of both individuals and society in the present. Mathews summarized this modernizing change in the goal of Christianity, asserting "[w]e may be decreasingly interested in the metaphysics of Jesus Christ, but we shall be all the more determined to show that his life and teachings reveal the divine purpose in humanity and therefore it is practicable to organize life upon his revelation of good will."[86] Christianity was the full and final revelation of Jesus Christ, superior to other religions, but the triumph of Christianity would be more ethical than religious. In this vein, *Re-Thinking Missions* held out the "supreme good" of humanity as the important goal of Christian missions.[87]

Although modernists denied that particular doctrinal statements were binding upon all Christians, they were not universalists in the sense that there were no boundaries to the Christian faith or that faith in Christ did not matter. Rather than use creedal statements to denote what makes one a Christian, modernists often affirmed that loyalty to Jesus Christ is the mark of Christianity. According to Mathews, being a modernist does not mean indifference to truth "that lies below doctrines." Being a Christian means not only personal loyalty to Jesus Christ, but also loyalty to the Christian movement and the Christian church.[88] Mathews wrote, "*We are Christians when this common effort* [for social good] *is controlled by the attitudes and convictions which from the days of its Founder have been the heart of the continuous ongoing Christian community*" (italics original).[89] For modernists, the boundaries of Christianity did not consist in determining who was saved or unsaved, but rather in looking for those who were moving towards loyalty to Christ and his purposes to help humanity.

---

upon the assumption that mission was primarily a conferral of the benefits of Western Christian civilization to the non-Western world. Stanley, *Christianity in the Twentieth Century*, 17.

86. Mathews, *Faith*, 175; Hocking, *Re-Thinking Missions*, 59.

87. Hocking, *Re-Thinking Missions*, 19.

88. Mathews, *Faith*, 172; Hocking, *Re-Thinking Missions*, 54.

89. Mathews, *Faith*, 173.

Modernists on the Mission Field

While there existed a global trend towards societal, political, and economic modernization, theological modernism was less prominent and not every place where theological modernism exerted influence turned into an arena of conflict with fundamentalism. The United States was the primary battlefield for fundamentalism and modernism, and China was second. There was some debate in India and Korea, but not as much as China. Missionaries in Egypt successfully sidestepped theological controversy and such debates were rare elsewhere in Africa as modernizing trends took hold more slowly in the absence of the type of economic, political, religious, and societal development gaining ground in other regions.[90] Even without the presence of conflict with fundamentalists, the impact of modernism can be measured from observation of the trends and emphases in communication and activity among those involved in Christian ministry. In this vein, Kevin Yao has noted that changes in missionaries' theology, though not loudly trumpeted, were a significant force behind changes in approach and methodology in China missions during the 1920s and 1930s.[91] Summarizing Hutchison, Yao pointed out "some of the major traits of liberal missionary thinking: first, the tendency to undercut the exclusivity of Christian claims to truth and enthusiasm for inter-religious dialogue and cooperation; second, the lack of premillennial expectation of the second coming and the sense of urgent direct evangelism; third, confidence in the coming Kingdom of God on earth and zeal for social service oriented missions."[92] To this list, Yao adds two features of liberal theology found among missionaries in China. First, God is the Father of all humans and secondly, the social and ethical implications of Christology, namely an emphasis on love and Christ as moral exemplar.[93]

Modernists retained traditional Christian activities such as worship services, preaching, and prayers, but increasingly emphasized social service ministries. Modernists were confident in humanity's ability to build the kingdom of God on earth, which found expression

---

90. See Stanley, "Christianity, Modernism, and Modernization," 25; Sharkey, *Americans Evangelicals in Egypt,*" 103–4.

91. Yao, *Fundamentalist Movement*, 39.

92. Not all conservatives were premillennialists. The majority of Presbyterians, for example, were postmillennialists. Hutchison, *Errand*, 102–11; Yao, *Fundamentalist Movement*, 12.

93. Yao, *Fundamentalist Movement*, 42–43.

in dedication of great amounts of time, personnel, and resources to schools, hospitals, and orphanages.[94] Although conservatives were often involved in social works as well, they experienced on-going tension in determining how these activities should be prioritized in relation to their primary mission of evangelism.[95] When modernists taught and preached, they tended to undercut the exclusivity of Christian claims to truth and expressed a disinterest in doctrinal formulations. Traditional beliefs were not necessarily repudiated directly, but they were neglected and obscured in favor of other emphases.[96]

On the mission field, modernists tended to favor inter-religious dialogue and cooperation over evangelism and the seeking of converts.[97] In *The Conversion of Missionaries*, Lian Xi points out that the biggest change among liberally minded missionaries in early twentieth century China was their enthusiasm for religious cooperation and inclusiveness.[98] Modernists displayed a lack of urgency in traditional evangelism that stressed repentance and personal commitment to Jesus Christ. The vocabulary of evangelism and salvation was increasingly redefined in terms of social rather than personal salvation.

Although both modernist and conservative missionaries of various types valued church unity, modernists were far more content than conservatives to enter into inter-denominational and church union organizations and institutions with minimal doctrinal bases.[99] Modernists were content with a unity primarily based on action and service in Christ's name rather than shared doctrines.[100] Modernists wanted peace, not division over doctrine. To that end, they wanted fundamentalists to simply be quiet so that everyone could get on with building a new social and religious order for the modern world.

---

94. Yao, *Fundamentalist Movement*, 12.

95. The contested relationship between education and evangelism in Thailand will be discussed in chapter 9.

96. Yao, *Fundamentalist Movement*, 70.

97. Hocking, *Re-Thinking Missions*, 58–59.

98. Xi, *Conversion*, 19.

99. Yao, *Fundamentalist Movement*, 194.

100. Mathews, *Faith*, 79.

3

Modernism and Fundamentalism in the Presbyterian Church in the U.S.A. and its Board of Foreign Missions

THE HOME DENOMINATION OF the American Presbyterian missionaries in Thailand was the Presbyterian Church USA (PCUSA), the oldest and largest American Presbyterian denomination. At the end of the nineteenth century, the PCUSA was a Northern denomination, having split with its Southern counterpart, the Presbyterian Church in the U.S., in 1861. The doctrinal standards of the PCUSA were the Westminster Confession of Faith and Catechisms. Second only to the Bible, these documents were the standard of orthodoxy for the denomination and specified what Presbyterians understood the Bible to teach. Yet starting in the late nineteenth century, doctrinal broadening resulted in various "camps" within the church.[1] While some conservatives insisted ministers strictly subscribe to the Westminster Standards, others advocated for looser interpretation of those standards.[2] Concerns about liberalism in the church prompted the General Assemblies of 1910 and 1916 to adopt measures requiring ministerial candidates to affirm "the fundamentals" of the faith, namely the inerrancy of the Bible, the virgin birth, substitutionary atonement, the bodily resurrection of Christ, and the miracle working power of Christ.

---

1. Revision of the Westminster Confession in 1903 and organic union the Cumberland Presbyterian Church in 1906 are two early indicators of increasing openness to doctrinal modification. Longfield, *Presbyterian Controversy*, 23–24, 61–62.

2. There was an abortive attempt to revise the Westminster Confession in 1893 and a subsequent successful effort in 1903. See Loetscher, *Broadening Church*, 39–47, 83–89.

The identification of these points as essential to the Christian faith was influenced by *The Fundamentals*, a series of books published between 1910 and 1915 which constituted a conservative re-statement of the fundamentals of the faith in the face of rising liberalism.[3]

THE BEGINNING OF CONFLICT AND DEFINING FUNDAMENTALISM

Conservative efforts to preserve traditional understandings of the Westminster Standards and historic Christian faith did not pass unnoticed by liberally-minded churchmen. In 1922, Harry Emerson Fosdick, a Baptist pastoring a Presbyterian church in New York, launched a frontal assault against conservatives, preaching what would become the most famous sermon of his career, "Shall the Fundamentalists Win?" Fosdick asserted that liberals were genuine evangelical Christians seeking to reconcile the traditional faith with modern knowledge. Fundamentalists, on the other hand, were intolerant of anyone who disagreed with their understanding of the faith, wishing to "shut the doors of Christian fellowship" against them. The sermon was widely distributed in print and Clarence Macartney of Philadelphia responded to Fosdick's sermon with a sermon of his own, titled "Shall Unbelief Win?" The ensuing controversy eventually led to Fosdick's resignation from First Presbyterian Church.[4]

It is notable that Fosdick chose the word "fundamentalist" in directing his attack and it is necessary to briefly outline the origin and use of this contested term.[5] Harkening back to the book series *The Fundamentals*, the term "fundamentalist" was coined by Curtis Lee Laws, a Baptist newspaper editor. Laws defined it as "a person ready to do battle royal for the Fundamentals."[6] The label "fundamentalist" was used as a term of self-identification from at least the 1920s onward, but even those who thought of themselves as fundamentalists did not use the label exclusively. Yao notes in the 1920s and 1930s, fundamentalists also referred to themselves as "evangelicals" or "conservatives."[7] The term "evangelical," however, was not a meaningful term in the theological debates of

---

3. Longfield, *Presbyterian Controversy*, 21, 25.

4. Longfield, *Presbyterian Controversy*, 9–11, 126–27.

5. The term "fundamentalist" is still in current usage today, albeit the definition has broadened to include reactionary elements within other religious groups, especially Islam. Bebbington and Jones, *Evangelicalism and Fundamentalism*, 2–3.

6. Marsden, *Fundamentalism*, 159.

7. Yao, *Fundamentalist Movement*, 283.

the inter-war period since both conservatives and liberals used it as a self-descriptor. "Fundamentalist," on the other hand, began as a positive identifying term for militantly anti-modern conservatives, but quickly became more common as a smear term intended to marginalize anti-modernists than it was as a self-identifier of people or of a movement.[8] As such, many whom their opponents called "fundamentalists" wanted to distance themselves from a label that had quickly become associated with obtuseness, intolerance, and bigotry. J. Gresham Machen, Clarence Macartney, and William Jennings Bryan were all labeled fundamentalists by others but failed to embrace the label for themselves.[9]

Historically, the identity of fundamentalists and the nature of fundamentalism has been murky, though in recent years scholars have brought greater clarity to the matter, most notably George Marsden, Ernest Sandeen, Joel Carpenter, and Michael Hamilton.[10] Marsden provided one of the most enduring and accepted definitions of fundamentalism when he described it as "militantly anti-modernist Protestant evangelicalism."[11] The exact origins and nature of Fundamentalism, however, are contested. Whereas Sandeen sees the roots of Fundamentalism in nineteenth-century millenarianism that rebranded itself in the twentieth century, Marsden sees millenarianism as a sub-movement that became part of a broader anti-modernist coalition, namely Fundamentalism, that originated after World War I. Joel Carpenter, questioning Marsden's postwar dating of the beginning of fundamentalism, sought to synthesize the views of Marsden and Sandeen. Carpenter advanced the thesis that Sandeen's millenarian movement was part of a broader interdenominational evangelicalism that preceded and succeeded the controversies of the 1920s and 1930s. More recently, Michael Hamilton has challenged these earlier theses, making the case there was not a fundamentalist movement per se, except in the eyes of liberals and in the wishful thinking of a small number of conservatives.[12] Instead of a movement, Hamilton saw a network of interdenominational evangelicals and denominational traditionalists, some of whom fought against modernism among Northern Baptist and American Presbyterian (Northern) churches but were never

---

8. Marty, *Noise*, 160–61; See Hamilton, "Interdenominational Evangelicalism."

9. See Hamilton, "Interdenominational Evangelicalism," 244–46.

10. Marsden, *Fundamentalism*; Sandeen, *Roots of Fundamentalism*; Carpenter, *Revive Us Again*; Hamilton, "Interdenominational Evangelicalism."

11. Marsden, *Fundamentalism*, 4.

12. See Hamilton, "Interdenominational Evangelicalism," 264.

able to effectively form coalitions to do so. There were a series of public conflicts over modernism and fundamentalism in these denominations but the majority of anti-modern conservatives did not militantly oppose modernists. Yet it was not uncommon for liberals to brand conservatives as fundamentalists with a broad brushstroke even though they may not have displayed the militancy which Marsden identified as a key element of fundamentalism. In a 1924 newspaper editorial, Quaker Walter C. Woodward argued that there are really very few extreme modernists or fundamentalists, but those who are make noise. Those labels, in his estimation, were thrown around too freely and caused division.[13] However, regardless of how many people in the interwar period qualified as fundamentalists according to Marsden's definition, it is necessary to understand the rhetorical importance of "fundamentalist" as a smear term used by those who wish to discredit and marginalize theologically conservative opponents. With these aspects of the history of "fundamentalist" in mind, I have used the term in this book without comment when found in primary and secondary sources, when a theological conservative was referred to as a fundamentalist in his own time, or when a given person fits Marsden's definition of a militantly anti-modernist Protestant evangelical. Unlike much common usage of the term, my use of "fundamentalist" is not intended to be derogatory.

PRESBYTERIAN CONTROVERSIES OVER MODERNISM AND FUNDAMENTALISM IN THE 1920S

Following on from Fosdick's initial volley, the Presbyterian Church U.S.A. endured nearly two decades of intermittent conflict over issues of modernism. The 1923 General Assembly saw William Jennings Bryan fail to convince the Assembly to prohibit the teaching of evolution in Presbyterian schools, and liberals represented by Henry Sloane Coffin rallied around Fosdick, against whom the Assembly directed the New York presbytery to take action.[14] In the six months following the Assembly, a group of liberal clergymen wrote a brief paper entitled *An Affirmation Designed to Safeguard the Unity and Liberty of the Presbyterian Church in the United States of America*. More commonly referred to as the *Auburn Affirmation*, named after the seminary affiliation of the initial drafter of the document, this statement asserted the right to liberty of conscience

---

13. Woodward, "Too Many Labels," 243–44.
14. Longfield, *Presbyterian Controversy*, 72–76.

in theological matters and became "the chief symbol of the liberal movement within the church."[15] At the 1924 General Assembly, conservative Clarence Macartney narrowly won the moderatorship but the majority of decisions were centrist. No action was taken against the Auburn Affirmation and the matter of two ministerial candidates who refused to affirm the virgin birth was referred to their presbytery for appropriate action.[16] Outside of annual Assembly meetings, tensions continued to percolate as liberals and conservatives preached and published to gather supporters to their cause. The 1925 General Assembly saw Charles Erdman of Princeton Seminary elected to the moderatorship. Although schism loomed as liberals seriously considered walking out, moderate conservative Erdman and liberal Coffin convinced them to wait.[17] In 1929, controversy that was building at Princeton Seminary came to a head. The faculty were divided over how much doctrinal tolerance should be allowed and the General Assembly voted to re-organize the administration and board of the seminary. Included on the new board were two men who signed the Auburn Affirmation. J. Gresham Machen saw this as a sure sign the seminary was headed in the wrong direction. Machen, along with a group of fellow faculty, clergymen, alumni, and concerned laymen established Westminster Theological Seminary in Philadelphia as an evangelical alternative that would continue the Old Princeton tradition.[18] The next phase of fundamentalist-modernist conflict would revolve around the Board of Foreign Missions, a story to which we will turn after a brief survey of the history and structure of the Board and its Missions.

THE BOARD OF FOREIGN MISSIONS OF THE PRESBYTERIAN CHURCH IN THE U.S.A.

The American Presbyterian missionaries in Thailand came under the jurisdiction of the Board of Foreign Missions, a PCUSA denominational entity tasked with administering and supervising foreign missions efforts. "The Board," as it was commonly referred to in correspondence and reports, was intimately connected with its "missions" in various countries. Among the American Presbyterians, "mission" was used in a dual sense to refer to both the organization of a group of missionaries in

15. Longfield, *Presbyterian Controversy*, 77–78.
16. Longfield, *Presbyterian Controversy*, 125–27.
17. Longfield, *Presbyterian Controversy*, 152–53.
18. Longfield, *Presbyterian Controversy*, 162–74.

a particular country as well as the Board's work in a particular country in an administrative sense.[19] Sometimes a single geopolitical country had more than one mission. China had seven missions and Thailand had two missions (Siam mission and Laos mission) until their unification in 1920.[20] A brief overview of the Board's history, organization, aims, and relationship to modernism and modernization will provide context for the Thailand-based missionaries' interactions with the Board that will appear in subsequent chapters.

Origin of the Board of Foreign Missions

At the dawn of the American foreign missionary enterprise in the early nineteenth century, Presbyterians did not have a denomination-wide organization for sending missionaries to foreign fields. As such, PCUSA churches sent missionaries under the auspices of other groups, especially the American Board of Commissioners for Foreign Missions (ABCFM), an inter-denominational mission board with a large representation of Congregationalists. In 1837, PCUSA formed its own denominational Board of Foreign Missions and established Missions in numerous countries around the world during the course of the nineteenth century.[21] Some of these were works begun under the auspices of the ABCFM prior to the formation of the Presbyterian Board, but most were new works.[22] The Board sent both ordained ministers and laypeople, and was responsible for the administration and finances of the missionaries, although not necessarily for their theological orthodoxy. An early objection to the Board was the claim that it was un-Presbyterian, namely it rivaled local churches, presbyteries, and synods as an extra-biblical church court. The Board sought to deflect this criticism by committing to send no ordained man to the mission field without the recommendation of his presbytery, while also recognizing supervision of a person's morals and doctrine was an ecclesiastical function, not to be exercised by the Board.[23] The 1854 Manual of the Board stated that the Board was a "Permanent Committee of the General Assembly" that is "general

---

19. Rycroft, *Ecumenical Witness*, 217.
20. Moffett, "Relation of the Board," 26.
21. Rycroft, *Ecumenical Witness*, 42–50, 55–57; Moffett, "Relation of the Board," 15–22.
22. Rycroft, *Ecumenical Witness*, 290–91, 294–95.
23. Moffett, "Relation of the Board," 12.

authority, supervision and control of the work of missions" but is only an executive agency of the General Assembly, not an independent entity. However, as Samuel Moffett noted, the Board of Foreign Missions was "historically and functionally" much "more than a permanent committee of the General Assembly."[24] Also, the Board was not able to remove itself entirely from questions of theology, nor did all members of the denomination believe it should do so, as would become clear during the era of fundamentalist-modernist conflict in the denomination.[25]

Organization of the Board and Its Missions

After its founding in 1837, the Board was administratively re-organized several times but the most significant change was a shift of responsibilities away from Board members to its secretarial staff.[26] The day-to-day business of the Board was handled by its secretaries while Board members merely reviewed and approved major decisions. From 1899 to 1922, the Foreign Department of the Board had three corresponding secretaries communicating with field missionaries. Following a merger in 1923 with the Women's Foreign Missionary Board, two of the secretaries, Robert E. Speer and Arthur J. Brown, were elevated and given responsibility for overseeing the entire work of the Board.[27] The Board and the missions they oversaw were in regular communication on issues of finances, personnel, and mission activity. Each mission met annually for meetings lasting several days. At these meetings, each missionary presented a report of their work and there were times of prayer, Bible study, and fellowship. They devoted many hours to budget planning and personnel requests for the upcoming year, which were then communicated to the Board. In fields where a national church had been established, national representatives were invited to attend one or more sessions of the mission meetings, though they were not direct participants in the budget and personnel planning. Missions and national churches often had fraternal and friendly relations but they were separate entities. As indigenous leadership developed, these leaders were increasingly consulted but a mission's obligatory partner in discussion and decision making

---

24. Moffett, "Relation of the Board," 13.
25. Longfield, *Presbyterian Controversy*, 181–208.
26. Moffett, "Relation of the Board," 24; Rycroft, *Ecumenical Witness*, 55.
27. Moffett, "Relation of the Board," 25–26; Schlect, "Onward Christian Administrators," 142–47.

was the Board, not the national church.[28] One example of increasing national involvement is the Siam Mission's decision to add Siamese Christians to its various committees in 1927.[29] Outside of the annual meetings, the missions were administered by an Executive Committee, consisting of a full-time Executive Secretary and other representatives elected by and from the members of the mission. The Executive Secretary was the primary point of contact and communication between the mission and the Board via the Corresponding Secretary assigned to the mission. All mission members were welcome to communicate directly with the Board's Corresponding Secretary for their mission, and many did regularly. However, matters affecting the whole mission, as well as particular personnel issues, were handled via the Executive Committee and its Secretary. To aid the missions in carrying out their work, Board secretaries would occasionally make overseas tours to get a better understanding of conditions in individual mission fields, encourage missionaries, consult with mission and national leaders on problems, and gather material for promoting the missions' work on the home side. This model of Board and mission organization predominated until the postwar period when a changed state of world affairs forced the Board and its missions to radically re-evaluate the relationship between themselves and the so-called "younger churches."[30]

Purpose and Works of the Board and Its Missions

The purpose and works of the Board and its Missions remained largely constant over the years, though varied in expression and emphases. In an 1846 letter to the Board's outgoing missionaries to Thailand, secretary Walter Lowrie reminded the missionaries that their activities should include direct preaching of the gospel, translation and distribution of the Bible and Christian literature, education for training indigenous leaders, and medical work. Their primary purpose, however, was to make "known the Gospel to the benighted heathen."[31]

A more developed statement of these basic purposes was given in the 1922 *Manual* of the Board, which defined the aim of foreign missions as follows:

28. Rycroft, *Ecumenical Witness*, 217–18.
29. Stewart, "Recommendations Made by Joint Committee, 1927."
30. Rycroft, *Ecumenical Witness*, 220–21.
31. McFarland, *Historical Sketch*, 354–57.

> The supreme and controlling aim of foreign missions is to make the Lord Jesus Christ known to all men as their Divine Savior and to persuade them to become His disciples; to gather these disciples into Christian churches which shall be self-propagating, self-supporting and self-governing; to cooperate, so long as necessary, with these churches in the evangelizing of their countrymen, and in bringing to bear on all human life the spirit and principles of Christ.[32]

In pursuit of this purpose, the Board *Manual* deemed "all methods and forms of missionary service legitimate in so far as they contribute to the realization of the aim stated" above, with recognition that the proportion and relation of various methods depended on varying conditions upon the mission fields themselves. The *Manual* specifically cited certain types of approved mission work, namely evangelistic or church work, medical work, literary work, and educational work. Concerning the latter, the threefold purpose of educational work was to evangelize non-Christians, leaven non-Christian society, and nurture Christian children.[33] These purposes of mission education, which mirrored the findings of Commission III of the 1910 World Missionary Conference in Edinburgh, will be discussed in chapter 9 in relation to their contested implementation in Thailand. In practice, there was considerable variety in how evangelistic, educational, and medical work were prioritized on mission fields. But the *Manual* was important as a unifying point of reference to which missionaries of all theological stripes had to relate.

The Board Amidst Fundamentalist-Modernist Controversy

As a denominational entity, the Board of Foreign Mission was no stranger to the conflicts over modernism that bombarded the PCUSA. From the early 1920s, the orthodoxy of the Board began to be called into question and controversy over the Board's claimed collusion with modernism did not finally subside until after the departure of J. Gresham Machen and the formation of the Orthodox Presbyterian Church in 1936.

Conflict over the Board began in 1921 when the English Anglican dispensationalist W.H. Griffith Thomas, returning from a recent tour of China and Japan, claimed there was rampant theological liberalism among

---

32. PCUSA, *Manual*, 1922, 5.
33. PCUSA, *Manual*, 1922, 69.

American Presbyterian missionaries in China.[34] He told of missionaries who held "loose views about the authority and inspiration of the Bible" and busied themselves with educational and social works, while leaving evangelism to the Chinese.[35] Board secretary Arthur J. Brown corresponded with Thomas, warning that his sweeping accusations would harm missions work, causing church members to withhold financial support.[36] There were several abortive attempts to get the PCUSA General Assembly to investigate but the issue was set aside when Robert E. Speer of the Board and Charles Erdman of Princeton Seminary assured the assembly of the Board's fidelity.[37] However, as a result of Thomas's report, John Leighton Stuart, a Presbyterian missionary to China and the first president of Yenching University, was tried for heresy in his home synod of Virginia for writing that Christianity is the fullest revelation but only one of many admirable faiths, "not different in kind from the revelation of earlier ages." He survived the trial and continued missionary work in China until he was appointed American ambassador to China in 1946.[38]

Concerns about modernism among the Board and its missionaries continued to surface in the years that followed. In 1923, Princeton seminary professor Dick Wilson wrote an article criticizing the Board for entangling itself in alliances with missionaries who did not hold Presbyterian doctrine and for hindering their missionaries from joining theologically sound organizations such as the Bible Union in China.[39] The 1924 conservative-controlled General Assembly successfully eliminated liberal clergyman William P. Merrill from the roster of nominees for the Board of Foreign Missions.[40] In 1925, the Board excised Sam Higginbotham and his Agricultural Institute from its North India Mission following complaints from fellow missionaries that he focused too much on providing social services, to the neglect of evangelistic activity. The Board, however, continued to support Higginbotham's Institute as

---

34. Marsden, *Fundamentalism*, 168.

35. Hutchison, *Modernist Impulse*, 260–61; See Thomas, "Modernism in China," 630–71.

36. Yao, *Fundamentalist Movement*, 81–84.

37. Marsden, *Fundamentalism*, 168.

38. Hollinger, *Protestants Abroad*, 318.

39. Rian, *Presbyterian Conflict*, 127; For a detailed account of the Bible Union of China, see Yao, *Fundamentalist Movement*, 55–100.

40. Longfield, *Presbyterian Controversy*, 126; Quirk, "Auburn Affirmation," 249; Longfield, "William P. Merrill," 66.

an independent project.⁴¹ In 1929, J. Gresham Machen wrote a letter to Robert E. Speer, senior secretary of the Board, asking "Can Evangelical Christians Support Our Foreign Board?" Machen asserted that the Board discriminated against militantly conservative missionary candidates. The language used in Speer's book *Are Foreign Missions Done For?* and in the Board *Manual* was, Machen alleged, "dishearteningly vague and evasive," such that even modernists could agree with it. He thought that the theological soundness of the Board was suspect because four of fifteen of the ministerial members of the Board, as well as the Candidate Secretary, signed the Auburn Affirmation. In reply, Speer defended the evangelical orthodoxy of both himself and the Board's missionaries, denying there was any bias in missionary candidate assessment. Speer claimed that he agreed with "almost all" of Machen's "great convictions," but nonetheless found fault with Machen's methods and extra-biblical language. For Speer, the controversy caused by Machen was a groundless waste of time that harmed Christian unity and the mission of the church.⁴² For the duration of his forty-six year career with the Board (1891-1937), Speer affirmed conservative theological beliefs yet advocated a broad vision for the social dimensions of Christianity not dissimilar to that of theological liberals.⁴³ He believed that Christian unity was essential for the furtherance of the evangelistic mission of the church and took a severe dislike to controversy. Because the PCUSA during the time of Speer's tenure had a conservative majority, Speer thought the presence of modernists was a lesser threat to the mission of the church than the controversy being stirred up by Machen and other fundamentalists.⁴⁴ Although publicly cordial to Machen, Speer spoke of him in disparaging terms privately, as did fellow Board Secretary Arthur J. Brown. In private correspondence, Speer referred to Carl McIntire as "one of Machen's henchmen" and Brown called Machen and his associates "fanatics."⁴⁵

A new episode of conflict over modernism and missions started in 1932 following the publication of *Re-Thinking Missions: a Laymen's Inquiry After One Hundred Years*.⁴⁶ Initiated and funded by Baptist lay-

41. Hollinger, *Protestants Abroad*, 67.
42. Longfield, *Presbyterian Controversy*, 181-83.
43. For a detailed survey of Speer's life and career, see Piper, *Robert E. Speer*.
44. Longfield, *Presbyterian Controversy*, 78, 186-99, 207-33.
45. Speer to Brown, January 29, 1935; Brown to Speer, January 31, 1935, PHS.
46. This book is variously referred to as *Re-Thinking Missions, the Laymen's Report, the Laymen's Inquiry,* and the *Report of Appraisal*.

man and business magnate John D. Rockefeller, *Re-Thinking Missions* was the report of an inter-denominational Commission of Appraisal that visited mission works in China, Japan, India, and Burma in order to assess the state of mission work in the contemporary world.[47] The report's theological principles were thoroughly modernist, suggesting the main opponent of Christianity is now secularism, materialism and naturalism, not other religions. The report asserted that Christianity should stand with non-Christian faiths in Asia for religion in general against secular, anti-religion philosophies.[48] The report claimed that religion cannot be handed on as a "finished doctrine" and both theological outlook and religious experience must be adjusted in light "of advance in scientific thought and of philosophical activity."[49] The aim of missions should be to "seek with people of other lands a true knowledge and love of God, expressing in life and word what we have learned through Jesus Christ."[50] The uniqueness of Christianity is in its simplicity and morality.[51] Mission work should put less emphasis on doctrine and denominations, and more on inspiration, social work, and church union.[52] The report lamented that most missionaries on the field today are second-rate workers and it gave numerous recommendations for improving various areas of mission work, such as education, literature, medical work, agriculture, industry, and administration.[53]

While liberal Christians praised the report, multiple denominations who initially supported it quickly distanced themselves from its more radical assertions.[54] Fundamentalist objections were many. The report was limited and superficial, not thorough and objective as it claimed. The preparers of the report were biased and unsound theological assumptions undergirded it. The report presented a relativist view of non-Christian religions and downgraded preaching and evangelism in favor of social

---

47. Longfield, *Presbyterian Controversy*, 199–200; Yao, *Fundamentalist Movement*, 239–41.

48. Hocking, *Re-Thinking Missions*, 29–32.

49. Hocking, *Re-Thinking Missions*, 18–19, 45.

50. Hocking, *Re-Thinking Missions*, 59.

51. Hocking, *Re-Thinking Missions*, 50–51.

52. Hocking, *Re-Thinking Missions*, 92–96.

53. Hocking, *Re-Thinking Missions*, 18–19, 114–15.

54. Longfield, *Presbyterian Controversy*, 200; Hutchison, *Errand*, 158–75; Baker, "Reactions," 379–98.

services.⁵⁵ Mission boards of multiple denominations issued statements on the report, including the PCUSA Board of Foreign Missions. In its statement, the Board re-affirmed the evangelical basis of mission and expressed confidence in the quality and devotion of its missionaries. Taken apart from "its theological basis," the report contained "many recommendations . . . which the Board believes to be right, and which it has sought and will continue to seek to carry out in the work under its care."⁵⁶ The American Baptist response was similar to the Presbyterians, while Methodists and Congregationalists were more enthusiastic. *Christian Century*, a theologically liberal journal, praised the report and published a laudatory article on it, authored by Presbyterian missionary and novelist Pearl Buck.⁵⁷ Buck effused enthusiasm for the report, calling it "the only book I have ever read which seems to me literally true in its every observation and right in its every conclusion."⁵⁸ In December 1932, the Presbyterian journal *Christianity Today* devoted several pages to the Laymen's Report and various responses to it, including Buck's article.⁵⁹ It was speculated that the Board would continue to make vaguely conservative statements in order to satisfy both its conservative and modernist constituencies, while simultaneously hoping Buck would quietly go away.⁶⁰

But Buck did not go away. In January 1933, speaking in New York to a group of Presbyterian women and members of the Board, Buck rejected several fundamental Christian doctrines and saw little future for foreign missions.⁶¹ The Board, however, did not take any action against Buck and fundamentalists wanted to know why the Board neither dismissed her for heresy nor more strongly denounced *Re-Thinking Missions*.⁶² On Jan 8, 1933, Clarence Macartney spoke against *Re-Thinking Missions* in a sermon at his Pittsburgh church. Shortly thereafter his church sent a letter to the Board wanting to know why the Board had

---

55. Yao, *Fundamentalist Movement*, 247–53; See Machen, "Modernism and the Board"; "Laymen's Foreign Missions Inquiry," 18–22.

56. "Laymen's Foreign Missions Inquiry," 20.

57. "Laymen's Foreign Missions Inquiry," 20–22.

58. Buck, "Laymen's Mission Report"; Longfield, *Presbyterian Controversy*, 201.

59. *Christianity Today* was published by Presbyterian and Reformed Publishing Company from 1930 to 1949. It is unrelated to the magazine of the same name started by Billy Graham.

60. "Laymen's Foreign Missions Inquiry," 18–22.

61. Longfield, *Presbyterian Controversy*, 201.

62. Speer to Brown, March 22, 1933, PHS.

not condemned the doctrinal statements of *Re-Thinking Missions*, and whether Buck was still associated with the Board. Charles Erdman replied on behalf of the Board, re-affirming its orthodoxy, and conceding that the Buck matter was "exceedingly difficult and perplexing." However, the Board was hoping she could be won back to the missionary cause.[63] Such was not to be. Buck submitted her resignation on May 1, 1933, which the Board accepted "with deep regret."[64] In a letter to journalist St. Clair McKelway, Board secretary Cleland McAfee explained that Buck resigned because she did not wish the controversy surrounding her to be an embarrassment to the Board and her resignation was "not provoked by differences with the Board." McAfee asserted that the Board "never resented her criticism of the work nor asked her in any way to retract anything she has said." She returned to China with the good wishes of the Board who welcomed "the increased number of persons who are not connected with the Mission organizations who continue to do Christian work as Mrs. Buck will do."[65]

In January 1933, Speer gave a lengthy critique of *Re-Thinking Missions* in the *Missionary Review of the World*, but this was not successful in deflecting fundamentalist criticism.[66] J. Gresham Machen was convinced that the Board was harboring modernists and in April 1933 presented an overture to the New Brunswick Presbytery requesting the General Assembly take action against the Board.[67] In Machen's overture, he asked that the General Assembly, 1) only elect to the Board those who will hold to the church's standards, especially fundamental doctrinal points, 2) not allow anyone who does not meet the criteria of the first point to be Candidate Secretary for the Board, 3) take care in the wording of application forms so there is no room for those who think progressive views are more important than faithfulness to God's Word, and 4) warn the Board of the great danger in union enterprises.[68] At the invitation of Presbytery, Speer was invited to speak to the overture and gave brief prepared remarks, affirming the faithfulness of the Board

---

63. Longfield, *Presbyterian Controversy*, 204–05.

64. Longfield, *Presbyterian Controversy*, 206; "Mrs. Buck Resigns; Board Accepts."

65. McAfee to McKelway, August 2, 1933, PUA.

66. Speer's January 1933 article was re-published as Speer, *Re-Thinking Missions Examined*.

67. Machen's overture and an explanatory document have been published in Carpenter, *Modernism and Foreign Missions*.

68. See Machen, "Modernism and the Board."

and claiming that of the fifteen hundred missionaries associated with the Board, only two have known problems, which were currently being addressed.[69] Machen's overture failed in the New Brunswick Presbytery. However, it was afterwards presented to the Presbytery of Philadelphia and passed. The Standing Committee at the 1933 General Assembly considered Machen's overture and brought majority and minority reports to the floor. The majority report affirmed the orthodoxy of Speer and the Board, and repudiated the theological statements of *Re-Thinking Missions*. The minority report maintained Machen's charges, reaffirmed the need to preach the true gospel, and nominated conservative candidates for Board. The majority report passed by an overwhelming margin and Machen responded by announcing the formation of an Independent Board for Presbyterian Foreign Missions.[70]

As the constitutionality of the Independent Board was called into question and found wanting, and judicial procedures commenced against Machen and others, criticism of the Board continued. Upon returning from a visit to Presbyterian mission stations in Asia, Presbyterian clergyman Donald Grey Barnhouse reported in October 1935 that although the majority of Presbyterian missionaries were spiritually and theologically sound, a minority denied or claimed ignorance of the truthfulness of key doctrinal points.[71] When Barnhouse presented his findings to the Board, they claimed to not know of any unfaithful missionaries but would make an investigation if evidence were supplied. Contrary to Machen, Barnhouse felt that the solution to unfaithfulness among Presbyterian missionaries was not the formation of an Independent Board, but rather reform of the existing Board. Barnhouse suspected, however, that the Board was not willing to admit there were problems, preferring to cover up any evidences of Modernism on the foreign field.[72] On April 8, 1936 he wrote an open letter to the Board, claiming it was "employing dilatory tactics in fulfilling the promise it made on November 18th last [1935] to give 'immediate and serious attention' to the conditions indicated in his Report of his visit to mission stations in Asia." While waiting for the Board to take action on

69. Longfield, *Presbyterian Controversy*, 205.

70. Longfield, Presbyterian Controversy, 206–7.

71. Barnhouse's visit to Thailand will be discussed in chapter 7.

72. Barnhouse, "Report of Dr. Donald Grey Barnhouse Concerning His Visit," 5–10; Executive Council, "Executive Council Comments on Barnhouse," 1–2, 7; Barnhouse, "Remarks by Barnhouse on the Comment," 8–9.

the modernism Barnhouse discovered in its Asia missions, Barnhouse was contacted by Presbyterian missionary Charles H. Dyke of the North India Mission. Dyke claimed that his fellow missionaries in the North India mission took all their "infidel" books off their shelves before Barnhouse's visit, having been warned that he was on a "heresy hunt." The Brahmin youth who told Barnhouse he wanted to become a Christian was put up to it. According to Dyke, the North India missionaries hid the true state of affairs and deceived Barnhouse well. Barnhouse wanted to know whether the Board would address the problems with modernism among its missionaries or merely continue its silence.[73]

The 1936 General Assembly defrocked Machen and several associates. On June 11, 1936, these men founded another Presbyterian denomination, soon to be called the Orthodox Presbyterian Church. With the departure of Machen and a number of his closest allies, a major critic of the Board of Foreign Missions was gone. Other critics, such as Clarence Macartney and Donald Barnhouse, remained in the Presbyterian Church U.S.A., but the height of the controversy had passed and a modicum of peace returned to the denomination.

---

73. "Is the Board Stalling?," 4, 14.

4

Modernization in Buddhist Thailand, 1820 to 1941

DURING THE NINETEENTH AND early twentieth centuries, Thailand experienced enormous developmental changes as modernization was both pursued by the country's elite and influenced by interactions with foreign nations. In order to better understand the ways in which American Presbyterian missionaries and Thai Christians encountered and responded to modernizing trends in Thailand, this chapter will provide a survey of the political, religious, and cultural context of Thailand with special attention to modernizing changes during this period.

FROM SIAM TO THAILAND

In the fourteenth century, the area of Central Thailand around the city of Ayuthaya was called Xian by the Chinese, which the Portuguese later changed into Siam. The terms "Siam" and "Siamese" thus came into subsequent usage, especially by foreigners.[1] From the sixteenth to the late nineteenth century, the kingdom of Siam extended across most of the area that is today central Thailand, including Bangkok. During that period, many regions of present-day Thailand were independent kingdoms which often related to Siam as vassal states with varying degrees of autonomy. As a result of French and British colonial claims in Southeast Asia, the area currently included in Thailand was determined to belong to Siam by the terms of the 1896 Anglo-French Declaration and the

---

1. Baker, *History of Thailand*, 8.

entirety of the country was known as the Kingdom of Siam until the nation's name was changed from Siam to Thailand in 1939.[2]

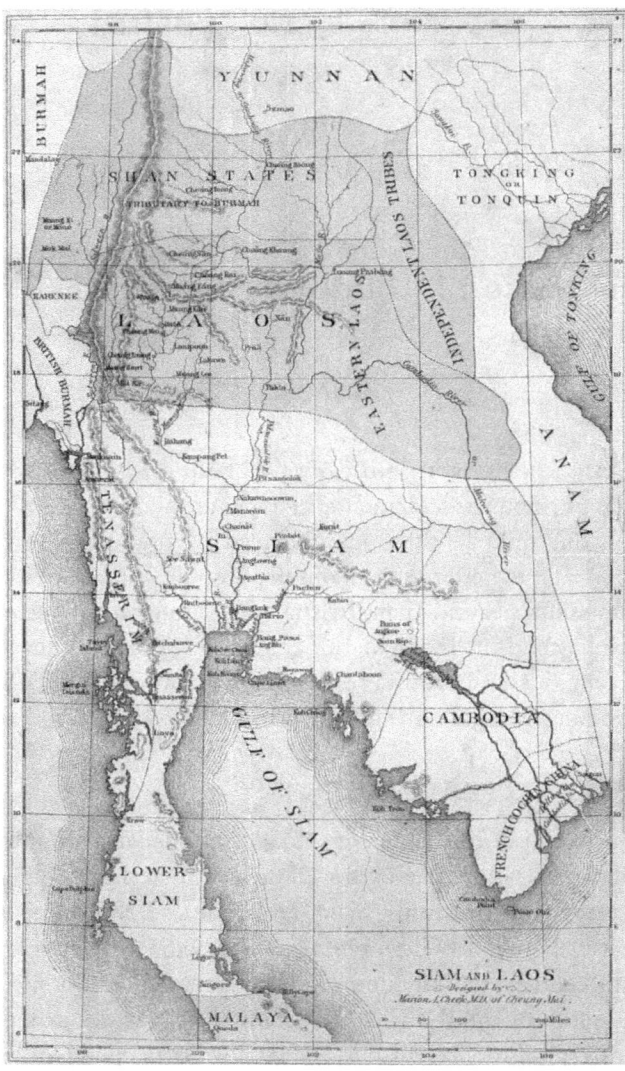

Map of "Siam and Laos" designed by Marion A. Cheek, as found in
Siam and Laos as seen by Our American Missionaries
(Philadelphia: Presbyterian Board of Publication), 1884.

---

2. Wyatt, Short History, 253; Jeshurun, "Anglo-French Declaration," 105–26; Winichakul, "Quest," 538; McFarland, *McFarland of Siam*, 103.

As a result, historical references to "Siam" and "Siamese" generally refer to the pre-World War II period, and references to "Thailand" and "Thai" predominate in the post-war period. In this book, the terms used in primary sources are retained when quoted. However, the terms "Thai" and "Thailand" will sometimes be used in historical retrospect to speak of the people and kingdom of Siam, and associated vassal states that became part of contemporary Thailand, even though those terms were not in contemporary usage.[3] Historically, the people in the central Thai region have referred to themselves in the Thai language as "Thai" even while foreigners were calling them Siamese.[4] The terms "Siam" and "Siamese" are not pejorative and even today are occasionally used by Thai people self-referentially.

THAILAND'S POLITICAL HISTORY TO 1941

The contemporary narrative of Thailand's history asserts that the Thai people have been ruled by kings dating back to at least the thirteenth century when King Ramkhamheng ruled from the then-capital of Sukhothai in present day Northern Thailand. The capital of what would become the kingdom of Siam progressively moved south from Sukhothai to Pitsanuloke, to Lopburi, to Ayuthaya, to Thonburi, and finally to Bangkok in 1782.[5] In that year, the first ruler of the Chakri dynasty ascended to the throne by means of a coup d'état. The Chakri dynasty has held the monarchy from that time to the present day. Starting with the third Chakri king, each monarch was given a regal name in addition to their personal name. In 1916, all the kings of the Chakri dynasty were retrospectively titled "Rama" followed by a number. Thus, Rama I, Rama II, Rama III and so forth.[6] Rama I, II and III were wary of foreigners, especially after the British victory in Myanmar in 1824.[7] King Mongkut (Rama IV, r.1851–1868) was more open to foreign learning and relations in comparison with his predecessors. King Mongkut and King Chulalongkorn (Rama V, r.1868–1910) are popularly credited with modernizing the country and defending the nation against the colonial

3. Baker, *History*, 131; House, "Ethnohistorical Study," 49–53; Cavendish, "Siam Becomes Thailand."

4. The modern Thai language is technically "Central Thai" or "Bangkok Thai," being differentiated from Northern Thai, Southern Thai, and Isaan (Northeastern Thai).

5. Marshall, *Kingdom*, 30–31.

6. For list of Chakri dynasty kings see Appendix 1 in Baker, *History*, 298–99.

7. Baker, *History*, 51; Aphornsuvan, "West," 407.

ambitions of Britain and France.[8] King Chulalongkorn is also remembered for ending slavery in his kingdom.[9] King Vajiravudh (Rama VI, r.1910–1925) continued the modernization program of Chulalongkorn and pursued national unity through reaffirming the importance of the monarchy and Buddhism. King Prajadhipok (Rama VII, r.1925-1935) ruled for only a short time before being made redundant by a coup d'état in 1932 that changed the form of government from absolute monarchy to constitutional monarchy. Rama VII abdicated in self-imposed exile in England in 1935, after which a nine year-old royal living in Switzerland, Ananda Mahidol, became King Rama VIII (r.1935-1946). The monarchy was eclipsed by the military and after years of internal dissension and further coups, Plaek Phibulsongkram emerged as prime minister of Thailand in 1938 and established a militaristic, nationalistic regime which lasted until nearly the end of World War II.[10]

RELATIONSHIPS WITH COLONIAL POWERS

In the 1820s, Siam began to be concerned about the encroachment of European powers into Southeast Asia. As the British asserted dominance over Siam's closest neighbor to the west in the Anglo-Burmese War, Siam signed a treaty with Britain in 1824 and another one with the United States in 1833.[11] Siam's political elite were quickly realizing that European powers, especially Britain and France, were forces that would need to be reckoned with. Formerly, the Mughal empire in India and the Qing empire in China were the major regional powers in Asia with which lesser countries had to relate. But as Britain extended its rule in the subcontinent and forced its way into China through successive "opium" wars, Siamese monarchs and elite turned their attention to the West.[12] The threat of the West was real and Westerners arriving in Siam in the 1820s were seen with suspicion. At the end of his life in 1851, King Rama III is reported to have said, "There will be no more wars with Vietnam and Burma. We will have them only with the West."[13]

---

8. Marshall, *Kingdom*, 32; Winichakul, "Quest," 532; Wyatt, *Thailand*, 180–212.

9. Aphornsuvan, "West," 426.

10. For a detailed study of Thailand's political history, see Baker, *History of Thailand*; Wyatt, *Thailand*; Terwiel, *Thailand's Political History*.

11. Aphornsuvan, "West," 407.

12. Winichakul, "Quest," 533–34; Aphornsuvan, "West," 406.

13. Baker, *History*, 38.

As the nineteenth century progressed, Britain continued to extend its rule in Burma on Siam's western border and along the Malay peninsula on Siam's southern border. Meanwhile, France sought to control Indo-China, first imposing protectorates over Tonkin, Annam and Cochinchina in Vietnam and then progressively moving into Cambodia and Laos. In 1893, tensions reached a breaking point. Siam and France came into direct conflict. France asserted her right to territory in the Lao states and Siamese forces defended their own claim to the same area. The Siamese mounted armed resistance to arriving French troops, killing the French commander. In response, France sailed gunboats into the mouth of the Chao Phraya River in Bangkok, aimed them at the Chakri palace, and demanded immediate submission to French land claims, an indemnity of three million francs, and punishment for those responsible for the death of the French commander. King Chulalongkorn and his government had no choice but to comply. The Siamese felt shocked and humiliated. They hoped the British would come to their aid, or at least apply diplomatic pressure on France. However, that assistance never materialized.[14] This defeat was especially painful for the Siamese because it highlighted both their inferiority to other sovereign kingdoms and the weakness of royal power.[15] Siamese pride in their progress towards being a modern, civilized nation was dashed and the fear of foreign threats to Siamese sovereignty took up a permanent place in the national consciousness.[16]

Siamese fear of European encroachment was not unfounded as France and Britain gained control of several regions formerly under Siamese rule in the following decades. Between 1867 and 1907, France claimed land in present-day Laos and western Cambodia on five different occasions and Britain gained control over four Malay states in the south that became part of British Malaya in 1909. These regions, to varying degrees, were under the suzerainty of the kingdom of Siam.[17] In total, Siam lost to European powers about 176,000 square miles (456,000 km2), an area equal to half of that under its rule at the end of

14. Winichakul, "Quest," 538; Wyatt, *Thailand*, 204; McFarland, *McFarland of Siam*, 100–102.

15. Winichakul, "Quest," 539.

16. Winichakul, "Quest," 538; Wyatt, *Thailand*, 204; This humiliating episode was later cited to justify Thailand's seizure of territory in Western Cambodia and anti-Catholic persecution in the early 1940s. Strate, "Uncivil State," 67.

17. Wyatt, *Thailand*, 207.

the reign of Rama III in 1851.¹⁸ By 1910, the borders of Siam took the shape of Thailand as it is today.

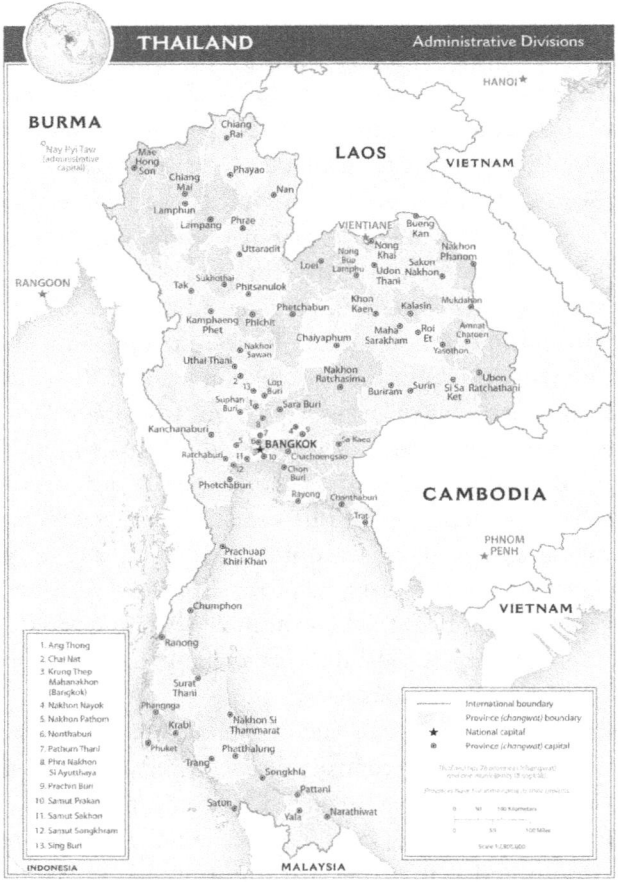

Map of Modern Thailand, 2013 (public domain)

However, Siam's losses might have been greater but for the Franco-British Declaration of 1896 which made Siam a buffer state between the two countries' competing colonial interests. Kings Rama IV and Rama V are credited with preventing colonization of Siam through forward-thinking modernization of the country and clever statecraft, but the role of the buffer state agreement should not be overlooked.¹⁹ At

18. Wyatt, *Thailand*, 208, 212.
19. Winichakul, "Quest," 538; McFarland, *McFarland of Siam*, 103; Marshall,

the same time, this agreement may not have been possible without the internal stability and security of the country brought about by Siam's on-going efforts to modernize.[20]

Modernization had been on Siam's agenda since the reign of Rama IV, in part because Siam's view of world powers changed in response to Britain's extending territorial control in India and commercial preeminence in China, the former superpowers in Asia. Siam needed to relate to the new superpowers in Europe, whose standard for worth and majesty was civilization.[21] Siam wanted not only to escape from being colonized, but also to be respected on the world stage as a powerful, civilized country in its own right. Modernization, or being perceived as modern or civilized, was a means to that end. There were other reasons for modernization too, as will be noted below. However, the motivation of the Siamese monarchs and elite to modernize the country cannot be uncoupled from their attempt to keep European powers at bay and gain their respect.[22]

THAI PURSUIT OF MODERNITY FOR THE THAI CONTEXT

In traditional Thai historiography, the motivation for modernization among Thai royals and other elite is a heroic tale of staving off colonial intrusion and preserving Thai independence. Some scholars, however, have disputed that interpretation, arguing that desires to dominate the indigenous populations within their European-defined boundaries and to promote a modern self-image to preserve power and status within Thailand were also significant motivators in modernization efforts.[23] Critical evaluation of Thai history has often been precluded by a strong sense of Thai cultural nationalism and exceptionalism as well as devotion to the monarchy, enforced by one of the strictest lèse-majesté laws in the world.[24] As such, scholars and journalists who wish to avoid having both their

---

Kingdom, 32.

20. Wyatt, *Thailand*, 208.

21. Winichakul, "Quest," 533–34; Cf. Aphornsuvan, "West," 406.

22. Winichakul, "Quest," 532; Aphornsuvan, "West," 419; Baker, *History*, 39; Peleggi, *Lords of Things*, 39.

23. For a summary of the challenges of Thai historiography, see Peleggi, *Lords of Things*, 46; Winichakul, *Siam Mapped*, 119; Loos, *Subject Siam*, 13–18.

24. Use of lèse-majesté law to suppress criticism began with King Vajiravudh's response to unfavorable newspaper articles in the 1910s and 1920s, and continues today, being employed to protect both current and historical monarchs. See Baker, *History*, 108; "Justice Minister Supports Vigilantism"; Prateepchaikul, "Sulak Lèse-Majesté Case."

writings and themselves banned from the country have had to tread very carefully in writing about Thai royalty, be it contemporary or historical figures.[25] Yet even with popular Thai sensibilities in mind, it is possible to present a coherent account of modernization efforts in the nineteenth and early twentieth centuries in Thailand.

Although the focus of this research is 1891 to 1941, it is necessary to go back to the 1820s to understand the trend towards modernization in Thailand. In 1824, the future King Mongkut (Rama IV) entered the monkhood, mostly likely to avoid a succession battle with his brother King Nangklao (Rama III) who recently ascended the throne. Mongkut wore the saffron robe for twenty-seven years, during which time he sought to reform Thai Buddhism and built relationships with foreigners, especially missionaries, who could help him learn English and Western science. Although Rama III was wary of foreigners and made little efforts to learn from them, Rama IV was fascinated with new learning and technology from abroad. He wanted to be both a man of the modern world and a traditional Thai monarch who upheld Buddhism as a pillar of Siamese society.[26]

King Mongkut's approach to astrology is illustrative of his attitude towards the modern and the traditional. Traditional Siamese astrology included both soothsaying and tracking of planetary bodies. King Mongkut never formally rejected the former, but he expressed no interest in it and did not believe the movement of stars and planets could affect human affairs. In 1858 and 1861, he rejected rumors of disasters accompanying the coming of comets. But Mongkut loved calculating planetary movements including eclipses, solar and lunar orbits, and positions of the stars. He contradicted fellow members of the Siamese elite, including former monks and King Rama III, citing their wrong understanding of the planets and stars. In 1868, the king predicted a solar eclipse and was confident it would happen where and when he predicted. The court astrologers calculated differently, using different books. The king wanted to prove himself and the superiority of his learning, so he made an expedition to the village of Wa Kor, Prachuap province to see the eclipse. When it happened at the time he said it would on August 18, 1868, he was ecstatic. Upon return to Bangkok, he berated as "vulgar" and "plebeian"

25. For examples of writings banned by Thai authorities, see Perlez, "Banned Book"; Itthipongmaetee, "Kinokuniya Pulls Oxford Researcher's Book"; "Thai Police Ban Scot's Book."

26. Baker, *History*, 36.

those who had not believed him.[27] King Mongkut did not hesitate to reject parts of traditional Buddhist cosmology and belief that seemed fanciful and unscientific. In the minds of Mongkut, his successors, and other Siamese elite, the pursuit of modern learning did not necessitate the rejection of Buddhism per se. Modernization in Siam was characterized by acceptance of nearly all aspects of Western science and development except for the retention of absolute monarchy and Buddhism, especially its ethical aspects. Scientific and other Western learning were first embraced by royals and other elites, and only slowly disseminated among the common people who were often looked down upon by the elite as ignorant, superstitious peasants.[28] During the second quarter of the twentieth century, political winds shifted against the monarchy for a couple decades before a significant revival of royalist sentiment occurred in the second half of the century. Thai devotion to Buddhism over against Western religion, however, remained unchanged. This sentiment is succinctly summarized in King Mongkut's reported statement to missionaries that, "The sciences I receive, astronomy, geology, chemistry,—these I receive; the Christian religion I do not receive."[29]

King Mongkut and his modernizing Siamese associates were happy to converse with foreigners on science, history, geography, and language. They heard them on religion as well and argued with them about it. King Mongkut and other members of the Siamese elite who styled themselves as modern and scientific rejected what they perceived as fanciful and magical in religion. Once these supernatural and superstitious elements were removed from religion, they believed Buddhism would appear as the more logical and rational of the two religions and thus in line with the modern world.[30]

Despite their aversion to the missionaries's religion, Mongkut and other members of the Siamese elite learned much from their foreign associates who in some cases became valued friends. Missionaries and the children of missionaries were often called upon to supply knowledge and expertise that the Siam elite wanted. Dan Bradley introduced modern printing and vaccination. Jesse Caswell taught English to King Mongkut. Samuel G. McFarland was invited by King Chulalongkorn to be headmaster of a school for sons of nobles. His son Edwin McFarland

27. Winichakul, *Siam Mapped*, 42–47.
28. Winichakul, "Quest," 534–37.
29. Presbyterian Board, *Siam and Laos*, 391.
30. Baker, *History*, 40.

developed a typewriter that printed Thai letters. Another son, George B. McFarland, and Heyward Hays developed modern medical practice and doctor training. A third son, William McFarland, helped develop modern military practice.[31] Missionaries were not the only foreigners who contributed to national development but as a group they were cited specifically by King Chulalongkorn, Prince Damrong, and Prince Mahidol of Songkla for their valuable contributions.[32] Thai scholar Thanet Aphornsuvan wrote without exaggeration that "the American missionaries became one of the most important agencies of modernization in nineteenth century Siam."[33]

The king and other Siamese elite did not form their ideas about modernity and Western learning from missionaries and other resident foreigners alone. Mongkut imparted his fascination with the modern and the foreign to his son Chulalongkorn, who ascended the throne upon his father's death in 1868. Chulalongkorn subsequently sought new avenues of learning about Europe and modernity, two ideas that were closely related in the minds of many. From the 1880s onward, a steady flow of information about Europe appeared in Siamese publications and formed popular opinion on what it meant to be *siwilai*, a Thai word borrowed from the English "civilized." At the end of the nineteenth and early twentieth centuries, the terms *siwilai* (civilized), *charoen* (development/progress) and *than samai* (modern) became commonplace in discussions of the Siamese elite as they negotiated their relationships to Western powers and the trajectory of their own country.[34] King Chulalongkorn was fascinated by Europe and desired to see it for himself. Such a journey was unprecedented for a Siamese king and Chulalongkorn thus first visited European modernity closer to home, in colonies at Java and Singapore. These visits whet his appetite for Europe itself, a journey which he made in 1897. The king visited Switzerland, Austria-Hungary, Italy, France and England, making note of what he saw in travelogues that were later published in Siam. While he enjoyed his experiences in Europe, the reality of the thing itself informed the image of Europe that had been formed from a distance.

31. Smith, *Siamese*, 24–25; McFarland, *Historical Sketch*, 16–19; McFarland, *McFarland of Siam*, 48–50, 70–71; McFarland, *Our Garden*, 48–52; Eakin, "Biographical Notes on Rev. and Mrs. McFarland."

32. Speer, *Report of Deputation*, 27–28; Freeman, *Siam*, 10; "Siam Is Progressive," 12.

33. Aphornsuvan, "West," 407.

34. Winichakul, "Quest," 529–31, 537.

As David Wyatt noted, the king's trip to Europe opened "his eyes to the unevenness of European modernity, the irrational persistence of local customs, and the extravagances and glaring inequities of European life."[35] In the king's mind, Italy, for example, was excellent for arts and crafts but was "a little dirty."[36] The king visited London's East End twice in order to see the poverty there.[37] Europe may have been the standard for civilization and modernity but it was far from perfect.

A firsthand view of both the glories and imperfections of Europe helped form a new line of thought in the king's mind, namely that it was not necessary to attempt modernization entirely on the European model which, as it were, had not been perfectly achieved even in Europe.[38] The best of Europe could be borrowed and adapted for Siam and the best of Siamese culture and institutions could be preserved, thus creating a Siamese form of modernity in the process.[39] Western science and technology could be readily employed to Siamese ends and certain superficial changes such as wearing Western-style clothing and striving for white teeth instead of betel-nut stained black teeth could create a greater appearance of civilization in the eyes of the West.[40] At the same time, the traditional Siamese institutions of Buddhism, the monarchy, and regional governing hierarchies still had important roles to play in a modern, independent Siam.[41] Though initially retained, polygamy was eventually abandoned when it became clear that its continuance was a major obstacle to Siam being considered civilized in the eyes of the West. King Chulalongkorn (Rama V) was the last king to have multiple wives and polygamy was legally abolished in 1935.[42]

With the aim of creating a distinctively Siamese modernity, King Chulalongkorn continued his father's efforts to modernize the country, developing the institutions of the monarchy, army, and civil service, as

---

35. Wyatt, *Thailand*, 211.
36. Winichakul, "Quest," 539.
37. Wyatt, *Thailand*, 211.
38. Loos, *Subject Siam*, 19.
39. Aphornsuvan, "West," 417.
40. Baker, *History*, 132; Winichakul, "Quest," 538; McFarland, *McFarland of Siam*, 130.
41. Wyatt, *Thailand*, 209–12; Winichakul, "Quest," 537–40.
42. Baker, *History*, 163; Winichakul, "Quest," 538; Winichakul, "Buddhist Apologetics," 79; Loos, *Subject Siam*, 7; Peleggi, *Lords of Things*, 4.

well as initiating educational, religious, and legal reforms.[43] Many modernizing developments begun under Chulalongkorn were continued and expanded to varying extents in the thirty years between his death in 1910 and the start of the Japanese occupation in December 1941.

Modernizing Education

Buddhist temple schools long existed in Siam as the only educational option, though their curriculum was limited and varied by locality. Modern schooling on the Western model was introduced by the first missionary schools in the middle of the nineteenth century.[44] While King Chulalongkorn valued these schools for their contribution to the country generally, he desired to promote education among the upper classes in particular and in 1878 invited American Presbyterian missionary Samuel G. McFarland to serve as headmaster of a school in Bangkok for the sons of princes and nobles.[45] This school was not long-lived but in 1887, Prince Damrong Rajanubhab was put in charge of the newly formed Ministry of Public Instruction and worked to expand the reach and quality of public education in Siam.[46] He recruited Edwin McFarland, son of missionary Samuel G. McFarland, to be his personal secretary, and Robert Morant, an Englishman, to help develop English-language programs, textbooks, and standardized examinations for elite schools. Prince Wachirayan, who was also influential in revitalization and standardization of Buddhism in the kingdom, promoted the foundation of village schools from 1898. He used standardized Bangkok Thai language, standardized syllabi and textbooks developed by the Ministry of Public Instruction in Bangkok, and introduced Western mathematics and science. The promulgation and influence of these standardized schools helped create greater uniformity in Siamese society.[47]

In 1902, King Chulalongkorn enacted the final educational reform of his reign, mandating two categories of education: general education and special/technical education. These two categories were divided into primary, secondary, and higher education. The goal of general education

---

43. Wyatt, *Thailand*, 223.
44. McFarland, *Historical Sketch*, 209–20.
45. McFarland, *McFarland of Siam*, 48–50.
46. Diskul, "Damrong Rajanubhab"; McFarland, *McFarland of Siam*, 75–76; Tanphaichitr, "Modernization," 158–59.
47. Wyatt, *Thailand*, 216–17.

was to make good citizens and the goal of special/technical education was to provide the skills needed for particular lines of work.[48] In 1921, a compulsory education law was passed requiring all children from seven to fourteen years old to attend school. This law, however, initially applied to less than half the country.[49] Implementation of educational standards lagged behind the legal requirement and education for boys was initially prioritized over that for girls. Women's education was promoted early on by Protestant missionaries but received a great boost in popularity and funding following the accolades received by Queen Saowapha Phongsi upon successful completion of her regency for King Chulalongkorn during his 1897 trip to Europe.[50]

The primary motivation for development of mass education, especially for the upper classes, was to develop men who could enter the civil service and thereby serve the cause of nation building. Foreign advisors were insufficient and often not in touch with the local situation in Siam. As such, progress was impeded by a lack of educated men for the civil service and administering the new infrastructure of provincial administration and government departments. The royal family were the first to be educated abroad and other Siamese elite were slowly catching up.[51] Education for the masses came gradually but preparation for government service was prioritized. To that end, Chulalongkorn University, Siam's first institution of tertiary education, was founded in 1917. One year after the Siamese revolution of 1932, the University of Moral and Political Sciences (later Thammasat University) was founded. Whereas Chulalongkorn University reflected its origin as the union of the School of Civil Servants, the Royal Medical College, and the School of Engineering, Thammasat University focused on politics and government administration, a newly important emphasis given the recent change in Siamese government from absolute to constitutional monarchy.[52] The People's Party, the architects behind the Siamese revolution, promised a full representative parliamentary assembly when

---

48. Suksod-Barger, *Religious Influences*, 58.

49. Wyatt, *Thailand*, 228–29.

50. McFarland, *Historical Sketch*, 78–79. For more on the influence of women's education and Christianity upon improving the status of women in Thai society, see Suksod-Barger, *Religious Influences*; Javani, "Changing Custom."

51. Wyatt, *Thailand*, 223–24.

52. Bovornsiri, "Higher Education," 30.

educational levels permitted it and thus increased spending on primary education fourfold between 1933 and 1938.[53]

Modernizing Medical Care

Modern medical care began in Siam through the agency of missionary doctors. The Pomeranian missionary Karl Gützlaff came in 1828 and administered some basic medical remedies, though he only stayed a couple of years.[54] Dr. Dan Beach Bradley, who arrived in 1835, left a more enduring impact upon medicine in Siam. He is credited with introducing vaccination and performing the first modern surgery. Bradley and other Western-trained doctors after him, both foreign and local, faced an uphill battle in convincing Siamese of the benefits of Western medicine. Bradley was often called upon only after herb doctors and spirit doctors failed to produce results. In 1928, American Presbyterian missionary doctor Edwin B. McDaniel estimated that up to seventy-five percent of the population still depended on "native doctors" using "ancient medical books," which he described as "a strange mixture of plant-lore, astrology, and spiritism."[55] Siamese royalty and other elite were the first to embrace Western medicine and the first Western-style hospital in Siam, a sixty-bed military hospital, opened in 1880 under the care of Thianhi Sarasin, a graduate of the American Presbyterian Boys School who completed a medical degree in New York City in 1871. In 1882, Dr. Ernest Sturge opened the first mission hospital in Petchaburi province.[56] In 1886, King Chulalongkorn wanted a new hospital to better respond to recurring cholera epidemics, and thus appointed a committee, granting them funding and lumber for the new hospital. Siriraj Hospital, named after the king's fifty-third child, Prince Siriraj, and often thought to be Thailand's first hospital, opened on April 26, 1888.[57] In 1890, American Presbyterian missionary Dr. Heyward T. Hays opened the first medical college at the invitation of the king, but the school closed within two years due to dwindling numbers of students and Hays' own limited

---

53. Wyatt, *Thailand*, 249.
54. Lutz, *Opening China*, 46–47.
55. McFarland, *Historical Sketch*, 195, 99.
56. Baker, *History*, 97; McFarland, *McFarland of Siam*, 67. Thianhi (or Thian Hee) was later bestowed the title of Phya Sarasin and became head of a wealthy Thai-Chinese business family who took the surname Sarasin.
57. McFarland, *McFarland of Siam*, 66–69; Baker, *History*, 66; Faculty of Medicine, "History."

language and cultural knowledge. Hays continued to practice medicine at Siriraj and later recommended that the king re-open the school under missionary Samuel G. McFarland's son George who was then finishing medical studies in the United States.[58] The king was familiar with the McFarland family and readily agreed. Dr. George B. McFarland assumed his duties on January 1, 1892 and remained an instructor at the college until his retirement in 1926.[59]

In the first years of Siriraj Hospital, there were two medical departments: Siamese medicine and Western medicine. The former initially received more patients and McFarland, Hays, and others committed to Western medicine were frustrated with the popular Siamese theory of disease that claimed all ailments are caused by an imbalance in one or more of the four main elements of the body: fire, earth, water, and wind. Public confidence in Western medicine was boosted in 1900 when Siamese medical college graduates and students worked to combat a cholera epidemic in Bangkok and saved many lives. Students at the college who wondered whether or not there were future career prospects for them in foreign medicine became convinced their studies were not in vain when the first graduating class quickly found government positions. Western medicine came to dominate the medical college and the two departments, Siamese and Western, were merged in 1907.[60] The Royal Medical College was absorbed into Chulalongkorn University upon its foundation in 1917.[61] The medical college saw further development in the 1920s as the Rockefeller Foundation was invited by the government to re-organize the college and thus provided funding and faculty to further develop medical education in Siam.[62] By 1920 there were two nursing colleges, one government and one mission-run.[63] However, until 1947 there was only one medical college for the entire country.[64]

In the early twentieth century, the development of medical care and facilities was aided by royal gifts to both government and mission hospitals, and the government's medical college was producing graduates who eventually replaced traditional doctors, the preferred option

58. McFarland, *McFarland of Siam*, 70–71.
59. McFarland, *Historical Sketch*, 201.
60. McFarland, *McFarland of Siam*, 139–41.
61. McFarland, *McFarland of Siam*, 147.
62. Shapiro, "Medical Education," 252; Landon, *Thailand in Transition*, 143–44.
63. McFarland, *Historical Sketch*, 202.
64. Shapiro, "Medical Education," 252.

by many people through the 1930s.[65] However, with basic health and hygiene practices still lacking in much of the country, the government issued codes for public health and established health clinics in more rural areas.[66] Yet the majority of doctors were located in Bangkok and most people continued to have limited access to modern health care.[67]

Social and Legal Modernizations

Several societal and legal reforms were also introduced to further modernization and nation building. Prince Raphi Phatthanasak, the first of King Chulalongkorn's sons to return from study in Europe, was charged with reforming Siam's law codes, which he based on the Napoleonic Code. He completed a limited criminal code for Siam in 1908 and a fuller reform was brought about in the 1930s under Pridi Phanomyong.[68] At that time, new law codes forbade polygamy, withdrew the need for parental consent to marry, and rescinded formerly recognized aristocratic privileges.[69]

Starting in 1873, royal decrees began to abolish slavery, a gradual process that concluded with the formal end of corvée labor in 1905.[70] The end of forced labor may have been hastened by the claim of Catholic missionaries that debt bondage was slavery. This accusation irked King Chulalongkorn because it tarnished the civilized image he wanted to portray to foreign powers.[71]

Universal military conscription was introduced in 1902, but the military played an auxiliary role to local police until after the 1932 Siamese Revolution when the government greatly increased military spending to develop modern armed forces, ostensibly to preserve an independent, sovereign Thailand.[72] In the early years of the twentieth

---

65. McFarland, *Historical Sketch*, 200; Landon, *Thailand*, 148–51.

66. Baker, *History*, 66.

67. As recently as 1992, it has been estimated that sixty percent of all doctors in Thailand are located in Bangkok. Shapiro, "Medical," 251. For more on the state of medical care in 1930s Thailand, see chapter six on "Medical Trends" in Landon, *Thailand*, 138–66.

68. Wyatt, *Thailand*, 210; Baker, *History*, 121–22. Prince Raphi Phatthanasak is listed by Wyatt as "Prince Rabi" and by Baker as "Prince Ratchaburi."

69. Baker, *History*, 121–22.

70. Wyatt, *Thailand*, 192, 210, 215.

71. Strate, "Uncivil," 65.

72. Wyatt, *Thailand*, 201; Landon, *Thailand*, 64–69.

century, the newly created army was most often deployed to quell internal rebellions as Siam sought to exert jurisdiction over its territory specified in the 1896 Anglo-French Declaration.[73]

At the beginning of the twentieth century, Siam was still yoked by unequal treaties with Western powers. Treaty stipulations included extraterritorial rights and the inability to raise import tariffs without requesting permission.[74] In 1937 Thailand was able to successfully negotiate new treaties with England, France, Germany, Italy, and the United States, granting Thailand "full and equal rights as an independent nation" and ending special privileges enjoyed by French and British subjects.[75]

Modernizing Communications, Transportation, Business, and Industry

Construction of telegraph lines began in the 1880s and the first telephone line was put into use by Prince Bhanurangsi Savangwongse in 1881.[76] Electric lighting was introduced to the palace in 1884 and the city of Bangkok in 1897.[77] The first Thai-language typewriter was developed in 1892 by Edwin H. McFarland, missionary son and private secretary to Prince Damrong Rajanubhab. Despite the fact it was missing two letters, the typewriter met with the approval of King Chulalongkorn who ordered forty machines for government use. Although Edwin died unexpectedly in 1895, his brother George inherited his typewriter business and developed it in succeeding decades.[78]

The first railway line opened in 1893, a short stretch of track from central Bangkok to the mouth of the Chao Phraya river. The second line ran from Bangkok to Ayuthaya, opening in 1894, and was extended to Nakhon Ratchasima (also known as Korat) by 1900. In 1903, a rail line to Petchaburi was opened, forming the first section of railway into Southern Thailand. By 1920, the railroad reached Chiang Mai in the North, reducing the journey time between Bangkok and Chiang Mai from eight weeks to

---

73. Baker, *History*, 64.

74. Reynolds, "Phibun Songkhram," 120; "King Asks Aid," 7.

75. Landon, *Thailand*, 72.

76. Wyatt, *Thailand*, 198; Baker, *History*, 78; Telecom of Thailand, "Birth of the Telephone."

77. Van Beek, *Royal Automobile Stables*, 15.

78. McFarland, *Our Garden,* 48–52; McFarland, *McFarland of Siam*, 191–95, 223–27.

three days.[79] The automobile was introduced to Thailand from Europe in the first years of the twentieth century and quickly became popular among Thai royalty and other elite who could afford such luxuries.[80]

At the dawn of the twentieth century, while the majority ethnic Siamese focused on rice farming, resident Chinese were largely responsible for building the modern sector of the economy. They spearheaded the digging of canals for transportation in the Bangkok area and built railways, shops, government office buildings, and bridges. The Chinese also developed banks and import-export services.[81] Alongside these private sector developments, the government expanded local government infrastructure and increased spending on roads, hospitals, and electricity generation.[82]

Modernizing Buddhism

Buddhism arrived in Thailand in the fifth century A.D. but was reasserted in the Theravada tradition in the thirteenth century when King Ramkhamhaeng (r.1279 – 1298) of Sukhothai sent monks for training in Sri Lanka. King Li-Thai, Ramkhamhaeng's grandson, invited a Singhalese monk to preside over the ordination of monks in Thailand in 1360 and Thai monks have since claimed a line of Buddhist orthodoxy stretching back to the Sri Lankan Buddhist Council of 70 A.D. The form of Buddhism that King Li-Thai promulgated included not only belief in the law of karma, nirvana, denial of self, and escape from suffering but also a belief in tiered realms for humans, animals, and ghosts, multiple heavens and hells, as well as a monarchical form of government.[83]

In the nineteenth century, King Mongkut and other members of the Thai elite sought to reform Buddhism for the modern world, reviving and modifying the religion in light of Western learning. As a monk, Mongkut founded the Thammayut Buddhist sect for the purpose of moral reform and cleansing Buddhism of superstitious and unscientific beliefs.[84]

---

79. Thailand by Train, "Thai Railway History"; Reichel, "Quarterly Letter—Chiang Mai," June 1920, PHS.

80. Van Beek, *Royal Automobile Stables*, 11–35; Chaloemtiarana, "Through Racing Goggles," 542–44; Baker, *History*, 68.

81. Wyatt, *Thailand*, 216–19.

82. Baker, *History*, 121–22.

83. Baker, *History*, 7; Boon-Itt, "Dialogue," 11–12.

84. Aphornsuvan, "West," 413; Winichakul, "Buddhist Apologetics," 78.

King Mongkut and other Thai elite revised their understanding of Buddhism, due in part to foreign criticisms of the more fantastical aspects of Thai cosmology, and emphasized the value of Buddhist teaching for life in this world.[85] Starting with Mongkut, Thai leaders sought to shift Thai Buddhism towards the life of the mind and away from an other-worldly focus upon obtaining nirvana. Previously, nirvana was hoped for by all people, but this goal faded from view for lay people. Nirvana now became reachable only for monks.[86] Among the educated and the elite, there was a decided attempt to refocus Buddhism for the modern world and to make it useful for the needs of a scientific age. Similar rational transformations of Buddhism were also occurring in Sri Lanka, where this new form of Buddhism has been referred to as "Protestant Buddhism," and in Myanmar, where it has been called "Buddhist modernism."[87] To preserve Buddhism for the modern world, Thai reformers employed what Thongchai Winichakul has termed, the "bifurcation intellectual strategy." Supernatural explanations of the natural world found in Hindu-Buddhist cosmology were rejected in favor of scientific explanations, yet for spiritual and ethical questions, Buddhist teaching was favored.[88] As such, the name "Buddhist modernism" is particularly apt because the way in which Thai elite modified Buddhism for the modern world is an intellectual trajectory similar to that of late nineteenth-century liberal biblical scholarship which separated the Jesus of History from the Christ of Faith. In both liberal Protestantism and the reformed Buddhism of the Thai elite, incredible sounding stories that seemingly conflicted with science were rejected, but the spirituality and morality of traditional faith were retained.

While Thai elite increasingly adopted a secularized, scientific form of modernity, the majority of the Thai population retained an enchanted worldview. At the popular level, "animistic" or primal beliefs and practices related to the spirit world were common throughout the nineteenth and twentieth centuries and remain so today. This mixture of animistic practices and Buddhism is sometimes called Folk Buddhism and has been the functional religious worldview of the majority of Thai up through the present day. Even as scientific explanations have gained popularity,

85. For a brief history of Thai Buddhist response to Christian critiques, see Winichakul, "Buddhist Apologetics," 78.
86. Boon-Itt, "Dialogue," 18–20.
87. Winichakul, "Buddhist Apologetics," 78–80.
88. Winichakul, "Buddhist Apologetics," 78.

supernatural beliefs have continued as part of an inclusive, enchanted Thai modernity that allows for varied local beliefs as long as people also participate in the Buddhist rituals of society at large.[89] Among Thai elite, however, Buddhism was promoted as a pathway to moral and successful living in this world. Beliefs about heavens and hells, the prophecy of *Phrasri-arn* (the Buddha to come), and supernatural explanations and solutions were deprecated.[90] In 1911, King Vajiravudh claimed that the "heart of Buddhism is that those who do good receive good and those who do evil receive evil."[91] The conception of Buddhism as primarily an ethical system became an increasingly important part of Thai national identity during the nineteenth and twentieth centuries.[92]

While varieties of Buddhist belief and practice continued to exist, Mongkut and his successors sought greater uniformity in Buddhism in Thailand. In the last years of the nineteenth century, Prince Wachirayan (1860-1921) sought to reform Thai Buddhism, establishing monasteries and stressing education of monks and the general populace. His reorganization of Thai Buddhism and promotion of the Thammayut sect over local variations in Buddhist belief and practice became a catalyst for greater integration of the northern, northeastern and southern parts of the country, thus enhancing the project of nation building.[93] Reformed Thai Buddhism was wedded to nationalism, and superstitious or so-called "non-orthodox" Buddhist practices were discouraged and sometimes punished.[94] The danger of unapproved beliefs was confirmed in the mind of King Chulalongkorn's government by several protests, uprisings, and millenarian rebellions in the north and northeast between 1895 and 1902, some of which were undergirded by belief "in a tradition of uprisings by *phumibun*, men of merit, who could overthrow the social order and usher in a better world."[95]

---

89. Boon-Itt, "Dialogue," 24–29.
90. Boon-Itt, "Dialogue," 18.
91. Vajiravudh, *Wild Tiger Sermons*, 85 in Boon-Itt, "Dialogue," 22.
92. Loos, *Subject Siam*, 22–23.
93. Wyatt, *Thailand*, 216.
94. Loos, *Subject Siam*, 22–24.
95. Baker, *History*, 55–56.

Thai Buddhism and Religious Toleration

Efforts to standardize Buddhist belief and practice across the nation notwithstanding, Thai people have long prided themselves on being tolerant of other beliefs and there has generally been freedom of belief and practice for non-Buddhist religions in Thailand.[96] Buddhist apologists have often re-iterated the point that "Buddhism never looks down upon other religions and their followers, and it never wages religious wars."[97] In a 1926 conversation with American Presbyterian mission secretary Robert E. Speer, Prince Wachirayan, Supreme Patriarch of Buddhism in Thailand, stated that proselytism "ought not to be," since the goal of all religions is the same. However, he believed, upon being asked pointedly, that a Christian son ought not to be forced by his Buddhist parents to enter the Buddhist monkhood and each person should be true to his own convictions. He further expressed the wish that the missionaries should stay in the country for a long time.[98] Speer did not expand on why the Supreme Patriarch hoped missionaries would stay, but from remarks made by other members of the Thai elite, it is highly likely that he valued missionary contributions to the modernization of Thai society. The comments of Prince Mahidol of Songkla, father of Kings Rama VIII and IX, are representative of the views of many in the Thai elite in the early twentieth century:

> King Vajiravudh is the only independent Buddhist sovereign in the world, and as such is regarded as the chief defender of the religion of the Buddha. Nevertheless no foreigners are more welcome to Siam than American Missionaries. They have done wonderful things for us. They come not to make money, but to spend it. They do not quarrel over the manner in which the Sacrament shall be administered. They teach, they minister to the sick, they build hospitals and schools. The Presbyterian Board has aided greatly our educational authorities. The work of the missionaries from America is constructive. They submit wonderfully to our laws. They do not interfere in our politics. They teach the young to be clean, honest and patriotic, not to the United States, but patriotic to Siam. We owe a great debt to

---

96. Landon, *Thailand*, 55–60.
97. Winichakul, "Buddhist Apologetics," 86; Aphornsuvan, "West," 422.
98. Speer, *Unfinished Task*, 144–45.

> the American Missionaries. Their deeds are the kind that will live after them, a constant inspiration for good.[99]

The positive view of missionaries expressed by Prince Wachirayan, Prince Mahidol and other Thai elites must be qualified. In spite of their valued contributions to Thai society, the religious freedom enjoyed by missionaries and other non-Buddhists did not include the freedom to criticize Buddhism.

In Thai society, it is commonly believed that criticisms of Buddhism are unacceptable and in certain cases constitute a threat to national security due to the role of Buddhism in creating and maintaining national identity and societal cohesion.[100] As such, studies in comparative religion in Thailand have rarely exhibited scholarly detachment, but have most often been conducted with confessional and apologetic aims, eager to demonstrate the superiority of Buddhism over other religions. Although secularization theory postulates that societies become less religious as they become more modern, elite Thai of the early twentieth century emphasized Buddhism as an essential aspect of modern Thai identity and employed it in the cause of nationalism. As such, critiques of Buddhism in Thailand have rarely been understood as merely viewpoints on religious truth, but are often seen as negative evaluations of Thai individuals, society, and the Thai nation as a whole.[101] Some tensions between Thai elites and missionaries in the latter's representation of Buddhism will be discussed in chapter 8.

Modernizing Governmental Administration and National Integration

Starting in the 1880s, the Siamese government sought to solidify control of vassal states in the northern, northeastern, and southern parts of what would become present-day Thailand. Siamese territorial claims in the North and West had long been at odds with Burmese ambitions in the same areas, often resulting in conflict during the eighteenth and early nineteenth century. In exchange for Siamese military protection against invading Burmese forces, local rulers in these regions allied themselves

---

99. Freeman, *Siam*, 10.

100. Winichakul, "Buddhist Apologetics," 97; Strate, "Uncivil," 65; Strate, "Sukhothai Incident."

101. For a detailed history of Thai responses to criticisms of Buddhism by Christians, especially Roman Catholics, see Winichakul, "Buddhist Apologetics," 76–99.

with Siam as vassal states. Siamese suzerainty over the northeastern states was recognized by local rulers, although French ambitions in Indochina, particularly Laos, threatened Siam's claim to the loyalty of that region. Despite Siam's paternal relationship with an unstable Cambodian kingdom in the early nineteenth century, that relationship weakened as French influence in Cambodia grew later in the century. In the South, Siam held suzerainty over several states, including some Malay states that bordered British-controlled Malaya.[102]

During the reign of King Rama I (1782 to 1809), Siam's vassal states enjoyed a high degree of local autonomy but by the end of the nineteenth century, Siam sought to exert more control over these territories.[103] British teak foresting was spreading into northern Thailand and the Siamese government wanted to ensure that the local ruler of Chiang Mai did not do anything to provoke a conflict with Britain. Starting in the 1880s, Siam appointed resident commissioners in several northern and northeastern cities. The progress of Siamese-appointed commissioners in wresting functional jurisdiction away from local rulers was gradual, but by the late 1880s, Siamese commissioners in Chiang Mai and Phuket started to take effective control of those regions, issuing laws and collecting taxes.[104] The southern island of Phuket was important to Siam for tin production, and Siam sought to extend its administrative control over not only Phuket but the entire southern peninsula between Bangkok and British Malaya. In a move reminiscent of the 1893 PakNam Incident, King Chulalongkorn dispatched a Siamese naval warship to the mouth of the Pattani River in southern Thailand to force the submission of local ruler Raja Abdul Kadir who was resisting Siamese authority and centralization reforms that would bring his region under greater Siamese control.[105]

Siamese efforts to integrate vassal territories into the kingdom of Siam proper were aided by re-organization of government administration. Inspired by European models, in 1888, Siam began transitioning to a government of cabinet ministers, a change that came into full force in 1892 when this group of ministers, together with the king, began to meet regularly. They could share information, consulting each other and the king, and were thus able to more efficiently shape national policy. Collection of revenue was centralized under the Ministry of Finance.

102. Wyatt, *Thailand*, 152–61.
103. Wyatt, *Thailand*, 158, 94.
104. Wyatt, *Thailand*, 201.
105. Loos, *Subject Siam*, 1–2.

Greater control of leasing timber rights was obtained in the North. A territorial army was organized in Nong Khai, a northeastern province bordering Laos, to subdue local rebellions and guard against French aggression.[106] Many government ministers and regional commissioners were princes and the growing national bureaucracy of Siamese appointed royals and elite commoners progressively displaced older, regional ruling hierarchies.[107] This new and growing centralized administrative infrastructure under the authority of the Siamese king was the foundation upon which other modernizations would be built. Modernizing changes in education, medical care, and Buddhism already mentioned would not have been possible without a modern, national administrative structure to establish them.

POLITICAL MODERNIZATION AND THAI NATIONALISM

King Vajiravudh (r. 1910 to 1925) continued with the modernization trajectory of his predecessors but added a strongly nationalistic bent. King Vajiravudh emphasized Thailand as a nation and produced a wide variety of literary and artistic output, including modern political essays. One of his most persistent themes was modernity and urging people to live in the modern way. He coined hundreds of surnames, established national holidays to honor King Chulalongkorn (October 23) and the Chakri dynasty (April 6), promoted sports, especially football, encouraged women to mix with men, and advocated monogamy over polygamy. King Vajiravudh founded the country's first university, Chulalongkorn University, and in 1921 introduced a compulsory education law for all children 7 to 14 years old.[108] King Vajiravudh also founded two military organizations, a unit to guard the royal residence and the Wild Tiger Corps, a nationwide paramilitary corps to defend "Nation, Religion, King." The latter was accompanied by a Junior Boy Scout movement with the same aim of promoting loyalty to "Nation, Religion, King." This tripartite formula was borrowed from England's "God, King, Country," with the notable replacement of "God" with "Religion," meaning Buddhism specifically.[109] In the king's mind, these three were inseparable. To love the nation was to love the monarch and to be Buddhist. King Vajiravudh stated:

106. Wyatt, *Thailand*, 200–201.
107. Wyatt, *Thailand*, 219–22.
108. Wyatt, *Thailand*, 228.
109. Wyatt, *Thailand*, 224–25.

Buddhism is the religion of our nation. We need to hold on to it out of gratitude to our parents and ancestors. Because I feel sure about this matter, I am able to stand here speaking to you all about Buddhism in the assured hope that you all who are Thai know now and realize that religion in these days is inseparable from the nation. Therefore, we who are Thais need to remain in our Buddhism which is our national religion.[110]

During the reign of King Vajiravudh, there was no move against Buddhism's dominant place in society, but the wisdom of absolute monarchy was starting to be questioned as increasing numbers of Siamese elite were exposed to democratic ideals while studying abroad. Beginning in the 1880s, Thai princes, and later other non-royal elites, were sent overseas to study a variety of subjects including European languages, diplomatic service, military warfare and strategy, forestry, education, and medicine. While the majority studied in Europe, namely England, France, Germany, Austria and Russia, some were sent to British colonies in Singapore and India, or to the United States.[111] Time spent abroad contributed to a growing dissatisfaction with the status quo of political rule in Siam. A conspiracy to stage a coup was dealt with swiftly in 1912 but the incident was an indicator that political winds were changing. Numerous officials suggested changes to the political order, particularly the monarchy, but King Vajiravudh rejected all calls for reform as "selfishly motivated, disloyal, and certain to bring ruin to Siam."[112]

Upon his death in 1925, King Vajiravudh's youngest brother ascended the throne, rather unprepared for the role suddenly thrust upon him. He inherited from Vajiravudh major economic problems and increasing calls for political reform.[113] King Prajadhipok was more open to considering political changes, but changes did not come fast enough for a group of about one hundred soldiers who staged a coup d'état on June 24, 1932. The coup resulted in only one casualty and was a *fait accompli* by noon time. The conspirators bluffed and immobilized other military units in the capital, rounded up chief government officials, and sent a letter to King Prajadhipok at his seaside palace asking him to submit to a

---

110. Boon-Itt, "Dialogue," 23; Baker, *History*, 106.
111. Suksod-Barger, *Religious Influences*, 48–50; Wyatt, *Thailand*, 219–20.
112. Wyatt, *Thailand*, 232.
113. Wyatt, *Thailand*, 234–35.

constitution. He replied he had been thinking about making this change already and would be content to serve the country under a constitution.[114]

The first years of the new government were chaotic as the elite, the military, and senior officials struggled to agree on how to structure a constitutional monarchy. King Prajadhipok went abroad in 1934 and abdicated in 1935, unhappy with the "undemocratic nature of the new regime."[115] A nine-year old royal living in Switzerland, Prince Ananda Mahidol, was appointed as the new king.[116]

The new government came to power at the worst point of the economic depression affecting the nation, which meant they received the credit when circumstances improved. Despite dissension in the infant government, great strides were made in promoting universal compulsory education and the development of the national military.[117] Following the 1932 revolution, Thailand pursued stronger cultural, political, and economic ties with Japan. Trade with Japan increased rapidly. Articles about Japan appeared in the Thai press and there were cultural exchanges between the two nations. In March 1938, a treaty between Thailand and Japan granted Japanese subjects full freedom to reside in Thailand with all the same rights as Thai people. Japanese in Thailand could legally engage in all types of employment and could own property for all kinds of purposes.[118]

With the 1938 election of Plaek Phibulsongkram as prime minister, a new era of intensified nationalism began. Phibulsongkram was a military man and favored a strongly nationalistic, militaristic regime. The beginning of his rule witnessed arrests of people suspected of political opposition and some were executed after trials of questionable legality. He banned display of pictures of King Prajadhipok and sued the former king for misuse of crown property. He used mass media, press censorship, and the government radio monopoly to promote devotion to the nation.

Phibulsongkram admired the rising regimes in Japan, Germany and Italy, and sought to create a great Thai empire on Hitler's model.[119] Pursuing this vision, in late 1940 he went to war with France in Cambodia to

114. Wyatt, *Thailand*, 241–42.
115. Wyatt, *Thailand*, 246–49.
116. Baker, *History*, 120.
117. Wyatt, *Thailand*, 249–50.
118. Landon, *Thailand*, 69–72.
119. Baker, *History*, 131; Reynolds, "Phibun Songkhram," 107–10.

retake provinces lost to France forty years earlier. Though ground conflicts were inconclusive, Thailand was successful in regaining her "lost territories" from French Cambodia through the assistance of the Japanese who helped negotiate a formal end of hostilities.[120] Phibulsongkram's campaign to retake territory from France was also accompanied by anti-French propaganda and government-sponsored persecution of Roman Catholics in Thailand who were associated with French missionaries. This persecution lasted from 1940 until 1944 when Phibulsongkram was ousted from power and an Allied victory seemed probable.[121]

The persecution of Roman Catholics was accompanied by increased pressure on other religious minorities, including Protestants and Muslims, to "return to Buddhism" to express their national loyalty. Although there was nationalistic pressure to be Buddhist during the reign of King Vajiravudh, Phibulsongkram ramped up the rhetoric, and civil servants and teachers were pressured to conform. In many cases, non-Buddhists lost their jobs when they declined to venerate a Buddha image. Lists of Thai people who re-converted to Buddhism appeared in the daily newspapers.[122]

Phibulsongkram's government enacted anti-Chinese measures also, due to fears of communism and anti-Japanese boycotts by Chinese residents in Thailand who were upset about the Sino-Japanese War that began in 1937. In July 1938, Wichit Wathakan, a prime architect of Phibulsongkram's nationalist propaganda, gave a speech vilifying the Chinese and pondering whether Thailand should enact against the Chinese policies similar to Hitler's against the Jews.[123]

People were discouraged from buying foreign products and "Thailand for the Thai" was the slogan for Phibulsongkram's nationalist economic campaign. As mentioned previously, the name of the country was changed from Siam to Thailand in 1939 in order to create greater national unity between the former kingdom of Siam and other regions now under her jurisdiction.[124] Between 1939 and 1942, twelve Cultural Mandates were issued, telling people what to buy, what to wear, and

---

120. Baker, *History*, 134; Wyatt, *Thailand*, 255–56. For a detailed account of the Thai-French conflict, see Strate, *Lost Territories*.
121. Strate, "Uncivil."
122. Smith, *Siamese*, 171–78, 199–202.
123. Wyatt, *Thailand*, 254; Baker, *History*, 128–29.
124. Reynolds, "Phibun Songkhram," 119–20.

how to behave. Phibulsongkram argued these were necessary to make Thailand a modern nation.[125]

On December 8, 1941, Japanese forces invaded Thailand because they wanted to use the nation as a passageway for movement of Japanese troops. Despite some short-lived battles, the Thai government quickly submitted to Japanese demands, realizing that it would be suicide to go to war with Japan and that aligning themselves with Japan would put them in a good position in the new world order in the likelihood that Japan won the war.[126]

CONCLUSION

In this chapter, we have seen the ways in which the Thai elite from the 1880s devoted new energy to modernizing their nation in a multitude of areas, incorporating developments from abroad with the Thai traditional institutions of monarchy and Buddhism. In doing so, they asserted equality with Western powers and simultaneously declared the validity of a Thai form of modernity. In the context of these changes in Thai society, the American Presbyterian mission and indigenous Thai churches grew and developed, sometimes adopting and other times diverging from modernizing trends around them. The next chapter will provide an historical overview of Christianity in Thailand, providing additional background context for understanding the impact of modernism among American Presbyterian missionaries that will be examined in chapters 6 to 9.

---

125. Wyatt, *Thailand*, 252–56.
126. Wyatt, *Thailand*, 256–58.

5

Missionary Work in Thailand Prior to World War II

ALTHOUGH MISSIONARIES CAME TO Thailand with primarily religious goals, their most recognized contributions to Thai society were in other areas. The history of Christianity in Thailand, especially Protestantism, is not only a story of religion but also a story of advancing modernity. This chapter will provide an historical overview of the development of Protestant Christianity in Thailand, tracing the progress of missionaries and Thai Christians towards their religious goals of conversion and church development as well as their achievements in propelling the modernization of Thailand.[1] As such, special note will be taken of foreign missionary contributions to Thai society in the advancement of scientific knowledge, printing, education, medical care, and the integration of the modern nation-state of Thailand. The missionaries were not only purveyors of modernity but were also influenced by modernizing trends around them, both those within Thailand and from abroad. The influence of one of those trends, theological modernism, will be examined in the second half of this book.

CATHOLIC BEGINNINGS, 1511–1828

Although notations in the journals of travelers suggest there was an East Syrian Christian presence in Thailand as early as 525 A.D., there is no

---

1. Portions of this chapter also appear in Dahlfred, "History of Christianity in Thailand" and Dahlfred, *Daniel McGilvary*.

archeological evidence to prove such a mission existed.² The start of documented mission and church history in Thailand begins with the arrival of Roman Catholic priests in 1511. These priests accompanied the Portuguese diplomatic mission which established an embassy in the city of Ayutthaya, the capital of Siam until it was sacked by the Burmese army in 1767. Two Dominican priests arrived in 1555 but were subsequently martyred in 1566 and 1569. Jesuits came in 1607 and the Paris Foreign Missionary Society in 1662.³ In the 1680s, a Greek Roman Catholic adventurer named Constantine Phaulkon came to prominence in the court of King Narai. However, Phaulkon was arrested and executed in 1688 by Siamese political enemies who feared both the conversion of the ailing monarch to Catholicism and French colonial ambitions that Phaulkon's political power might enable.⁴

Following the Phaulkon affair, French soldiers and missionaries were expelled from the country and British and French merchants left Ayutthaya.⁵ Siamese suspicions of Catholics persisted through the end of the eighteenth century, and the small Catholic community in Siam experienced insignificant growth during this period. In the minds of Siamese rulers, the Christian religion was associated with Western culture and politics, and therefore suspect. The kings of Thailand from the late eighteenth century through the middle of the nineteenth century were generally wary of Westerners. It was only with the ascent of King Mongkut to the throne in 1851 that there was renewed openness to Westerners and their potential contributions to Thai society. Prior to this, the priests who came to Thailand largely ministered among the foreign community and made few converts among native Siamese. In 1785, the Roman Catholic church in Siam reported a total of 1372 Catholics in the country, of whom 413 were Siamese of Portuguese origin, presumably the progeny of marriages between Portuguese settlers and local Siamese.⁶

    2. Smith, *Siamese*, 13.
    3. Smith, *Siamese*, 9.
    4. Smith, *Siamese*, 13; Baker, *History*, 13; Boon-Itt, "Dialogue," 33–34; Aphornsuvan, "West," 405–6.
    5. Boon-Itt, "Dialogue," 34; Baker, *History*, 17.
    6. Smith, *Siamese*, 9.

PROTESTANT BEGINNINGS IN SIAM, 1828–1840

The first Protestant efforts to reach the Thai were those of the Baptist missionary Ann Judson who evangelized Thai prisoners of war and their descendants in Burma. Encouraged by her husband Adoniram, Ann Judson learned the Thai language and translated into Thai a Burmese catechism, a tract, and the Gospel of Matthew.[7] The first record of a Siamese convert to Protestant Christianity is Moung Shway-pwen in Burma.

The first resident Protestant missionaries in Thailand were Karl Gützlaff and Jacob Tomlin who arrived in Bangkok on August 23, 1828.[8] Karl Gützlaff was a Prussian who formerly worked under the auspices of the Netherlands Missionary Society.[9] Jacob Tomlin was an Englishman working under the London Missionary Society.[10] The pair were welcomed by the Portuguese Consul and the Siamese foreign minister. Gützlaff already spoke Chinese and the pair set to learning Siamese. Gützlaff and Tomlin translated the four Gospels and Romans into Siamese and produced an English-Siamese dictionary up to the letter R.[11] They engaged in distributing Christian books in Chinese, which attracted considerable interest from locals, especially Chinese, as well as opposition from Catholic priests. Though Tomlin's journal includes multiple accounts of people who read at least portions of the missionaries' books, it is probable that many eagerly received the free books because of their novelty since the printing press had not yet arrived in Siam and literacy was not widespread.[12] Protestant missionaries in Thailand from Gützlaff and Tomlin onward were strong proponents of literacy but some were unsure about the evangelistic effectiveness of literature distribution. In 1858, American Presbyterian missionary Stephen Mattoon commented that "we fear it is only a desire to satisfy curiosity or the love of acquisition" that led people to receive Christian books.[13]

Tomlin left Bangkok on May 14, 1829 to collect his family in Singapore and to restore his failing health. Gützlaff later followed Tomlin to Singapore where he married Maria Newell of the London Missionary

---

7. Smith, *Siamese*, 12–13.
8. Farrington, *Early Missionaries*, 8–10.
9. For more on Gützlaff's career, see Lutz, *Opening China*.
10. For a brief summary of Tomlin's career, see Sibree, *London Missionary Society*, 26.
11. Smith, *Siamese*, 14–15; Phra Klang is a title, not a personal name.
12. Tomlin, *Journal*, 53, 55.
13. Pongudom, "Apologetic and Missionary Proclamation," 110.

Society. The newly married couple returned to Bangkok on February 11, 1830. A year later, Mrs. Gützlaff died in childbirth, her twin daughters dying shortly thereafter. Tomlin had not yet returned from Singapore, and a heartbroken Gützlaff set sail for China on June 3, 1831, never to return to Siam.[14] Following Gützlaff's short ministry in Thailand, he proceeded to China, where he spent twenty years itinerating up and down the Chinese coast. Tomlin returned to Bangkok on June 30, 1831 to discover he had missed Gützlaff by only a month. Without his co-worker, Tomlin stayed in Siam only six more months, leaving for good on January 7, 1832. Gützlaff and Tomlin's efforts resulted in several inquirers but only one baptized convert, a Chinese man named Boon Tee (Koë Bun Tai).[15]

While together in Singapore, Gützlaff and Tomlin sent letters to the American Board of Commissioners for Foreign Missions (ABCFM) and to the American Baptist mission in Burma, appealing for more missionary workers for Siam.[16] The letter to the United States was carried on the same ship transporting the Siamese Twins, Chang and Eng, whose itinerant exhibitions brought the country of Siam to the attention of the American public.[17] These letters bore fruit in the appointment of three missionaries to work in Siam. The ABCFM sent David Abeel to Siam, accompanied by Jacob Tomlin, and the American Baptist mission in Burma designated John Taylor and Eliza Grew Jones to work in Siam.[18]

David Abeel arrived in Siam in 1831 and stayed less than a year, during which time he struggled with fever. When John and Eliza Jones arrived in 1833, the couple set to work learning Siamese and John Jones translated the New Testament from Greek into Siamese, which was printed in 1843. John and Eliza Jones are noteworthy for being the first Protestant missionaries to come to Siam specifically to reach the Siamese. Previous missionaries and many of those arriving after the Joneses came to reach the Chinese, not the Siamese. A number of missionaries, such as Gützlaff and Tomlin, worked among the Siamese as

---

14. McFarland, *Historical Sketch*, 34.

15. Smith, *Siamese*, 15–16; Lutz, *Opening China*, 52. For more on Chinese immigration and Chinese Protestant Christianity in Thailand, see Blanford, *Chinese Churches in Thailand*.

16. Lutz, *Opening China*, 52.

17. Smith, *Siamese*, 15; Wallace and Wallace, *Two*; Sources available to the author did not specify which American churches received Gützlaff's letter.

18. McFarland, *Historical Sketch*, 27, 59.

they were able, although the Siamese were not their main objective.[19] This situation changed after China became more open to foreigners at the end of the first Anglo-Chinese (Opium) War in 1842, but it should be borne in mind that during the initial period of Protestant mission in Siam from 1828 to the early 1840s, many missionaries in Siam were merely using Siam as a stepping stone to China.[20]

After the arrival of the Joneses in 1833, a small number of other Baptist missionaries arrived in the following decades and there were several conversions among the Chinese in Bangkok. In 1837, a small group of Chinese converts were formed into Maitri Chit Church, the first Chinese Protestant church in Asia. The first Siamese convert was reported in 1849, and by 1850 the congregation increased to 35 members.[21] However, after several missionaries died and others relocated from Siam to China, the American Baptist mission officially ended their work in Siam in 1868.

After the departure of David Abeel in 1832, several more ABCFM missionary couples arrived in the 1830s and 1840s, although many of these missionaries met tragic deaths and others left after only a short time. Drowning, fever, and diseases such as tuberculosis were common causes of death.[22] The ABCFM missionaries saw few conversions as the result of their work, but two of them are nonetheless of historical significance: Jesse Caswell and Daniel Beach Bradley.

Jesse Caswell bears the distinction of having been English language tutor to Prince Mongkut, the future King Rama IV of Siam (r. 1851-1868).[23] In 1845, Prince Mongkut, who was then living in a Buddhist temple as a monk, invited Caswell to instruct him in English. As an enticement to accept this invitation, Caswell was offered use of a room at the temple for preaching and tract distribution following the conclusion of lessons. This arrangement continued for a year and a half. Smith notes that the high respect given to teachers in Thai culture contributed to the future king's positive view of Christian missionaries in successive years.[24]

19. Aphornsuvan, "West," 409.
20. Smith, *Siamese*, 53–56; McFarland, *Historical Sketch*, 36.
21. Smith, *Siamese*, 21–22; Maitrichit Chinese Baptist Church, "History of the Church."
22. Smith, *Siamese*, 23–24.
23. Regarding the title "Rama," see Baker, *History*, 298.
24. McFarland, *Historical Sketch*, 19–21; Smith, *Siamese*, 24.

Dan Beach Bradley may be the most well-known missionary in Thai history, having distinguished himself in medicine and printing. A medical doctor by training, Dr. Bradley and his wife Emilie arrived in Bangkok in 1835, thus making Bradley one of the earliest Protestant medical missionaries and a contemporary of Peter Parker in China. Like several other Presbyterians at the time, they worked under the auspices of the ABCFM. Bradley brought with him a printing press which was set up a year after his arrival. Mr. Robinson of the ABCFM produced the first printed page in Siam using Siamese font upon this press, a sheet tract containing the biblical account of the giving of the law at Sinai, the Ten Commandments with explanations, a prayer, and three hymns.[25] The printing quality was deemed unsatisfactory, however, and both the American Baptist mission and the ABCFM obtained better presses. Upon one of these presses the first printed document of the Siamese government was published in 1839, an edict banning opium.[26] Bradley spent substantial time over his thirty-eight years in Thailand printing various materials, including not only religious literature but also Siamese government documents and Siam's first newspaper, *The Bangkok Recorder*. Through their printing endeavors, Bradley and other missionaries facilitated the modernization of Siam by promoting the dissemination of both printing technology as well as a diversity of information published using that technology. Though the Siamese government eventually acquired their own printing presses, they relied heavily on mission presses at first. When the American Presbyterians founded a press in Chiang Mai in 1892, the mission press played a major role in modernization in the North, printing government literature and spreading new ideas. When the Presbyterians in Chiang Mai developed their printed Sunday school lessons into a monthly newspaper in 1903, this periodical was the only news publication in the North for a long time. Containing national, international, and church news as well as Sunday school lessons, this newspaper furthered the modernization and integration of northern Thailand which the Siamese government desired.[27]

Bradley also became renowned for his contributions to modern medical practice in Siam. Shortly after his arrival, Bradley opened a

---

25. In the seventeenth century, Catholic missionaries in Thailand used the printing press to publish religious materials, albeit using Romanized rather than Thai script. See "Twenty Years Ago."

26. McFarland, *Historical Sketch*, 16.

27. Swanson, *Krischak*, 52–53.

medical dispensary, treating patients and giving out medicines for free. As he acquired the Siamese language and indigenous helpers, Scripture verses and prayers were included in the free offerings of his clinics. Outbreaks of cholera and smallpox were common occurrences in Siam and Bradley is credited with introducing vaccinations which reportedly greatly reduced the annual death rate due to preventable diseases. He is thought to have performed the first modern surgery in Siam, amputating the arm of a Buddhist monk who was injured when a cannon exploded at a temple festival. His medical successes earned him favor with Thai royalty and he trained royal physicians in vaccination techniques during the reign of King Rama III.[28]

After the death of his wife, Bradley and his children returned to the United States in February 1847, leaving Caswell and his brother-in-law Asa Hemenway as the only ABCFM representatives in Siam. In the United States, Bradley resigned from the ABCFM due to his belief in the possibility of obtaining entire sanctification in this life. Bradley and Caswell strongly advocated for this belief among their fellow missionaries in Bangkok, giving rise to considerable interpersonal conflict which directly influenced Bradley's resignation and the ABCFM's decision to close their mission in Thailand.[29] After resigning from the ABCFM, Bradley joined the American Mission Association (AMA) and became their sole representative in Siam, together with his second wife Sarah whom he met in Oberlin, Ohio. The newly married couple and Bradley's children returned to Siam in 1850 and continued in mission work until Dan Bradley died in 1873. His wife survived him by twenty years and several of Bradley's children and grandchildren worked as missionaries in Siam through the early twentieth century. Jesse Caswell died in Siam while Bradley was in the United States, thus leaving Asa Hemenway as the last ABCFM missionary in Siam. When Hemenway left in 1849, the ABCFM closed its work in Siam.[30]

Not long after Dan Bradley returned to Siam with his second wife, a unique opportunity opened up for the new Mrs. Bradley and a couple of other missionary wives. Despite the general neglect of women's education in mid-nineteenth century Siam, in 1851 King Mongkut invited Mrs. Mary Mattoon (APM), Mrs. Sarah Bradley (AMA), and Mrs. Sarah

28. Smith, *Siamese*, 24–25; McFarland, *Historical Sketch*, 16–17.

29. ABCFM, *Siam Mission and Messrs. Bradley and Caswell*; Bradley, *Abstract of the Journal of Rev. Bradley*, 68; Lord, "In His Steps," 133–43.

30. Smith, *Siamese*, 24; McFarland, *Historical Sketch*, 19–21.

Jones (Baptist) to teach English to his wives and other women in the royal palace.[31] Accepting the king's invitation, for more than a year the three missionary women visited the palace six days per week, each woman taking two days. Teaching temporarily stopped in December 1852 after the illness and death of one of the young queens. When it recommenced in 1853, the teaching became more evangelistic than previously, due in part to interest shown by the palace women themselves. The Mattoons's 1854 annual report recorded that very little was done in English during the previous year, the majority of instruction being Christian content in the Siamese language.[32] Just two days previous to the writing of this report, on September 28, 1854, King Mongkut summoned all the missionaries and European residents of Bangkok to question them about a scathing article about himself that appeared in *The Straits Times* a couple of weeks earlier. The king was very angry about the article and felt certain that one of the missionaries was the unnamed source for the Singaporean newspaper article.[33] Servants and employees of missionaries were arrested and then released after a brief detention, and the king nearly ejected all missionaries from the country. At this time the three missionary women temporarily ceased teaching, though after a few days, Mrs. Mattoon and Mrs. Smith returned to their teaching in the palace. This was short-lived however, and not many days later, no one would open the gate of the palace to let in the missionary women. The exact reason for the termination of their teaching sessions is unclear. However, King Mongkut's subsequent employment of a private teacher, Mrs. Anna Leonowens, to teach the palace women and children indicates a strong possibility the king was displeased with the missionary women's prioritization of teaching religion over English. In a February 26, 1862 letter inviting Anna Leonowens to come to Bangkok, the king wrote:

> We are in good pleasure, and satisfaction in heart, that you are in willingness to undertake the education of our beloved royal children. And we hope that in doing your education on us and our children (whom English call inhabitants of benighted land) you will do your best endeavor for knowledge of English language, science, and literature, and not for conversion to Christianity; as the followers of Buddha are mostly aware of

---

31. After the death of his second wife, John Taylor Jones married Sarah Sleeper. Trakulhun, "Among a People of Unclean Lips," 1217–18.

32. Smith, *Siamese*, 40–41.

33. Bradley, *Journal*, 173–76; "Siam," 5.

the powerfulness of truth and virtue, as well as the followers of Christ, and are desirous to have facility of English language and literature, more than new religions.[34]

It is evident from the experience of the three missionary women and the subsequent terms of employment for Anna Leonowens that King Mongkut, while valuing what missionaries could offer, was only content to accept the help of foreigners if they gave the type of assistance he desired. Missionaries were welcome in Siam as long as they contributed to national development and modernization in ways desired by the Thai elite, and eschewed proselytization in certain contexts.[35]

AMERICAN PRESBYTERIAN BEGINNINGS, 1840–1860

Previous to 1840, American Presbyterians worked in Siam under the auspices of the ABCFM. However, after the Presbyterians founded their own Board of Foreign Missions, as discussed in chapter 3, the new board sent Robert Orr to Bangkok in 1838 on a survey trip to evaluate the possibility of opening up a mission work among the Siamese and the Chinese. It was decided to pursue this plan and William P. Buell and his wife were sent to Bangkok in 1840. The Buells were on their own for nearly four years until Mrs. Buell became ill and the couple returned to the United States.[36]

The departure of the Buells in 1844 left the American Presbyterian mission without any personnel in Siam until the arrival of Stephen and Mary Mattoon, and Samuel Reynolds House on March 22, 1847.[37] Although William Buell learned Siamese well enough to preach, the work of the Presbyterians in Thailand was established in earnest by these new arrivals. On August 31, 1849, House, Mattoon, and Stephen Bush who arrived in April 1849 formally organized the first Presbyterian Church of Bangkok at Samray. The church was composed entirely of missionaries but shortly thereafter was joined by Sin Saa Qua Kieng, a Chinese convert who transferred from the ABCFM whose work recently closed.[38] During the first twenty years of the American Presbyterian

---

34. The non-standard grammar in this quote is original. Leonowens, *English Governess*, v–vi.

35. Watson, "Missionary Influence," 158; Aphornsuvan, "West," 409–17.

36. Son, "Christian Revival," 41–42; Smith, *Siamese*, 26; McFarland, *Historical Sketch*, 35–36.

37. McFarland, *Historical Sketch*, 37.

38. Smith, *Siamese*, 26–27; McFarland, *Historical Sketch*, 36–42.

work in Siam, namely 1840-1860, the missionaries saw only a small handful of converts. Their first Siamese convert was Nai Chune, who was baptized in 1859 and subsequently took over teaching responsibilities from Sin Saa Qua Kieng at the Presbyterians' mission school.[39] With the change in teachers, the language of instruction changed from Chinese to Siamese.[40] The first female Siamese convert was Nang Esther Pradipasena who joined the church in 1860.[41]

During the initial years of their Thailand mission, APM missionaries dedicated themselves to medical work, preaching in a mission chapel, and book and tract distribution. However, their work was not impressive to some outsiders. On a visit to Bangkok in 1855, the British diplomat and Unitarian Sir John Bowring commented on the lack of results from Christian mission work, pointing out that in regard to the Chinese, in twenty-seven years of Protestant missions the missionaries did not have even twenty-seven converts.[42]

PRESBYTERIAN EXPANSION OUTSIDE OF BANGKOK

Until 1861, all missionary activity in Siam was limited to Bangkok.[43] Itinerant trips to other areas were allowed but foreigners were not permitted to take up residence outside the capital. By the early 1860s, four new missionary couples joined the American Presbyterian mission: Daniel and Sophia McGilvary, Jonathan and Maria Wilson, Samuel and Jane McFarland, and Noah A. McDonald and his wife. Of these new missionaries, the McGilvarys and McFarlands were the first to live outside Bangkok. In 1861, the two couples moved 75 miles southwest of Bangkok to establish a new work in Petchaburi province. Samuel McFarland preferred school work and taught the lieutenant governor's son while Daniel McGilvary focused on evangelistic work. In the 1870s, Jane McFarland opened in Petchaburi an industrial school for women and older girls, teaching them to sew, crochet, and knit. Around the same time, missionary Harriette House began an industrial school for girls in Bangkok. When sewing machines were introduced to the country by missionaries, both women

---

39. "Nai" is the Thai equivalent of "Mr."
40. McFarland, *Historical Sketch*, 50.
41. McFarland, *Historical Sketch*, 46. "Nang" is the Thai equivalent of "Mrs."
42. McFarland, *Historical Sketch*, 47.
43. Smith, *Siamese*, 57.

used them in their schools.[44] The use of sewing machines by Mrs. McFarland apparently became quite prominent, for John A. Eakin reported in 1928 that Petchaburi had become known as the "sewing machine town."[45] In this way, American Presbyterian women helped pioneer modern education for women in Thailand. A church was established in Petchaburi in 1863 and a Siamese man was licensed to preach there in 1867.[46] The church experienced slow growth for many years but saw a sharp upturn after McFarland left to assist the Siamese government with educational work and was replaced by Eugene P. Dunlap. Under Dunlap's leadership the church increased to thirty-two members by 1879.[47]

THE BEGINNING OF THE LAOS MISSION, 1867

While in Petchaburi, Daniel McGilvary preached to Lao war captives relocated from Korat in northeast Thailand to serve as forced labor in government works projects at Petchaburi. While living in Bangkok, McGilvary met the Lao ruler Chao Kawilorot and was intrigued by his language and culture. Chao Kawilorot was sovereign over his realm but Chiang Mai and the other Lao states were vassal states of the Siamese king to whom they were required to pay tribute.[48] McGilvary's encounter with Kawilorot and his ministry among the Lao in Petchaburi kindled in McGilvary a desire to visit the Lao homeland. The Presbyterian mission was not yet ready to establish a station in the Lao city of Chiang Mai, but the newly organized Presbytery of Siam gave him permission to make an exploratory trip in autumn 1863.[49] Arriving in Chiang Mai on January 7, 1864, many people came to see the novelty of these white foreigners and ask why they came. After this initial ten-day visit in Chiang Mai, the missionaries returned to Bangkok. Even though it was only a brief visit, McGilvary became convinced his life's work should be in that region.

After a three-year delay due to missionary personnel changes in Bangkok, McGilvary moved to Chiang Mai in January 1867 to open a new mission station there. From 1867 to 1921, the American Presbyterian

44. Suksod-Barger, "Religious Influences," 126–30; McFarland, *McFarland of Siam*, 40–43.

45. McFarland, *Historical Sketch*, 94–95.

46. McFarland, *Historical Sketch*, 52.

47. Swanson, *Towards a Clean Church*, 4.

48. "Chao" means lord or ruler.

49. The spelling "Chiang Mai" is used on modern maps but other historical transliterations include "Chieng Mai," "Chiangmai," and "Chiengmai."

mission maintained two independent missions within Thailand, the Siam mission, covering the Bangkok area and the southern Peninsula, and the Laos mission, covering Chiang Mai and other areas of present-day northern Thailand. At the urging of Prince Damrong, the Laos mission was renamed the North Siam mission in 1913, a change in line with the Siamese government's desire to integrate the North into the kingdom of Siam. At this time, the Siam mission was renamed, "South Siam mission." In 1921, the North Siam mission and South Siam mission were combined into a single administrative unit, namely the Siam mission, a change facilitated by improved communications and transportation.[50] However, when McGilvary founded the Laos mission in 1867, it took forty-nine days to travel from Bangkok to Chiang Mai and the Lao states of the North were ruled by feudal princes.[51] Five of these Lao states (Chiang Mai, Lampun, Lakawn, Prae, Nan) were later incorporated into present-day Thailand and the sixth (Luang Prabang) is part of modern Laos. The region that McGilvary called "Laoland" has since become northern Thailand. The descendants of the people with whom McGilvary worked have linguistically and culturally assimilated into mainstream Thai culture. Yet in McGilvary's time, the Lao states were little known in Bangkok and were almost another world. Before McGilvary, only one other Westerner ever visited Chiang Mai. The missionaries were given a small plot of land in Chiang Mai in 1868 and set down roots in the north. With their strong connections to Bangkok, McGilvary and other missionaries who followed came to play an important role in the eventual integration of the north into the kingdom of Siam, pioneering modern education, medical care, and printing in Chiang Mai and neighboring areas.

The first Lao converts came in 1869 through McGilvary's evangelization of conscripted laborers who came into Chiang Mai to work at building projects for the ruler of the city. Nan Inta, a former Buddhist abbot, was the first man to be baptized. His faith in Buddhism was shaken when McGilvary accurately predicted an eclipse in contrast to the claims of his pseudo-scientific Buddhist books about cosmology and geography. In addition to proclamation of the gospel, McGilvary's apologetic strategy included rationalistic attacks upon local supernaturalism and spirit beliefs, and the promotion of Western science and medicine in their place. McGilvary and some of his converts engaged

---

50. Swanson, *Krischak*, 154–55; House, "Thai Christians," 212; Callender to Brown, December 16, 1913, PHS.

51. McGilvary, *Half Century*, 63.

in debunking tours of caves, hill tops, and other places where evil spirits were believed to dwell, seeking to show people that their fears were unfounded. McGilvary believed people would acknowledge the truth of the gospel and the falsehood of their traditional beliefs if presented with superior evidence. Though this strategy bore fruit in convincing Nan Inta to re-consider his beliefs, it was largely ineffective in winning additional people to the Christian faith. Nevertheless, when Siamese resident commissioners began to settle in Chiang Mai and promote greater integration with Siam, they appreciated the missionaries' opposition to local "superstitions," as such a stance dovetailed well with Bangkok's modernizing emphasis on an ethically focused and civically useful Buddhism.[52] The Buddhist cosmological beliefs that led Nan Inta to believe that eclipses are caused by a monster eating the sun had already been abandoned by King Mongkut. The king, like McGilvary, predicted the 1868 eclipse using modern scientific learning, and was observing it at the predicted time in distant Prachuap province on the southern peninsula of Thailand.[53] Abandonment of Buddhist cosmology was already in progress among Siamese royals and other elites in Bangkok but had not yet begun in the north. In that context, so distant from Bangkok, Nan Inta's conversion opened the way for more professions of faith and gave greater respectability to the missionaries and their religion.

PERSECUTION AND TOLERATION IN THE NORTH

As more converts were made, Chao Kawilorot, the ruler of Chiang Mai, felt threatened. In early 1869, he sent a letter to Bangkok asking the U.S. Consul to remove the missionaries because they caused a recent rice famine in the area. The U.S. Consul told the ruler of Chiang Mai that they did not cause the famine and would not be removed. However, he promised to order the missionaries not to cause any such famines. Kawilorot was unhappy with that reply and ordered all Christians to be arrested. This was an extremely tense time and both the Lao Christians and the missionaries were in peril. Most Lao Christians fled but two were captured and, refusing to recant their faith, were tortured and murdered. For a long time, no one would tell the missionaries what happened because they feared for their own lives. Eventually someone secretly told the missionaries about the martyrdoms and the missionaries sent word

---

52. Zehner, "Thai Protestants," 297–301.
53. Winichakul, *Siam Mapped*, 42–47.

to Bangkok, not knowing whether this would be their last communication this side of heaven. Acting U.S. Consul Noah McDonald, who was also a Presbyterian missionary, and a royal commissioner appointed by the Siamese regent traveled together to Chiang Mai and informed Kawilorot that he could do whatever he wanted to his own servants (namely, the Lao Christians) but the missionaries must not be harmed. Kawilorot was very upset at this and threatened to banish the missionaries. Once he calmed down, he consented for the missionaries to stay as long as they only distributed medicine and did not preach Christianity.[54] Kawilorot opposed McGilvary and other missionaries not only because of the new religion they preached, but also because they were becoming, perhaps unintentionally, rivals to Kawilorot and other Lao patrons. The missionaries' superior resources, such as the anti-malarial quinine and strong connections to authorities in Bangkok, made them attractive patrons in the eyes of Chiang Mai residents.[55]

In 1869, the Siamese commissioner only had limited ability to enforce the will of Bangkok in Chiang Mai. However, as Siam progressively expanded its authority over northern rulers, the missionaries' requests for assistance provided opportunities for Siamese commissioners to exert their authority over local rulers.[56] Though not all Siamese commissioners who served in the North were supportive of the missionaries, these foreigners were valuable nonetheless for their contributions to the integration of Chiang Mai into the kingdom of Siam. While the Laos mission initially focused on evangelism, in the late 1890s their priorities shifted to activities that encouraged societal modernization and national integration, a development that will be discussed shortly.

Following the martyrdoms and the departure of the consul and commissioner, it seemed that the mission station in Chiang Mai would have to be closed. However, McGilvary was confident that God would prevent it. The ruler of Chiang Mai went to Bangkok to pay tribute not long after this, and while there he became sick and died on the return trip. After Kawilorot's death in 1870, Bangkok exerted its influence to pass over logical successors to the Chiang Mai throne and appointed Chao Intanon, who was expected to be friendlier to Bangkok policies than Kawilorot had been.[57] The new ruler was also friendlier to the

54. Smith, *Siamese*, 66–69.
55. Zehner, "Church Growth," 28–29.
56. Zehner, "Church Growth," 25–28.
57. Wyatt, *Thailand*, 194.

missionaries. However, it was three years before local Christians became confident enough to follow Christ openly. Some new converts were made but these new believers were mostly older men living on the mission compound, working there, or coming for medical attention. Church growth was slow in this period and a number of converts returned to the spirit practices of Lao folk Buddhism. Still, a trickle of people continued to profess faith in Christ, increasingly those outside of the missionaries's employ. Some were treated in the "hospital" of the missionary Dr. Cheek, and some were relatives of one of the martyrs.

By 1877 the church in Chiang Mai had eighteen members. In 1878, the viceroy of the king of Siam, with the king's implicit consent, issued an edict of religious toleration at the urging of the missionaries. The edict only applied to certain Lao states in the North and displeased the Lao king and officials, but benefitted Lao Christians who had been forced to work on the Sabbath, accused of witchcraft, or denied legal recognition of their marriages. For the church, this edict meant that theoretically no person could be punished for becoming a Christian. The edict also encouraged more people from the lower classes to publicly inquire about Christianity. Swanson noted although McGilvary thought the edict marked the end of supreme authority for the ruler of Chiang Mai and the transfer of effective authority to Siamese officials, it was more modestly just one more event in a continuing power struggle between northern rulers and the Siamese government.[58] In autumn 1882, the edict of toleration was repealed and Lao authorities in the North "issued a proclamation forbidding intercourse with the missionaries."[59] This prompted increased opposition to the gospel but soon thereafter one of the most ardent and powerful enemies of Christianity within the Lao administration died and the former atmosphere of toleration more or less returned. However, there was continued opposition on the local level. It was not uncommon for Christians to be accused of witchcraft, threatened with family disinheritance, imprisonment, or other punishment. Some converts later turned from the faith and left the church or were disciplined and sometimes excommunicated for performing spirit rites, drinking alcohol, or smoking opium. Some of those disciplined, however, were later restored to full church membership.

58. Swanson, *Krischak*, 28–29.
59. Smith, *Siamese*, 73.

EDUCATIONAL WORK AND CHURCH GROWTH

In the early nineteenth century, the only schools in Thailand were temple schools whose curriculum was reading, writing, and Buddhism with the aim of preparing boys for monkhood. Modern education on the Western model was largely unknown and the first missionaries began their educational efforts by taking students into their homes as private pupils, sometimes paying them to come. On September 13, 1852, Mrs. Mary Mattoon started the first Western-style school in Bangkok, teaching a small group of girls. On September 30, 1852, Sinsaa Ki-eng Qua-Sean, a Chinese mission assistant, opened a boarding school on mission premises beside Wat Cheng temple and taught in Chinese. This school moved to a larger location in 1857 and changed the language of instruction to Thai in 1860. The curriculum was philosophy, mathematics, geography, composition, and astronomy. In 1890, Presbyterian missionaries John B. Dunlap and John A. Eakin joined the teaching staff. Eakin stayed at the school fifteen years, overseeing its development and relocation to bigger premises on the east side of the Chao Phraya river in 1901. This school, which developed into a primary and secondary school, was eventually named Bangkok Christian College and was the APM's leading school for boys in Bangkok. Founded in 1875, the mission's leading school for girls in Bangkok was Wattana Wittaya Academy, a primary and secondary school that moved into its current location in 1921, still further east of Bangkok Christian College on the outskirts of the city at that time.[60] In Chiang Mai, the APM's educational efforts began with Mrs. Sophia McGilvary who gathered some girls in her home as private pupils in 1875, a group that developed into Dara Wittaya Academy, the APM's leading girls school in the North. The first boys' school in the North was organized by David G. Collins in 1887, renamed in 1906 by King Vajiravudh (Rama VI) as "Prince Royal's College" in recognition of the significant role that the school was playing for education of boys in northern Thailand.

During the late nineteenth and the early twentieth centuries, there was a marked increase of mission schools in both the Laos mission (northern Thailand) and the Siam mission, though the two missions developed along different lines and held divergent philosophies of mission education. Hugh Taylor, Presbyterian missionary to the Lao from 1888-1934, summarized and compared the philosophies and results of the Laos and Siam missions, noting that the Laos mission evangelized and then

---

60. McFarland, *Historical Sketch*, 209–14.

educated whereas the Siam mission educated in order to evangelize. Taylor drew a correlation between strategy and results, concluding that the Laos mission had many more converts though admittedly less educated, while the Siam mission had few converts but "a few well-educated, outstanding leaders."[61] Although it is difficult to say with certainty whether the difference in educational philosophy between the two missions, which will be examined in greater detail in chapter 9, was as significant for church growth as Taylor believed, the difference in membership growth between the two missions is remarkable. In 1913, two years after McGilvary's death, the church in northern Thailand had over six thousand members compared to only six hundred in Bangkok and southern Thailand.[62] After 1914, growth continued through the start of the Japanese occupation in December 1941, but at a slower pace. Throughout the whole period the majority of church membership remained in the North.[63]

Why was there such a stark difference between the two missions? Although both the Laos mission and the Siam mission were part of the American Presbyterian mission, the two missions were geographically distant and developed along different lines in different contexts. Though educational and evangelistic philosophies were likely contributing factors, anthropologist Edwin Zehner has suggested four additional reasons that help explain the disparity in evangelistic growth between the Laos mission and the Siam mission. Firstly, the Laos mission's Bangkok connections strengthened their local position as the kingdom of Siam increased its control over the North. Secondly, Bangkok's effort to assert itself in the North created social disjunctions that opened the way for religious change. Thirdly, the Laos mission first offered access to Siamese literacy when its advantages were just becoming apparent.[64] Fourthly, it was not uncommon for missionaries in northern Thailand to be seen as patrons. They had language (English and Siamese) and medicine, could represent people in court, and could provide jobs. On this final point, it is true that the Siam mission also offered these benefits but in Bangkok, in contrast to the North, they were not the only ones able to do so. In Bangkok,

---

61. Taylor, "Missionary in Siam," 74–76, 162–64; Smith, *Siamese*, 94–95.

62. Smith, *Siamese*, 92–93.

63. Smith, *Siamese*, 92.

64. From the early days of the Laos mission, the missionaries and some of their converts taught the Central Thai language as they assumed Central Thai would come to displace Northern Thai. See Zehner, "Thai Protestants," 301; House, "Thai Christians," 67; Swanson, *Krischak*, 26.

the missionaries were not exerting influence as rival patrons and were not the only ones with medicine or with Siamese language. They were, in short, less distinctive and less attractive to the common people and this may partially account for the difference in church growth between north and south.[65] The Laos mission was at the forefront of modernization in the north, whereas the Siam mission centered in Bangkok was being overtaken as the leaders in modernization by the Siamese government whose advances came first to the capital before being progressively implemented nationwide. Some APM missionaries also insinuated that modernist re-interpretations of evangelism and an accompanying failure to preach the gospel were to blame for lack of church growth in the Siam mission. Their views will be discussed in chapter 9.

65. Zehner, "Thai Protestants," 300–302.

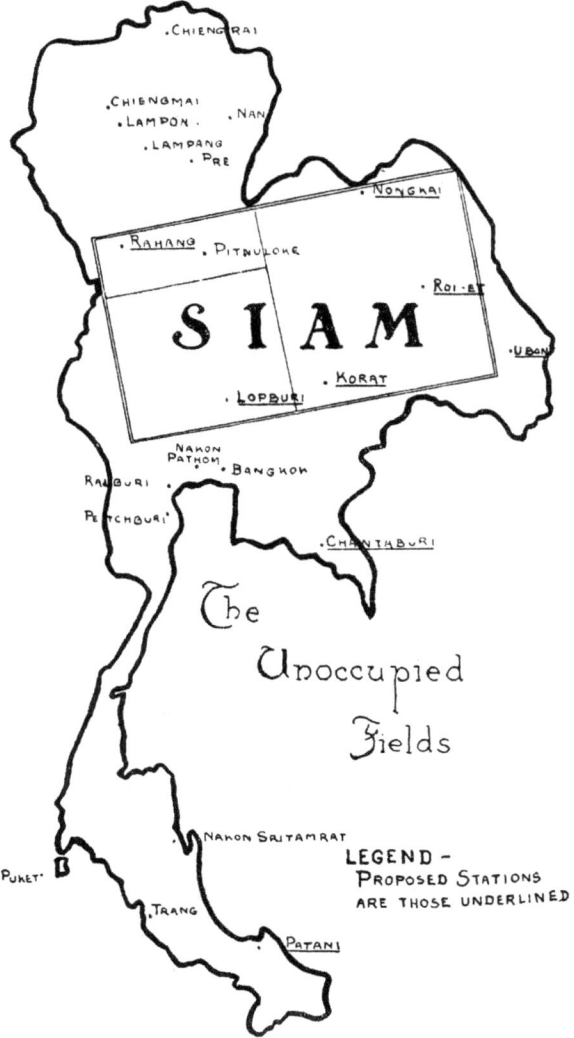

American Presbyterian Mission map of "Siam ~ The Unoccupied Fields" (1928)

Annual Meeting of the Laos Mission, 1906
(Courtesy of the Presbyterian Historical Society, Philadelphia)

THE NEVIUS METHOD AND STUNTED LEADERSHIP DEVELOPMENT

In spite of positive church growth trends during the 1884-1914 period, largely in the North, there was also a retardation of leadership training and indigenization resulting from a botched implementation of the Nevius Method. This method, developed by Presbyterian missionary John Nevius and widely used in Korea, theorized that churches should be self-propagating, self-supporting, and self-governing as quickly as possible for the benefit of their own growth and that of evangelization[66] In 1893 and 1894, a handful of Northern Thai (Lao) Christians were ordained as clergy, many of these paid evangelists of the Laos mission at the time of their ordination. At the meeting of the Northern Laos Presbytery in December 1894, decisions were made to simultaneously appoint a number of northern Thai clergy as pastors of churches and to require these churches to pay their salaries. None of the churches previously had pastors, having been led by lay elders and benefitting from the labors of paid evangelists of the Laos mission. The missionaries had not educated church

---

66. Nevius, *Planting and Development of Missionary Churches*.

members on the role and necessity of a pastor and it seemed beyond the means of many churches to provide a pastor's salary. In addition to this, the men stepping into these roles saw a drastic reduction or elimination of their former income as paid evangelists because they became pastors. The decisions made by the missionaries in Chiang Mai who dominated the presbytery meeting were not well communicated either with other missionaries at outlying stations or with local Christians and churches. As a result, resentment and misunderstanding developed. During the annual presbytery meeting in 1895, northern Thai pastors formed the majority and reversed the decisions of the previous year. They voted to greatly increase the salaries of pastors, up to double the previous amount in some cases, and required the mission to fund those salaries instead of the churches. When these actions were known among the missionaries, many of whom could not attend the meeting, they were not received warmly. Although opinions varied, many missionaries viewed the actions of their Thai co-workers as a "revolt." They suspected the pastors of being greedy and doubted whether they were truly ready for leadership. As a result, there was a lack of trust between missionaries, Thai pastors, and churches for a number of years and serious efforts at training indigenous leadership were curtailed.[67] Following the 1895 "revolt," it was nearly twenty years before the Laos mission again organized formal theological training for Thai Christians, founding the Thailand Theological Seminary (later renamed McGilvary Theological Seminary) in 1912.[68] This institution would produce a modest number of Thai Christian leaders until its closure just before the outbreak of World War II.

THE SHIFT TOWARD INSTITUTIONAL WORK

In the early twentieth century, American Presbyterians in the Siam and Laos missions shifted away from prioritizing direct evangelism and church work, favoring instead educational and medical work, which paralleled the Siamese government's efforts towards universal education and expanding access to medical care. Kenneth Wells, who taught at Prince Royal's College in Chiang Mai from 1927 to 1941, believed this "modern movement toward universal education" largely owed its origin to Christian influence in the world, and founding schools was included in Christ's

---

67. See Swanson, "Pastors' Revolt," 106–11.
68. McFarland, *Historical Sketch*, 229–31.

command to make disciples of all nations.⁶⁹ The dramatic growth of mission schools can be seen in the table below.⁷⁰

Year	Schools	Students
1899	7	528
1913	14	676
1932	52	3764
1938	65	5500

APM Mission Schools in Thailand

As the needs of the schools increased, an increasing proportion of missionary personnel were assigned to them. New missionaries on the field were assigned to the schools and when there were insufficient foreign staff, Thai and missionary evangelists and church workers were assigned to educational work as well. By 1939, only 18 percent of national workers were employed in evangelistic work while the remaining 82 percent were engaged in educational, medical, or other work.⁷¹ Even while the overall number of Presbyterian missionary personnel in Thailand was declining, the APM in Thailand increased the number and quality of their schools over the course of the early twentieth century.⁷² This was done in part to compete with the growing number of government schools that were being established. But another important motive in institutional build-up was ostensibly evangelistic. Some mission leaders were convinced that the most effective way to reach the Thai for Christ was through the schools. Paul Eakin, executive secretary of the APM Thailand mission from 1930-1941, claimed that the schools were "our most successful method" for evangelism.⁷³ This claim was contested by some of his fellow missionaries, a point of tension that will be examined further in chapter 9.

In addition to a dramatic increase in mission schools, there was an accompanying increase in APM commitment to modern medical care. In 1938, Presbyterian missionary John L. Eakin, son of John A. Eakin and brother of Paul, noted the massive growth of the APM's medical work in

69. McFarland, *Historical Sketch*, 229–31.

70. Suksod-Barger, *Religious Influences*, 133; Smith, *Siamese*, 159–60.

71. Son, "Christian Revival," 70.

72. Smith, *Siamese*, 179; Wells, Actions Taken by Executive Committee, December 15–21, 1936, PUA.

73. Smith, *Siamese*, 168.

Thailand since 1910. Unlike mission educational work, the increase in medical work was notable not in terms of number of hospitals but rather better and more well-equipped hospitals, and a large increase in number of in-patients. Mission hospitals treated 890 in-patients in 1908, 1,759 in-patients in 1914, and 4,999 in 1936. Even more people received medical assistance through mission dispensaries, rising from 17,777 in 1908 to 44,626 in 1938.[74] By 1939, the number of Christian-affiliated hospitals was slightly greater than the number of government hospitals. At that time, the Thai government maintained eleven hospitals, the American Presbyterian mission nine hospitals, the Roman Catholics two hospitals, and the Churches of Christ in Great Britain one hospital.[75] Compared with mission schools, the impact of hospitals and dispensaries upon the assignments of missionary personnel was not as great since the smaller number of medical institutions were largely staffed by an increasing number of Thai doctors and nurses.[76] This fact explains in part the reason why the role of the schools became a point of contention in the APM Thailand mission whereas hospitals did not.

Various factors explain the great increase in mission institutions. Firstly, the APM Thailand mission maintained three departments of work in Thailand, namely evangelistic, educational, and medical.[77] The mission's goal was to see each mission station include a full set of mission institutions, namely a church, two schools (boys and girls), a hospital, and a dispensary.[78] This ideal was rarely achieved and was difficult to maintain where it was due to personnel and financial limitations. In seeking institutional growth, the APM Thailand mission was not primarily striving to contribute to nation building or modernizing the country, although they were not displeased to be recognized for their achievements in those areas. The APM Thailand mission hoped its institutions would contribute to evangelism, the development of indigenous churches, and equipping Thai Christians and churches to thrive in a rapidly modernizing world.

---

74. Smith, *Siamese*, 164–66.
75. Smith, *Siamese*, 166; McLeish, *To-Day in Thailand*, 26.
76. Smith, *Siamese*, 164.
77. Taylor, "Missionary in Siam," 164.
78. Swanson, *Krischak*, 52.

THE CHURCH OF CHRIST IN THAILAND (CCT)

The early 1930s saw the genesis of the first Thai Protestant church denomination, the Church of Christ in Siam (later Thailand). A national indigenous denomination was in the minds of missionaries for more than ten years but did not have enough support to make such a move feasible.[79] However, with rapidly progressing integration and modernization of the country, the union of the South Siam and North Siam missions in 1921, and the international Christian trend towards ecumenism and indigenization as promoted by the International Missionary Council, the time was ripe for the formation of the first indigenous Thai church denomination.[80] Following meetings in Bangkok led by John R. Mott, a Siam Christian Council was formed in 1930, the body which laid the groundwork for the formation of the Church of Christ in Siam in 1934.[81] The new national church was composed of churches started by the American Presbyterians and American Baptists. Other churches considered joining but remained separate from the new national church body, namely the British Churches of Christ, the Christian and Missionary Alliance, the Seventh Day Adventists, the Christian Brethren, and some independent Chinese churches.[82] Although the new denomination did not include all Protestant churches in Siam, this organizational union of the majority of churches across the country contributed to a greater sense of national consciousness among Thai Christians that was in line with the government's national integration efforts.

---

79. Pongudom, *History*, 51.

80. Treloar, *Disruption*, 246–47, 250.

81. Pongudom, *History*, 57; McFarland, *Our Garden*, 73–79; Smith, *Siamese*, 181–84; Boon-Itt, "Dialogue," 46–48; Hopkins, *John R. Mott*, 671.

82. Smith, *Siamese*, 183.

Rev. Pluang Sudhikam, first moderator of the Church of Christ in Thailand, 1934 (Courtesy of the Presbyterian Historical Society, Philadelphia).

WORLD WAR II ENDS MISSIONARY WORK IN THAILAND

As war broke out in Europe, and Japan extended its reach into China, many Thai believed their nation was safe from the aggressions of imperial Japan. This was a mistaken hope. Japan invaded Thailand on December 8, 1941 and the Thai government quickly conceded. With the beginning of Japanese wartime occupation, all missionary work in Thailand came to a halt. Missionaries living in the Bangkok area, along with other Westerners, were arrested and interned at the University of Moral and Political Science. They were repatriated in 1942. Missionaries living in northern Thailand, however, fled into Burma, and then

India, which was under British control. The missionaries were gone and Thai Christians were now on their own to face nationalist and Japanese opposition through the end of the war.[83]

CONCLUSION

The narrative of the American Presbyterian mission and the Church of Christ in Thailand was one of religious conversion, church growth, and societal modernization. Missionaries in particular contributed to the advance of scientific knowledge, printing, education, medical care, and the integration of the modern nation-state of Thailand. American missionaries were not only mono-directional contributors to Thai modernity but were also influenced by modernizing trends around them, within and outside the church, both within Thailand and from abroad. The next four chapters constitute the heart of this book and will examine to what extent, and in what ways, theological modernism impacted the American Presbyterian mission in Thailand.

83. Smith, *Siamese*, 199, 207.

6

Dimensions of Modernism in the American Presbyterian Mission in Thailand

DURING THE COURSE OF the late nineteenth and early twentieth centuries, the Presbyterian Church in the U.S.A. (PCUSA) affirmed a conservative theological consensus even as modernist theological views were gaining influence and becoming a point of conflict within the denomination. From the 1920s forward, modernism was increasingly tolerated within the PCUSA, a development that was reflected to various degrees among Presbyterian foreign missions. However, specific social and mission contexts influenced the ways and extent to which modernist theological views impacted particular foreign fields. Modernism did not affect all corners of the church equally and the fundamentalist-modernist tensions in the PCUSA that resulted in intense controversies in the United States were not necessarily mirrored overseas. Among Protestant mission fields, China experienced the greatest amount of fundamentalist-modernist division, and some other fields experienced similar controversies on a smaller scale.

In Thailand, American Presbyterian missionaries maintained an essentially conservative consensus up to the outbreak of the Second World War, yet modernism was present among them and was increasingly tolerated, especially from the 1920s onward. The current chapter explores various dimensions of modernist theological influence among these missionaries and the responses that these views prompted. The four dimensions to be examined are 1) responses to modern biblical criticism, 2) the influence of theological revisionism in the west, 3) the encounter with Thai Buddhism and its implications for Christian uniqueness, and 4) the desire to modernize Christianity to appeal to Thailand's educated elite. Each dimension represents a key area in which modernism either entered into the thinking of missionaries or became a factor in the spread of modernism among them. The influence of modernist theology among Thai Christians will be mentioned in passing, yet due to a paucity of data definite conclusions are impossible. After discussion of these four dimensions, the chapter will conclude by examining APM Thailand missionary responses to the *Laymen's Inquiry* in order to illustrate how the missionaries sought to uphold a conservative consensus even while modernism was affecting their mission.

THE PROTESTANT MISSIONARY CONSENSUS IN THAILAND

Before discussing the first dimension of modernist influence in Thailand, it is necessary to understand the nature of the conservative consensus that the APM Thailand mission sought to maintain. Until the early years of the twentieth century, there was a consensus among American Protestant missionaries around the world that consisted of four broadly held convictions. First, the controlling aim of missions work was to proclaim the gospel of Jesus Christ, to persuade people to become disciples of Christ, and to gather them into self-governing, self-supporting, and self-propagating churches. Secondly, there was doctrinal unity on the divinity and uniqueness of Jesus Christ. Thirdly, even though evangelism was seen as the primary task of missions, social service with the aim of societal transformation was an important and legitimate aim of missions. There was no dichotomy between evangelism and social service ministries. Fourthly, Protestant missionaries valued pragmatic cooperation between church bodies for the sake of furthering Christian mission goals.[1] This consensus on the nature and purpose of Protestant missions was manifest at major pan-Protestant missions conferences such as the 1907 China Centenary Missions Conference and the 1910 World Missionary Conference in Edinburgh.[2] Starting in the 1920s, however, this consensus among Protestant

---

1. See Patterson, "Loss of a Protestant Missionary Consensus," 73–91.

2. Yao, *Fundamentalist Movement*, 34–36; Stanley, *World Missionary Conference*, 320.

mission groups broke down on multiple mission fields amidst rising tensions connected to modernism and fundamentalism.

Even as it was being lost elsewhere, the American Presbyterian mission sought to maintain this missionary consensus in Thailand, a task at which they were largely successful up until the years just before the Second World War. Those late divisions among missionaries in Thailand will be discussed in chapter 7 when the impact of John Sung's revival meetings in Thailand is examined. However, up until the late 1930s, the APM Thailand mission maintained the former Protestant missionary consensus. They were able to maintain this consensus, in part, due to the fact that American Presbyterians were the only statistically significant Protestant mission operating in Thailand and thus felt uniquely responsible for the Christianization of the country.[3] Maintaining this consensus and maintaining unity within the mission were essential to making progress in Christianizing Thailand, a goal which was threatened by the specter of possible modernist-fundamentalist conflict.

MODERNISM AND THE SPECTRUM OF THEOLOGICAL VIEWS

As the dimensions of modernist influence in Thailand are considered in this chapter, it must be acknowledged that it is difficult to assess accurately the theological beliefs of individuals due to partial information, possible bias in the sources, and ambiguity in emerging theological positions during the time period under consideration. William Hutchison has noted that the majority of missionaries could not be easily classified as liberal or conservative, though theological tendencies were sometimes evident from words and actions.[4] The word "tendencies" is important because it is often more accurate to talk about theological tendencies or leanings among missionaries than it is to definitively label and categorize people. To do the latter runs the risk of limiting and defining them unnaturally and fails to appreciate the messy complexity of the lived reality of individual people within the broader scope of cultural, intellectual, and religious trends. That said, theological labels necessarily appear in the following pages because the people under consideration used them, albeit often in imprecise ways that sometimes

---

3. Eakin, "Siam, A Presbyterian Responsibility"; Hooper, "Enlarged Program," 243–46; McFarland, *Historical Sketch*, 249–69; "Thailand," 789–93.

4. Hutchison, *Errand*, 103.

make it challenging for the historian to determine if a given label is an accurate description of a person's views or simply a pejorative generalization. Theological labels can be helpful at times in identifying a person's leanings, but few of the missionaries left written documentation of their convictions on specific doctrinal matters. In many cases, the most that can be done is to make tentative conclusions based on the evidence available and to hold such labels lightly.

The focus of this chapter is views that would be considered modernist when contrasted with traditional conservative theological positions, yet it must be kept in mind not all affirmations of the modern necessarily qualify as modernist. Protestants across the theological spectrum embraced many aspects of modernity, though there was not agreement about the extent to which specific modernizations should be embraced or rejected.[5] In the Thailand context, for example, the American Presbyterian mission rejected the modernist theological conclusions of the *Laymen's Inquiry* while embracing the report's exhortations to improve their efforts at modern education and medical services on the mission field. Similarly, both conservatives and liberals became more respectful in their religious communication over time, a modernizing change reflected in APM Thailand missionaries' interaction with Buddhism, a topic discussed in chapter 8. Modern does not always imply theological modernism but in the following pages, "modernism" will serve as shorthand for theological modernism while the term "modern" will generally refer to the broader movement of progressive development in social organization, economic and political institutions, transportation, and communication driven by rational thought and scientific inquiry. Also, it should be kept in mind that in this book, "modernist" is sometimes used retrospectively and interchangeably with "liberal." This is done consciously and with the caveat that, as noted in chapter 1, modernism as a label and an identifiable phenomenon did not develop until the interwar period. In the 1890s, modernism was still unknown as a theological term, yet liberal positions beginning to be expressed at that time, like salvation of non-Christians and denial of biblical inerrancy, would later come under the umbrella of modernism. It is with that later development in mind that some positions are classed as "modernist" even though the people involved would not have used that label.

---

5. Treloar, *Disruption*, 67–90.

DIMENSION 1 ~ RESPONSES TO MODERN BIBLICAL CRITICISM

The first dimension of modernist influence in the American Presbyterian mission in Thailand concerns the missionaries' varied responses to modern biblical criticism. As previously discussed in chapter 2, during the final decades of the nineteenth-century, new approaches to biblical scholarship were developing, causing scholars and lay Christians to rethink the ways in which the text of the Bible assumed its present form. This scholarship raised significant questions about the accuracy and authority of the biblical text. Responses to this scholarship varied. While some concluded that the Bible was neither inerrant nor authoritative as previously thought, others believed that aspects of modern biblical scholarship were useful and compatible with belief in an inerrant and authoritative biblical text. As modern biblical scholarship became known, debate ensued in many churches and seminaries, sometimes prompting dichotomistic arguments that Christian faithfulness in the modern world entailed either full embrace or full rejection of biblical criticism. In the American Presbyterian mission in Thailand, the majority of missionaries proceeded on the assumption that the Bible was true and authoritative. Some of them may have embraced selective aspects of modern biblical criticism alongside a traditional view of the supreme authority of Scripture, though it is impossible to be certain because most missionaries did not record their views on this topic.[6] However, a minority of missionaries embraced biblical criticism and came to modernist conclusions about the accuracy and authority of the biblical text. When those convictions became known, they often prompted disapproval from fellow missionaries.

The Resignation of Evander McGilvary, 1894

The earliest instance of tension over modern biblical scholarship in the American Presbyterian mission in Thailand centers on the person of Evander McGilvary who worked as a missionary with the Laos mission from 1891 to 1894. The events surrounding McGilvary's resignation need to be recounted at some length because they help establish a baseline for understanding subsequent APM Thailand responses to modernism,

---

6. The terms "inerrant" and "infallible" were largely interchangeable during the time period covered in this research though modern biblical criticism was beginning to prompt more precise definitions.

especially the priority which mission leaders repeatedly placed upon unity over theological homogeneity.[7]

The son of Daniel McGilvary, missionary founder of the Laos mission, Evander was born in Bangkok and went to the United States for his education when he was nine years old. Following his studies at Princeton Theological Seminary, McGilvary returned to Thailand specifically to translate the New Testament into Lao, a related yet distinct language from the Thai spoken in Bangkok.[8] To produce a quality translation, McGilvary told Board secretary Arthur Mitchell that he would need assistance from his mother whose mastery of colloquial Lao was better than his own, as well as additional money to purchase critical commentaries on the Bible, which McGilvary said were in extremely short supply on the mission field.[9] In the two years following his arrival in 1891, McGilvary made sufficient progress in Lao language to begin Bible translation work in earnest. Living in the city of Chiang Mai in Northern Thailand, he also took on responsibilities as the Laos mission's treasurer in addition to some pastoral and evangelistic work.

While McGilvary and his wife were settling into life on the mission field, portentous events were underway in the Presbyterian Church USA that would directly impact their future. In 1892, the church courts grappled with how to respond to the views of Charles Briggs, a Presbyterian minister and lecturer at Union Seminary who denied biblical inerrancy based on use of higher critical methods for studying the Bible.[10] At their 1892 General Assembly, the PCUSA adopted a statement affirming biblical inerrancy. The Portland Deliverance, as it came to be called, read in part, "Our Church holds that the inspired Word, as it came from God, is without error . . . All who enter office in our Church solemnly profess to receive them [i.e., "the sacred Books"] as the only infallible rule of faith and practice. If they change their belief on this point, Christian honor demands that they should withdraw from our ministry."[11] In 1893, the General Assembly re-affirmed their inerrancy statement and unanimously adopted a resolution declaring "the Bible as we now have

---

7. For an extended account of McGilvary's resignation, see Dahlfred, "Evander McGilvary."

8. Document 1108—Memorial Resolution on the Death of E. B. McGilvary, PUA; Interview with Ellen Zimmerman Hocker, PUA.

9. Evander McGilvary to Mitchell, January 7, 1892, PUA.

10. For a detailed account, see Loetscher, *Broadening Church*, 48–62.

11. Loetscher, *Broadening Church*, 56.

it, in its various translations and versions, when freed from all errors and mistakes of translators, copyists, and printers, is the very Word of God, and consequently wholly without error."[12]

When Evander McGilvary received news of the 1893 General Assembly's resolution on inerrancy and the conviction of Charles Briggs on heresy, he concluded he was obliged to withdraw from the Presbyterian ministry. It is unclear as to how and when McGilvary's views on inerrancy and higher criticism developed, but it is likely his views developed during his education in the United States. Aside from his time in Thailand as a child, McGilvary's cumulative experience in Thailand was less than two years, and it is likely he became familiar with the theories and methods of modern biblical scholarship while studying at Princeton Seminary. McGilvary recognized that his views were substantially similar to those of Briggs, and thus unacceptable to the church at large. McGilvary also came to the conviction it was not necessary to believe in Christ in order to be saved, a point that will be discussed later in this chapter.[13] With his convictions as they were, sometime during late summer or early autumn 1893, McGilvary decided he was honor-bound to resign and tendered a formal letter of resignation to the Board of Foreign Missions.[14]

While waiting to hear back from the Board in response to his resignation letter, McGilvary presented a paper on his views on inerrancy to the North Laos Presbytery at their annual meeting in December 1893. He wanted the Presbytery to decide whether, in light of his views, he should remain a member of the Presbytery or withdraw. It seems McGilvary wanted an official severance of relation with the Presbytery so that he and his wife could move on with the next stage of their life. However, the Presbytery tabled the matter until their next annual meeting in December 1894. The unofficial consensus of the Presbytery was that no one wanted McGilvary to leave, and it was hoped that in the intervening year he would re-consider his resignation and remain on the mission field.[15] Jonathan Wilson, a senior member of the Laos mission and long-time friend of Evander's father, begged the younger McGilvary not to leave the work he was especially suited for, namely Bible translation. Wilson felt a compromise could be justified because of the

12. Stated Clerk, *Minutes of the General Assembly of the PCUSA* 1893, 169.
13. Phraner et al. to Daniel McGilvary, May 15, 1894, PUA.
14. Evander McGilvary to Dulles, May 11, 1894; Elizabeth McGilvary to Mother, March 21, 1894; Phraner et al. to Daniel McGilvary, May 15, 1894, PUA.
15. Peoples to Speer, May 21, 1894; Taylor to Speer, May 14, 1894, PUA.

work needed to be done. Wilson thought the senior McGilvary could perhaps persuade his son to change his views. Daniel McGilvary, who was on furlough at the time, was deeply disappointed when he heard that his son decided to resign. Nonetheless, he "sympathized with his [Evander's] position, and respected his motives."[16] Later reflecting on his son's resignation and the trial of Henry P. Smith for heresy related to higher criticism, a trial which he witnessed in person at the 1893 PCUSA General Assembly, Daniel McGilvary expressed his disapproval of church courts passing judgment on such matters. He wrote,

> I doubt whether critical and scientific questions are proper subjects for trials before such a body. If tried at all, such questions should be tried by a commission of experts. Biblical criticism and science will go on, and the questions involved will be decided according to their own lines of evidence, quite irrespective of the decrees of Popes, Councils, and General Assemblies. I am much mistaken if the good sense and temper of the church would now sanction heresy trials on such questions.[17]

Like Daniel McGilvary, Jonathan Wilson also regretted that such a question had come before a church court. It would have been better if the younger McGilvary had not presented his views to Presbytery at all. If he kept quiet about his views and not shared them with others, then he could have easily continued in his translation work without issue. However, McGilvary's views were now known among the missionaries, and to some degree among the Lao Christians.[18] Although Presbytery action on McGilvary's views was delayed, he was not prohibited from sharing them with others, including the Lao Christians, in the interim. This failure to refrain from teaching his views would become an important factor in subsequent discussions among Laos mission members regarding continuance or departure. In the view of his fellow missionaries, the fact that McGilvary held such views was not nearly as problematic as the harm they might do to the peace and harmony of the church when they became known.[19] For their missionary work to be successful, it was not necessary to have theological homogeneity but it was necessary for the mission to present a united front in their teaching. In the minds of many of the missionaries,

---

16. McGilvary, *Half Century*, 370–71.
17. McGilvary, *Half Century*, 371–72.
18. Taylor to Speer, May 14, 1894; Wilson to Speer, June 12, 1894, PUA.
19. Thomas to Speer, May 24, 1894; Wilson to Speer, June 12, 1894, PUA.

modernist rejection of inerrancy was dangerous because it might cause disunity, not primarily because it was incorrect in itself.

Shortly after the North Laos Presbytery voted to table action on McGilvary's views until the following year, McGilvary received a telegram from the Board of Foreign Missions informing him that his resignation had been accepted. It seemed the decision was settled. McGilvary would leave. However, letters between Thailand and the United States crossed in the mail and the Board only learned of the North Laos Presbytery's decision to delay action on McGilvary after the Board already accepted his resignation. Since the Board's preference had always been to defer to the presbytery, this new information put McGilvary's resignation letter in a new light. The Board changed its mind and decided to withdraw its acceptance of his resignation. McGilvary was notified of its new decision by telegram, which he received on April 2, 1894.[20]

The Board's decision, however, was not unanimous. Two members of the Board, Dr. Booth and Dr. Paxton, did not vote for the withdrawal of the acceptance of his resignation. On the contrary, they suggested the Board should present McGilvary's case to the General Assembly to be prosecuted for heresy. They also suggested that the North Laos Presbytery should likewise be brought up on charges.[21] The Board itself did not have jurisdiction to make such theological judgements, a fact which greatly relieved Board treasurer William Dulles who thought it would have been a disaster if the Board was dragged into theological controversy.[22] Although the recommendations of Booth and Paxton did not carry the day, they do indicate the mood of some in the Presbyterian Church at the time. Had the recommendations of Booth and Paxton been enacted, the names of Evander McGilvary and the North Laos Presbytery may well have become well-known in the annals of theological controversy in the Presbyterian Church USA. In the 1890s, modernist views were starting to spread among American Presbyterians but those who held them were still a very small minority.

When McGilvary received the Board's telegram on April 2, 1894 notifying him that acceptance of his resignation had been withdrawn, some of his fellow missionaries asked if the way was now clear for him to stay. It was

20. "Rev. E.B. McGilvary," 27.
21. Phraner et al. to Daniel McGilvary, May 15, 1894, PUA.
22. Dulles to Evander McGilvary, March 1, 1894, PUA.

not. Within two weeks of receiving the Board's telegram, he sent a second resignation letter to the Board, hoping this one would be final.[23]

Nevertheless, opinions among his fellow missionaries in Northern Thailand were still divided. Those in favor of McGilvary's departure were concerned that his liberal views might have a harmful influence on the Lao Church and the missionary community. Lao Christians did not have the educational background to understand issues of higher criticism, and teaching them about it would just cause confusion, thus disrupting the peace and harmony of the church.[24] Several members of the Laos mission wrote to the Board asking that for the sake of harmonious relationships in the missionary community, the Board should send no more liberals but only "those men whose views are known to be in accord with the General Assembly and with the great body of the Church at large."[25] Aside from the question of peace and harmony, some members of the Presbytery were also concerned that if McGilvary did not leave, the General Assembly might take action against them for retaining in good standing a minister with heretical views. In a letter to Board secretary Robert Speer, Samuel Peoples explained that some members of the mission were sympathetic to McGilvary's views, and there was "a very decided sentiment of liberality toward those holding such views." As such, it was unlikely McGilvary would be dismissed by the Northern Laos Presbytery. Peoples concluded that the "probable result would be to set the Presbytery in open and conspicuous antagonism to some of the late actions of the General Assembly."[26] Those who wished for McGilvary to stay cited his particular suitability for translation work and concluded that since his statement of views was tabled by the Presbytery, there was no imminent danger of adverse action by the General Assembly. In fact, even those who thought it would be best for McGilvary to leave would actually have preferred for him to stay if the obstacles to his continuance could be resolved.[27] In theory, if McGilvary's views had been kept an open secret among the missionaries and he had spoken of them to neither the Lao Christians nor brought up the question to the North Laos Presbytery and the Board, he could have remained in the Laos mission and continued with his much valued work in Bible translation. Though there is no conclusive evidence that any other

23. Phraner et al. to Daniel McGilvary, May 15, 1894, PUA.
24. Wilson to Speer, June 12, 1894; Thomas to Speer, May 24, 1894, PUA.
25. Phraner et al. to Board, May 24, 1894, PUA.
26. Peoples to Speer, May 21, 1894, PUA.
27. Taylor to Speer, May 14, 1894, PUA.

missionary in either the Laos mission or the Siam mission agreed with his views on inerrancy and the salvation of non-Christians, neither did any missionary wish him to leave. However, after much internal wrangling in the Laos mission and a confusing correspondence of letters between Thailand and the United States, the Board accepted his second resignation letter and Evander McGilvary left the Laos mission in June 1894.[28] Returning to the United States, McGilvary taught philosophy and moved away from the Christian faith, eventually becoming agnostic.[29]

Paul Eakin, a Fallible Bible, and Miracles

Between the departure of McGilvary from the mission field and the First World War, it is uncertain whether there were other Thailand missionaries who embraced modern biblical scholarship to the point of denying the infallibility of Scripture. However, the issue did not go away and by the 1920s, there were again missionaries who had come to modernist conclusions about the Bible. Paul Eakin, born and raised by missionary parents in Thailand, was a missionary with the APM Thailand mission from 1913 to 1949 and held numerous modernist views. Eakin embraced higher criticism and believed the Bible was "not infallible." Everyone had different interpretations of Scripture and even the biblical authors John and Mark disagreed with each other, claimed Eakin. He thought the Bible was valuable, not as a final authority or something literally true, but rather as a source of inspiration. The Bible was not a revelation from God, but merely a record of God's revelation, which is Jesus Christ. The Bible's truth had to be verified. Eakin reasoned that whenever the Bible and the ideas of religious leaders are in accord with facts established by experience and reason, then the Bible's truths should be accepted.[30] It is uncertain to what degree his fellow missionaries understood Eakin's views on biblical criticism, but his modernist conclusions about the Bible manifested themselves in various ways.

Although it is impossible to determine if Eakin's belief in a fallible Bible led to his rejection of miracles, or if his rejection of miracles led to his denial of infallibility, the two beliefs hung together harmoniously in Eakin's worldview. In an undated sermon, most likely from the

28. Eakin, "Biographical Notes on Evander McGilvary."

29. Swanson, interview with Ellen Hocker, PUA.

30. Eakin, "Road of Approach to Non-Christians"; Eakin, "What Can We Believe?"; Eakin, "My Reasonable Faith."

late 1920s or early 1930s, Eakin told listeners that in order to interpret Christianity for people of today, some old ideas must be laid aside. These included young earth creationism, God's supernatural intervention in the natural order, and God revealing himself through "abnormal trances" and other similar ways.[31] Although rejection of young earth creation is not a certain indicator of modernism since there were conservatives who also rejected a young earth, Eakin's dismissal of God's supernatural intervention through miracles and direct revelations reflected his modernistic convictions on the Bible. In a similar vein, Eakin believed speaking in tongues in the New Testament was a psychological, not a supernatural phenomenon, that had "no moral value."[32] Eakin did not completely reject the bodily resurrection of Christ though he hesitated to affirm it. He believed that Christ convinced his disciples that he had survived death. "In some way," wrote Eakin, "through a body or spirit or a new substance, He showed His presence" to his disciples. Though he believed in the incarnation, full affirmation of the bodily resurrection of Christ seemed a bridge too far.[33] As already noted, Eakin thought the truths of the Bible needed to be verified by other sources in order to be accepted and most supernatural events in the Bible apparently failed to meet Eakin's criteria for external verification. For Eakin, an infallible Bible and a miracle-working God were not a necessary part of Christian belief. Rather, Eakin thought the essence of Christianity lay in the belief that God was the spiritual reality behind all of life and the source of power for living in today's world.

---

31. "New Situation and a New Task" in Eakin, *Sermon Outlines*.
32. Eakin, "Question," PUA.
33. Eakin, "My Reasonable Faith."

Rev. Paul Eakin, 1912
(Courtesy of the Presbyterian Historical Society, Philadelphia).

Thai Christians and Biblical Criticism

Eakin's views on the Bible and miracles most likely had an impact on the thinking of Thai Christians though a paucity of evidence makes firm conclusions impossible. There are, however, indicators that he did not hide his views from them. Kenneth Landon, a fundamentalist-leaning APM Thailand missionary with whom Eakin had a tense relationship, claimed that a Thai leader told Landon that studying with Eakin "caused him to doubt the inerrancy of scripture and resulted in the confusion of his faith."[34] Landon did not name the Thai leader who said this, but it was probably Rev. Charoen Sakulkan who will be discussed in chapter 7.

34. Landons to Board, October 9, 1940, WCSC.

Aside from Charoen Sakulkan, there were two other Thai leaders who were sympathetic to modernist conclusions about the Bible, though they were likely influenced by seminary director Carl Elder and their own theological studies abroad rather than Paul Eakin. Banchop Bansiddhi and Prasert Intaphantu were teaching at the mission's seminary in Chiang Mai when an effort was made to get Elder removed from the seminary due to his opposition to Chinese evangelist John Sung. Among other issues, Elder was criticized for using books at the seminary that made a positive presentation of modern biblical scholarship.[35] In a letter to Paul Eakin, Elder's colleagues Banchop and Prasert explained that Elder was just teaching according to the course of the seminary. "True," they admitted, "he may have opinions that differ from others regarding some interpretations; but that is common among preachers, but such differences are minor and in no way injure the faith of the students."[36] The exact nature of Elder's views on modern biblical criticism is unknown, as is the extent of Banchop and Prasert's agreement with them. But whatever his views were, his colleagues did not see them as problematic, despite the protestations of fundamentalist-leaning Thai Christians and APM Thailand missionaries. In the face of criticism, Paul Eakin also stood by Elder, writing to him, "I believe in you and what you really stand for."[37]

In considering the impact of modern biblical criticism in the American Presbyterian mission in Thailand, it is safe to say that embrace of modern biblical scholarship to the point of rejecting belief in an infallible Bible was a minority viewpoint. However, modernist conclusions on biblical criticism had an impact on the mission. Such views were an immediate reason for Evander McGilvary's resignation and had an influence on the teaching and preaching of Paul Eakin who directed the mission throughout the 1930s. The extent to which modern biblical criticism impacted Thai Christians is more difficult to determine, though the accusation that Carl Elder had a modernist understanding of the Bible became a point of contention among pro-Sung and anti-Sung missionaries and Thai Christians in the late 1930s.

In comparing the responses to biblical criticism among APM Thailand missionaries from the 1890s to the 1930s, a difference emerges. In 1894, though members of the Laos mission professed to be in agreement with the resolutions of the General Assembly affirming inerrancy,

---

35. Hanna to Elder, September 15, 1939, PUA.
36. Bansiddhi and Intaphantu to Eakin, October 25, 1939, PUA.
37. Eakin to Elder, October 18, 1939, PUA.

they simultaneously did not wish to move against those who were not in agreement with the Assembly. They disagreed with Evander McGilvary's position but hoped to find a way for him to remain in ministry in Thailand. Although their stated theological convictions were not substantially different than those of so-called fundamentalists of 30 years later, they lacked the hostility towards theological liberals that came to be associated with fundamentalism. Essentially moderate conservatives, their desire for peace and for completion of practical ministry tasks, such as the Lao New Testament, trumped their desire for every minister to conform theologically. In principle, missionaries should have correct doctrine. But in cases such as McGilvary's, it was the practical implications of those views rather than the views themselves that were problematic. The missionaries would have preferred to not deal with academic debates that were not pressing issues in their local area, but McGilvary's decision to announce his views forced their hand. The situation in the 1920s and 1930s, however, was quite different from the 1890s. Modernism as a recognizable phenomenon had emerged and found ways to sustain itself within the Presbyterian Church USA, thus taking some pressure off missionaries who held modernist views. Whereas McGilvary felt compelled to resign, there are no indications that either Paul Eakin or Carl Elder feared they would be forced out of the mission due to their theological views. Ironically, Evander McGilvary felt he must resign in spite of the wishes of fellow missionaries that he stay, yet missionaries such as Eakin and Elder felt they could stay in spite of rising fundamentalist opposition to views like theirs.

DIMENSION 2 ~ THE INFLUENCE OF THEOLOGICAL REVISIONISM IN THE WEST

A second dimension of modernism relates to the influence of Western intellectual trends. The majority of American missionaries in Thailand and elsewhere were born and raised in the United States and received their education in the West. This being the case, they received their formative intellectual formation in a Western cultural context, which included modern assumptions about the value of rational inquiry and science. Christians receiving their education in the West would have been aware of the challenges to traditional beliefs then being presented by modern education. Those who studied at theological schools, especially theologically liberal institutions, would have been particularly familiar with questions raised by modern biblical scholarship, evolution, and scientific challenges to the miraculous aspects of the Bible. Kevin Yao has noted that from at least the First World War, many newer missionaries in China received liberal ideas from the Bible colleges and seminaries they attended in the West.[38] Gretchen Boger has similarly contended that mission fields in India and China functioned as a mirror reflecting trends in American Christianity.[39] Albert Wu has sought to make the case that Chinese Christians were a primary factor in pushing German missionaries in China towards modernist theological views yet even then the source of influence was Western since the Chinese Christians in question had been "trained, for the most part, in an American-inflected liberal Social Gospel theology."[40] Hee-Mo Yim has observed that modern, namely liberal, theological ideas came into Korea through universities in Korea teaching Western ideas, foreign missionaries, and Koreans who studied abroad in the West, especially the United States.[41] Modern liberal theology in Japan likewise developed through contact with the West. Western learning was disseminated in Japanese universities and foreign missionaries introduced liberal theological ideas. These factors influenced, but did not determine, the trajectory of indigenous Japanese theologizing.[42]

In the Thailand context, two stories serve to illustrate how modernist views developed through encounter with Western intellectual influences and how modernism was being received by the APM Thailand mission and Board of Foreign Missions. These are the resignation of William Perkins (1924) and the last-minute decision of Cornelia Gillies not to return to Thailand as a missionary (1932).

The Resignation of Dr. William Perkins, 1924

An example of the roots of modernism in Thailand in Western liberal theology comes in the resignation of Dr. William Perkins. Appointed by the Board as missionaries on October 6, 1919, William and Barbara Perkins arrived in Nan province in Northern Thailand on January 3, 1920 where Dr. Perkins immediately started seeing patients. The urgent pull of medical work was such that the doctor and his wife had little time for

---

38. Yao, *Fundamentalist Movement*, 41.
39. Boger, "American Protestantism," 4.
40. Wu, *From Christ to Confucius*, 257.
41. Yim, *Unity Lost*, 29–46.
42. Jennings, "Theology in Japan," 145–56.

language study, a fact which he later regretted. Over the next two years in Nan, followed by several months in Chiang Mai, Dr. Perkins showed himself a dedicated physician who sought to keep medical work and the gospel united through Christ-like compassionate service to the people of Thailand, regardless of class, economics, or education.[43] It was Perkins's hope that through medical work and the Christ-like living of local Christians that Thai people would also believe in Christ.[44]

The longer Perkins spent in Thailand, however, the less confidence he had in the gospel message he had been sent to make known. At the time, he did not think his difficulty had to do with any doctrinal differences between himself and the Presbyterian church. Rather, he thought his doubts about certain doctrinal questions were merely a personal weakness. The practical result of his private doubts was that he found it increasingly difficult to affirm and teach publicly beliefs he was no longer sure about. Perkins said his doubts developed as a result of listening to other Presbyterian missionaries teach "views and beliefs that are incompatible with reason and stretch the faith beyond credulity." These doubts, however, did not arise in response to brewing fundamentalist-modernist controversy in the United States. "In Siam," wrote Perkins, "I heard practically nothing of the controversy between Fundamentalism and Modernism except indirectly through the Bible Union formed in China."[45] He had "no idea a certain amount of freedom in interpretation of the Scriptures was not allowable" since freer interpretations such as his went unchallenged while he worked in Thailand.[46] For Perkins, and many other missionaries, theological controversy over modernism was far removed from their everyday life and work. In her study of missionary thinking in China and India, Gretchen Boger noted that many missionaries did not have to think about fundamentalist-modernist controversy more than once per month when their missions magazine arrived in the post.[47]

When Perkins and his wife went on an emergency furlough in August 1923 due to ill health, he had a number of concerns on his mind

---

43. Eakin, "Biographical Notes on Dr. and Mrs. Perkins," PUA; Strong, "Nan, Siam Station Report," PHS.

44. Perkins, "Personal Report," PHS.

45. The Bible Union of China was a coalition of conservative missionaries in China. For a detailed account, see Yao, *Fundamentalist Movement*, 55–100.

46. Perkins to Brown, December 31, 1923, PHS.

47. Boger, "American Protestantism," 18.

regarding the Thailand mission, though none of them had to do with his personal beliefs or theological controversy in Thailand.[48] Though some of his fellow missionaries questioned the wisdom of his return to Thailand after furlough due to concerns about financial mismanagement of medical work in Nan, their letters to the Board regarding Perkins did not mention doctrinal matters.[49] However, shortly after arrival in the United States, he received a "Statement Regarding the Evangelical Loyalty of the Board of Foreign Missions and the Missionaries" which was passed by the Board on November 19, 1923. The statement of evangelical loyalty was ostensibly issued in reaction to recent criticism of the Board for their participation in theologically questionable union bodies on the mission field, and for not allowing Presbyterian missionaries to join the Bible Union in China.[50] "The importance of this document to me," wrote Perkins to Board secretary Arthur J. Brown, "has superseded all other considerations relative to my return to the mission field." Perkins affirmed that his beliefs were orthodox when he signed the missionary application questionnaire in 1919. At that time, Presbyterian doctrine went unquestioned in his own conscience. Nevertheless, he could no longer give affirmative answers to what he formerly believed. Confessing that he was at wide variance with the beliefs of the Presbyterian Church, Perkins recounted the matters he could no longer affirm in two letters and in personal meetings with Arthur Brown, Robert E. Speer, and other Board members.

Perkins rejected special creation and affirmed evolution. He thought that God imbued man with a soul only at a later stage of evolutionary development. Perkins doubted the Virgin Birth and believed Jesus was merely a chosen instrument to reveal God through natural channels. He asserted that Christ died for people only in the sense of martyrdom and God did not plan for Christ to atone for our sins or to assume our place as a substitution, nor to suffer vicariously. He believed that the resurrection of Christ was a superfluous belief. Perkins asserted that salvation consists in using the power given to us to overcome the natural sins of the flesh.[51]

---

48. Brown to Siam mission, Board Letter# 227, October 2, 1923, PUA; Perkins to Brown, February 5, 1924, PHS.

49. McDaniel to Brown, October 1, 1923; McClure to Brown, December 18, 1923, PHS.

50. Rian, *Presbyterian Conflict*, 127–28.

51. Perkins to Brown, December 31, 1923; Brown to Ewing and Stevenson, January 11, 1924; Perkins to Board, January 14, 1924, PHS.

Dimensions of Modernism in the American Presbyterian Mission

Dr. William Perkins, 1919
(Courtesy of the Presbyterian Historical Society, Philadelphia).

Given his variance with Presbyterian doctrine, Perkins submitted his resignation, concluding, "I do not think that the Church wishes to have doubting teachers on its border provinces and so, dear friends, I must here by my own conscience and before God, ask to be relieved from my former field of service under the Board of Foreign Missions of the Presbyterian Church."[52] Arthur Brown accepted Perkins' resignation letter of January 14, 1924 as conclusive of the matter, and told fellow Board members J.C.R. Ewing and J. Ross Stevenson that meeting with Perkins

52. Perkins to Board, January 14, 1924; Perkins to Brown, February 5, 1924, PHS.

further would be fruitless.[53] Brown similarly wrote to Francis M. Fox, minister of Perkins' home church in Germantown, Pennsylvania. Fox too regretted losing Perkins and wondered if he was influenced by his wife who, Fox said, came from a "strictly German family" that "doubtless sticks to the German theology."[54] Though Fox did not elaborate, his reference to "German theology" likely meant higher critical theories of biblical composition associated with German scholarship.

Perkins did not specify how or why several of his theological views changed within only a few years' time, although given his own statements, it appears that disillusionment with the conservative preaching of his fellow missionaries and reflection arising out of his American upbringing were the most likely sources. Perkins' Thai language ability was minimal, so it is unlikely that he became very conversant with the religious thinking of Thai Buddhists, and the doubts he expressed to the Board related to matters arising from Western scientific inquiry and learning, not questions of religious pluralism and the salvation of non-Christians. However the change in his thinking came about, the necessity of resignation was settled in Perkins's mind, and the Board regretfully accepted the resignation and notified the Thailand mission.[55] Perkins still had an interest in Thailand, however, and in 1926 he moved to Bangkok to work at Siriraj Hospital under the Rockefeller Foundation.[56]

The change in beliefs that led to Perkins' resignation was formed in relation to Western intellectual trends, and it was internal ecclesiastical wrangling in the United States that led to his resignation, not concerns arising from the mission field itself. When Perkins parted ways with the Board and the Thailand mission in January 1924, changes were afoot in the way in which theological diversity was negotiated by the Board. Modernism was gaining momentum in the Presbyterian Church USA as the New York Presbytery continued to ordain men who held views condemned by the General Assembly and numerous ministers were calling for greater freedom of doctrinal interpretation with the publication of the Auburn Affirmation.[57] Caught in the crossfire between emerging liberal elements and their conservative critics, the Board sought to stay in the

53. Brown to Ewing and Stevenson, January 17, 1924, PHS.
54. Fox to Brown, January 24, 1924, PHS.
55. Brown to Siam mission, Board Letter# 230, January 25, 1924, PUA.
56. Eakin, "Biographical Notes on Dr. and Mrs. Perkins," PUA.
57. Longfield, *Presbyterian Controversy*, 77–79; Longfield, "William Merrill, the Brick Church, and the Fundamentalist-Modernist Conflict," 65.

good graces of all parties by presenting a conservative public image while privately working to retain missionaries who found it difficult to uphold traditional Presbyterian doctrine. If concerns about modernism in the denomination, and in the Board especially, had not arisen in 1923, the Board conceivably would not have felt it necessary to pen a statement of evangelical loyalty for their missionaries to re-affirm. In the absence of such a statement at the time Perkins went on furlough, the question of his theological views would have likely gone unchecked for many years to come. But in the light of criticism, the Board felt compelled to present an orthodox face to its American Presbyterian constituency. At the same time, they wished to retain the support of liberal Presbyterians. Thus, when news of Perkins' resignation came to the attention of Henry Sloane Coffin, a prominent liberal Presbyterian minister, Arthur Brown sought to assure him that the Board was not sending out "reactionary questions" nor "putting on doctrinal screws," as Coffin accused them of doing.[58] The Board wanted to be all things to all people, pushing forward in united Christian service on the mission field through avoiding alienating any of the theological camps within the PCUSA. Though wrangling over modernism was not a concern for the majority of American Presbyterian missionaries in Thailand, they were directly affected by the American context, both in the formation of their theological views and the shifting attitudes towards doctrine among their American constituency.

Cornelia Gillies' Lack of "Evangelistic Feeling," 1932

The loss of yet another missionary for the Thailand field provides a second example of the influence of Western intellectual currents on the formation of modernist views. Born in Chiang Mai to missionary parents, Cornelia Gillies completed a bachelor's degree at Flora Macdonald College in 1928 and was appointed as a missionary of the Board of Foreign Missions on December 1, 1930 while doing graduate work at the Teacher's College of Columbia University.[59] On October 19, 1931, she was appointed to the Thailand mission, where she hoped to work as both a school teacher and as a trainer of teachers in mission schools. Having grown up in Thailand, she would be returning to Chiang Mai where she was well known and where her parents still lived and worked.[60] Shortly

---

58. Coffin to White, April 25, 1924; Coffin to Brown, May 3, 1924, PHS.
59. McAfee to Siam mission, Siam mission Letter #357, December 8, 1932, PHS.
60. Eakin, "Biographical Notes on Dr. and Mrs. Roderick Gillies," PUA; McAfee to

after her appointment to the Thailand mission, however, Cornelia wrote her parents to tell them she changed her mind about becoming a missionary. "My reasons are several," she told her parents, "but the chief one is that I no longer feel able to subscribe to the beliefs of my church." Her parents talked with Cornelia so that she would be clear about the difference between the essential points of the faith, as compared to more minor points about which she might have doubts. They did not want her doubts about secondary doctrinal matters to prevent her from becoming a missionary. However, they told her plainly that they "did not want her to come to Siam on any other ground than as a convinced Christian desiring to promote the knowledge of Christ and Christian living, whatever doubts she may feel concerning points of doctrine usually taught by the evangelical churches."[61] On February 14, 1932, Cornelia wrote to Board secretary Cleland McAfee to express her indecision. He urged her to take time to think things over.[62] She later told him that she felt "wretched and unhappy" and requested to meet with him again to talk the matter over.[63] The two likely met in person in early March 1932.[64] Cornelia then wrote McAfee again on March 22, informing him honestly about her current religious convictions and stating that she wished to go to Thailand as a missionary if her stated positions were acceptable. She wanted to be frank and told McAfee she was having great difficulty making up her mind, confessing "I do not have any evangelistic feeling nor do I want to convert anyone . . . My only desire is to help people help themselves, and to do the best job that I can of teaching and helping others to teach." She didn't know if that was enough warrant to become a missionary and asked McAfee, "Do you feel that it is right for me to go like this?"[65] Apparently he did because six days later, McAfee wrote to the Thailand mission announcing that Cornelia Gillies had confirmed her appointment and expected to sail to Thailand in the summer.[66]

As a secretary of the Board, McAfee would have known that the Board manual stated that the "supreme and controlling aim of Foreign Missions is to make the Lord Jesus Christ known to all men as their

Siam mission, Siam mission Letter #357, December 8, 1932, PHS.

61. R. Gillies to McAfee, February 17, 1932, PHS.
62. McAfee to C. Gillies, February 18, 1932, PHS.
63. C. Gillies to McAfee, February 22, 1932, PHS.
64. Kilmer to C. Gillies, March 8, 1932, PHS.
65. C. Gillies to McAfee, March 22, 1932, PHS.
66. McAfee to Eakin, March 28, 1932, PHS.

Divine Saviour and to persuade them to become His disciples."⁶⁷ Cornelia's stated position that she had no interest in evangelism or converting people stood in stark contrast with that primary purpose of missionary work, yet McAfee managed to convince himself that her purpose in going to Thailand was sufficiently in line with the manual. Writing to her parents, McAfee said that when he "pressed to know whether her fundamental purpose in going to the field was the bringing of Christ to the people whom she touched, both by her life and work, she was as quick to say Yes." He got her to assent to something that could be deemed acceptable. As a result of talking with her, McAfee concluded that her primary reason for hesitating to be a missionary was fear of remaining single, and that doubts about "a traditional idea of a missionary's purpose and plan of work" were only secondary. He told her parents, "I satisfied myself quite fully that she is ready to go to the field."⁶⁸

The Thailand mission was glad to hear this news as they were experiencing a personnel shortage in mission schools in Northern Thailand and were eager to have Cornelia Gillies back on the field. It is probable that pressure from the Thailand mission to send more personnel influenced McAfee's decision to endorse Gillies. On May 19, the Thailand mission cabled the Board asking them to urgently send her as soon as possible, and decided that Cornelia would be assigned to Dara Wittaya Academy in Chiang Mai after her first year's language study.⁶⁹ The Thailand mission, however, would be disappointed. In late June 1932, McAfee cabled Paul Eakin to tell him Cornelia had decided definitely she would not come, and her appointment was officially cancelled on June 20, 1932.⁷⁰

Writing to McAfee in July, her parents confessed that they did not know why their daughter changed her mind at the last minute. They suspected, however, that she was spending too much time with "young people who think they can believe nothing at all in the sphere of religion."⁷¹ Cornelia did not explain why her faith had changed, but her education in the United States and the secularizing influence of classmates may

67. Roy, "Overseas Mission Policies," 209–10.
68. McAfee to R. Gillies, April 13, 1932, PHS.
69. Eakin to Executive Committee, April 25, 1932; Eakin to Executive Committee, May 12, 1932; Eakin to Executive Committee, June 4, 1932; McAfee to Eakin, June 22, 1932, PUA.
70. McAfee to Eakin, June 22, 1932; McAfee to Siam mission, Siam mission Letter #363, July 15, 1932, PUA.
71. R, Gillies to McAfee, February 17, 1932, PHS.

have been responsible for the modernist direction of her theological convictions. Her convictions may have also been influenced by her friend Margaret Neuber who recently resigned from the Thailand mission after coming to the conclusion that Buddhism was better suited for the Thai than Christianity.[72] Cornelia's missionary parents were disappointed that she would not be coming back to Thailand as a missionary but felt that "if her Christian conviction was not sufficiently full and clear, possibly she did the right thing."[73] They believed she would eventually "come out all right in time," but their daughter's faith needed to be firm in order for her to be part of the Thailand mission. The convictions of her parents stand in contrast to those of Cleland McAfee who was satisfied with a vague affirmation of wanting to touch people for Christ in spite of a clear statement from Cornelia she did not want to evangelize or seek to persuade Thai people to become Christians. In his mind, the desire to meet social needs, such as education, in the name of Christ was apparently adequate missionary motivation. McAfee's assessment of Cornelia Gillies' preparedness for missionary service suggests the Board was open to modernist conceptions of the nature and purpose of mission work and no longer strictly requiring all its missionaries to hold evangelism as their primary goal. Changes to the Board manual in 1927 allowed for a broader conception of the goals of mission work yet retained conversion as the primary goal.[74] However, as the case of Cornelia Gillies illustrates, the Board allowed, at least in some cases, for these other purposes of mission to functionally replace the primary goal of winning and making disciples, as field personnel needs dictated.

In considering the above examples, it may be seen that one dimension of modernism among Thailand missionaries was exposure to Western intellectual influences, perhaps especially Western education. Dr. William Perkins developed doubts about traditional Christian beliefs, by his own testimony, in reaction to the preaching of his fellow American missionaries. Perkins' statement of doubts and the current status of his beliefs to Arthur Brown reflected Western challenges to the miraculous aspects of Scripture, something not being questioned by Thai Christians. Cornelia Gillies' doubts about the salvific aims of missionary service

---

72. Neuber's case will be discussed later in this chapter. C. Gillies to McAfee, March 22, 1932; Barnhouse "Travel Notes," January 3 and 11, 1935, PHS.

73. R. Gillies to McAfee, July 7, 1932, PHS.

74. Roy, "Overseas Missions Policies," 211.

seem to have developed during her education in the United States rather than her earlier years in Thailand.

Outside of missionary circles in Thailand, modernist re-evaluations of religion also came through exposure to Western intellectual influences. In nineteenth- and early twentieth-century Thailand, the first Thai to question the supernatural aspects of religion were King Mongkut (r.1851-1868), King Chulalongkorn (r.1868-1910) and other elite Thai who pursued Western learning and sent their sons to Europe and America for education.[75] Journalist Charles Selden, whose visit to Thailand will discussed in chapter 7, noted with approval this move towards a type of "modernist Buddhism" in Thailand even while many missionaries remained conservative.

Concerning Thai Christians and exposure to Western intellectual influences, it is significant that during this time period there were extremely few Thai Christians receiving a Western-style education outside of what was offered them at Presbyterian primary and secondary schools in Thailand. Missionaries with modernist views within the Thailand mission seem to have often kept their views to themselves and Thai Christians likely had little exposure to such ideas. In the 1930s, some Thai church leaders began to study in the Philippines and the United States, having been identified and sponsored for further studies abroad by the Thailand mission.[76] Of these, some studied education, some medicine, and others theology. Among these was Banchop Bansiddhi who completed theological studies in the Philippines. His higher education abroad likely contributed to his willingness to defend the orthodoxy of seminary director Carl Elder when he was accused of compromising biblical truth for the sake of modern biblical scholarship. Also, though Thai pastor Charoen Sakulkan did not study abroad, doubts he expressed about the veracity of the Bible most likely came from Western influence in the form of Thailand mission executive secretary Paul Eakin.[77] There is little evidence of modernist ideas among Thai Christians before the Second World War, which might be largely explained by their lack of exposure to such ideas through the medium of a Western education, especially at the university level or above.

---

75. Landon, *Thailand*, 134–36; Suksod-Barger, *Religious Influences*, 48–50.

76. Indhabhan, "Siamese Students," 126–27; Singhanetra, "Public Health," 201–4.

77. Landon to Cort, December 27, 1934; Landons to Board, October 9, 1940, WCSC.

DIMENSION 3 ~ ENCOUNTER WITH THAI BUDDHISM AND ITS IMPLICATIONS FOR CHRISTIAN UNIQUENESS

A third dimension of modernism among missionaries in Thailand and other Asian mission fields was the influence of living in a majority non-Christian society. This influence sometimes led to questioning or abandonment of the exclusivity of Christ for salvation and to greater openness to other religions. For some missionaries, this religious pluralism eventuated in their self-abnegation from the mission field. For other missionaries, modernist views on the relationship between Christianity and other religions led them to retreat from conversion as the primary goal of missionary work, favoring instead societal influence as an equally valid metric for missionary success.

Factors Influencing Missionary Attitudes Towards Buddhism in Thailand

Thailand missionaries who moved towards modernist views as the result of living in Thai society will be discussed momentarily, but it will first be helpful to note how the social and mission context in Thailand was different from that of China and thus fostered different results among the missionaries vis-à-vis religious pluralism. In the Chinese context, Lian Xi has called attention to the liberalization of religious views among missionaries in China as a result of their encounter with Chinese culture, a theme also highlighted by David Hollinger.[78] Xi attributes this liberalization among China missionaries to three factors, only two of which are relevant for Thailand. The three factors named by Xi are missionary appreciation for Chinese culture due to long residence there, the relativist implications of liberal theology (which the missionaries presumably received through exposure to Western intellectual influences), and the rise in China of a rationalist and materialist modern culture as the chief rival of Christianity which pushed missionaries to seek common ground between Chinese traditional religions and Christianity.[79] In Thailand, nationalism did not manifest in the same ways as it did in China, and thus had a different effect upon missionaries and indigenous Christians relative to modernism. In China, nationalism turned against both Confucianism and Christianity in favor of democracy and science, thus

---

78. Xi, *Conversion*; Hollinger, *Protestants Abroad*.
79. Xi, *Conversion*, 14–17, 171–206.

prompting missionaries who sympathized with nationalistic assertion of Chinese culture to doubt the traditional missionary goal of conversion. Chinese culture and religion have inherent value, they reasoned, so who are we to urge them to abandon it by converting to Christianity? In Thailand, nationalism was not anti-religion as it was in China. Thai nationalism embraced Buddhism as a pillar of national identity, and anti-foreign nationalist sentiment was largely directed at the Chinese, not Europeans. It was not until the late 1930s that Thai nationalism began to view Christianity as a threat to national identity and unity, much later than the emergence of comparable anti-Christian sentiment in China. Unlike China, secular and scientific materialism in Thailand did not push Christianity and the majority religion, in this case Buddhism, closer together against a common enemy. Even amidst mounting nationalism, American Presbyterian missionaries in Thailand continued to see Christianization as part of the solution to Thai woes, not part of the problem. This was true of both conservative and modernist-leaning missionaries. In Thailand, there was no societal move against religion in general. Thus, conservative and modernist-leaning missionaries still had more in common with each other in pursuing Christianization of the nation, however they conceived it, than they did with Thai Buddhists who sought an alternative modernity that gave Buddhism pride of place among the many religions tolerated in Thailand.

Also, as compared to China, missionaries in Thailand were slower to take an interest in studying indigenous religious traditions. This lack of interest was due to various factors. Firstly, the Buddhist scriptures, also known as the Pali canon, did not have a central role in religious teaching in Thailand as did the Confucian classics in China or the Bible in Western cultures. The Pali canon, as well as other manuscripts, were used for teaching Buddhism in monasteries in Thailand, though the actual content of teaching was often an eclectic mix of written and oral traditions, local beliefs and folktales, and indigenous spirit beliefs. Thai monasteries held diverse collections of manuscripts written on palm leaves. Some of those were only in Pali while others were bi-lingual manuscripts written in Pali and Central Thai, Northern Thai or any of a number of other regional languages.[80] Manuscript collections varied from one location to another and were selectively and creatively used in Buddhist instruction. Most monks would not learn Pali in the way a Protestant minister would learn Greek

---

80. "Northern Thai Literary Tradition."

and Hebrew to study the scriptures in the original language. Rather, both then and now the meaning of chosen Pali words have often been "lifted," as Justin McDaniel puts it, from texts "both canonical and noncanonical, and then creatively engaged with and explained by teachers based on their own experiences."[81] For missionaries who wished to study Buddhism, there were texts available to them, but the Pali canon itself was not the focus of dedicated study for Buddhists to nearly the same degree as the Bible was for Christians, nor the Confucian classics for Chinese. Writing in 1926 on the Christian approach to Buddhism, Robert Speer noted that thoughtful Buddhists in Thailand were few, and many Buddhist monks were unfamiliar with Buddhist teaching and texts. If even many monks did not know the Buddhist scriptures, it is not difficult to see why Christian missionaries did not see the need to study them in order to engage in discussion with Thai Buddhists.[82] The role of Buddhist texts was also changing from the mid-nineteenth century, being promoted by Thai royalty as sources of ethics and social instruction rather than a foundation for cosmological explanations.[83] Secondly, Buddhism in Thailand was often a combination of Theravada Buddhism and indigenous spirit practices. As compared to Bangkok and central Thailand, this was even more true of northern Thailand where indigenous spirit beliefs were often more influential than Buddhism in the lived religion of most people. As such, the religious practices missionaries commonly saw had their source in local beliefs and practices that often relied upon sacred charms and holy men as much as, or perhaps more than, Theravadin Buddhist teaching. For these reasons, much of what was called "Buddhism" seemed to be mere superstition in the eyes of most missionaries, and thus without value. William Briggs, for example, summarized Thai Buddhism as a "compound of Agnosticism, Demon worship and superstitious idolatry."[84] Thirdly, according to Maen Pongudom, lack of interest in studying Buddhism can be explained by the missionary belief that Buddhism was a man-made religion in decline that would soon crumble under the superiority of Christianity and American culture.[85]

These factors notwithstanding, a handful of missionaries in Thailand chose to study Buddhism. Some studied Buddhism for the purpose

81. McDaniel, *Gathering Leaves*, 3–9.
82. Speer, *Unfinished Task*, 146.
83. Lorgunpai, "World Lover, World Leaver," 176.
84. Briggs to Board, March 27, 1894, PUA.
85. Pongudom, "Apologetic and Missionary Proclamation," 58–65.

of finding evangelistic points of contact to use for evangelism rather than genuine interest in the Buddhism or Thai culture. In Northern Thailand, for example, William A. Briggs and William C. Dodd often used a well-known prophecy about a coming Messianic reincarnation of the Buddha to solicit interest in their message about the Christian Messiah.[86] Yet other missionaries took a genuine interest in Buddhism, which in some cases became the path of their exit from missionary service. However, in other cases it contributed to modification of the ways in which they pursued Christianization of Thailand, namely through societal improvement rather than explicit proselytization.

Evander McGilvary's Denial of Eternal Damnation of the Heathen, 1894

As mentioned earlier in this chapter, while working in Northern Thailand in the mid 1890s, missionary Evander McGilvary came to the conviction that it was not necessary to believe in Christ in order to be saved. The "heathen" would not be eternally lost. When a fellow missionary asked whom he meant, McGilvary cited his Northern Thai language helper as an example, a staunch Buddhist who thought Christianity and Buddhism were the same.[87] It is unknown how McGilvary came to the conclusion that profession of faith in Christ was not necessary for salvation, but it is likely his experience of living and working in the majority Buddhist context of Northern Thailand led to a modification of his views. His work in Bible translation would have involved many discussions of religious terms and concepts with his Buddhist language helper and may have also been a significant influence since McGilvary specifically cited this man when asked for an example of a "heathen" who would not be lost. As noted earlier, McGilvary's departure from the traditional view on the salvation of non-Christians together with his denial of biblical inerrancy led to his self-abnegation from mission work in Thailand. Though McGilvary's views were unique in Thailand at the time, similar views were expressed in the 1890s by ABCFM missionaries in India and China who argued against the damnation of the "heathen" based on their encounter with intelligent Hindus and Chinese.[88] Overt affirmation of the possibility of salvation

---

86. Dodd, *Tai Race*, 67–68; Brown, "Results of Missions," 339–43.
87. Phraner et al. to Daniel McGilvary, May 15, 1894, PUA.
88. Xi, *Conversion*, 208–11.

apart from Christian profession would not become permissible among American Presbyterian missionaries in Thailand until the 1960s.[89]

The Ambiguous Faith and Buddhist Idols of Carl Hansen, 1909

Fifteen years after Evander McGilvary departed for the United States, another member of the Laos mission also left, at least in part, due to modernist views that developed as a result of his encounter with Thai Buddhism. Dr. Carl C. Hansen and his wife Lillian arrived in Thailand in 1897 and for fourteen years worked in the northern Thai province of Lampang.[90] Hansen was the sole doctor at the Charles T. Van Santwoord mission hospital and was well liked by both local people and missionary colleagues. Hansen was financially generous, perhaps to a fault, and gained a reputation as one of the finest surgeons in the Laos mission.[91] However, when the Hansens left for furlough in September 1908, a question mark hung over their return to the field.

While the Hansens were on furlough in the United States during 1908–1909, it was decided they would not go back. Mrs. Hansen's health was the official reason the Board did not return them to the field.[92] However, letters from fellow missionaries indicate other factors, including Hansen's views on Buddhism and Christianity. Though Hansen's missionary application in 1895 indicated that he knew the Bible well and held zealously to the Westminster Confession, something apparently changed in his religious views and practices during his time in Thailand.[93] Hansen was very fond of language study and dedicated more time than many of his colleagues to the study of Buddhism, which eventually included collecting Buddha images. Fellow missionary David Collins thought that none of the great evangelists of the Thailand mission, such as Daniel McGilvary and Roderick Gillies, spent time studying Buddhism. However, those few who did "read and study the sacred Buddhist books see a lot more good in the teaching of Buddhism than some of the rest of us who the never had the time for such study."[94] In the period before World War II, the only other missionaries who seem to have

---

89. McLean, "Thai Protestant Christianity," 164–166.
90. Eakin, "Biographical Notes on Dr. and Mrs. Hansen," PUA.
91. Collins to Brown, August 31 1908; R. Gillies to Brown, October 8, 1909, PUA.
92. Daniel McGilvary to Brown, August 13, 1908, PUA.
93. Mathena to Gillespie, July 10, 1895, PHS.
94. Collins to Brown, August 31, 1908; R. Gillies to Brown, October 8, 1909, PUA.

taken a serious interest in studying Buddhism were Paul Eakin, Kenneth Wells, and Sinclair Thompson. Only in the post-war period would more American Presbyterians take a greater interest in studying Buddhism, which led to an interfaith lecture series featuring Buddhist and Christian presenters at the McGilvary Theological Seminary in Chiang Mai during the 1960s.[95] In 1908, however, Hansen's keen interest in Buddhism made his missionary colleagues uncomfortable. David Collins wondered if Hansen "perhaps thinks too much of some of his valuable idols." Roderick Gillies likewise "fear[ed] his large traffic in Buddhist idols was from every point of view a very undesirable thing."[96] Because of his value as a surgeon and personal fondness for the Hansens, his fellow missionaries wished him to stay. However, they regretted he had very little interest in evangelism.[97] His hesitancy to evangelize was likely related to his appreciation for Buddhism. Shortly after the Hansens left for furlough, fellow missionary Roderick Gillies wrote to Arthur Brown of the Board to lay out the pros and cons of the Hansens returning. Gillies cited the positive qualities of Dr. Hansen already mentioned but he also called into question the soundness of Hansen's faith:

> [O]ne has often *wondered whether Dr. Hansen is a Christian or a Buddhist or something* else. He dabbles in philosophy but I fear only enough to get himself muddled. Probably he regards God as operating in all religions alike, the only distinction between them being that of higher and lower; and he would probably accord to Christianity the highest place. But it appears he has persistently extolled Buddhism and left a very misleading impression. He has *never done anything directly in evangelistic* work. And I rather think the fact of conversion in the evangelical sense has no place in his view of things at all.[98]

It is unknown to what extent Gillies' letter influenced the decision of the Board but, as with McGilvary, the seemingly relativistic religious views of Hansen caused some of his fellow missionaries to question Hansen's suitability for missionary service. However, unlike McGilvary, Hansen and his wife did not want to leave Thailand. Following their resignation from the

---

95. Eakin, *Buddhism and the Christian Approach to Buddhists*; Wells, *Theravada Buddhism*; "W.J. Sinclair Thompson Memorial," PHS.

96. Collins to Brown, August 31, 1908; R. Gillies to Brown, October 8, 1909, PUA.

97. Daniel McGilvary to Brown, August 13, 1908; Collins to Brown, August 31, 1908, PUA.

98. R. Gillies to Brown, October 8, 1909, PUA.

American Presbyterian mission in 1909, they moved to Bangkok where Dr. Hansen opened a medical dispensary and worked as a physician until his death in 1929.[99] Though Mrs. Hansen's health was the official reason for the discontinuation of their service with the Board, the couple's subsequent twenty years of residence in Bangkok makes one wonder if her health was really the primary reason. It is likely that a more significant reason for their departure from the Laos mission was concern about Dr. Hansen's ambiguous faith, large collection of Buddhist images, and lack of evangelistic zeal. Unlike many of his missionary colleagues, Hansen made a serious investigation of Thai Buddhism which led to changes in his thinking and behavior in a modernist direction, putting him unacceptably out of step with his fellow missionaries.

Margaret Neuber: Buddhism is Better Suited Than Christianity for the Thai, 1930

In addition to McGilvary and Hansen, there were a handful of other missionaries in the prewar period who left Thailand as a result of their encounter with Buddhism. While meeting with missionaries in Bangkok in 1935, Donald Barnhouse, whose visit will be discussed in chapter 7, heard the story of Margaret Neuber, an APM Thailand missionary teacher at a girls' schools in Northern Thailand, who did not see any difference between a good Christian and a good Buddhist. Missionary Ruth Case related to Barnhouse that Neuber "was discouraged and didn't know where she stood." According to Case, after Neuber went on furlough in 1930, "the Board would not send her back because she was not evangelical."[100] In a separate discussion, Lucy Starling, director of a mission school for girls in the northern province of Lampang, affirmed many of these same details to Barnhouse. "She was all at sea," recounted Starling; "[Neuber] concluded that Buddhism is just as good, if not better, than Christianity for the people of Siam," a reflection apparently borne from Neuber's experience with Thai Buddhists while teaching in Northern Thailand. Neuber was not, however, the only missionary in the living memory of the APM Thailand missionaries in 1935 whose faith had been unsettled by living in Thai Buddhist society. Graham Fuller told Barnhouse that Neuber was just one of a number of young

---

99. "Dr. C.C. Hansen," 391.

100. Barnhouse, "Travel Notes," January 3, 1935, PHS; Eakin, "Biographical Notes on Margaret Neuber," PUA.

people who came out to Thailand as missionaries but returned home shortly thereafter, lacking the spiritual resources to sustain their faith in a non-Christian country. Starling thought that part of the responsibility for such departures lay with other members of the Thailand mission. Regarding Neuber, Starling said, "[p]art of the failure is ours. Certainly we missionaries should have been able to lead her to Christ."[101]

The assessments of Neuber by Fuller and Starling reflected the belief of several experienced missionaries that younger missionaries without a sufficient foundation of faith were likely to move away from the Christian faith when immersed in Thai Buddhist society. Another such case was Dr. John and Mrs. Julia Horst who resigned from the Thailand mission in 1932 when they developed religious doubts after being "unable to answer the questions of intelligent Siamese" Buddhists.[102] In the context of China, Lian Xi noted a similar trend, citing Pearl Buck as an example of the "tendency toward self-abnegation" on the part of missionaries who moved away from traditional Christian beliefs.[103] Conservative critics of modernism claimed that the loss of belief in the exclusivity of Christ and uniqueness of Christianity "cut the nerve of missions," namely destroying the foreign missions movement by eliminating the motivation of saving people from hell. Modernists denied this was the case, but there are numerous examples, such as Margaret Neuber, where this is exactly what happened.[104] Instances of missionaries becoming more conservative as a result of encounter with Thai Buddhism were rare. My research has only turned up one instance of a missionary becoming more conservative on the mission field. Missionaries of the Chiang Mai station told Donald Barnhouse that Carl Elder, who had recently become the director of the theological seminary in Chiang Mai, "was more or less liberal when he came to the field, but that under the necessities of actual conditions here has rapidly been becoming more conservative." Exactly what Elder's former views were, and how they had changed, were not specified in Barnhouse's notes. However, Elder stands as an exceptional case.[105]

---

101. Barnhouse "Travel Notes," January 11, 1935, PHS.

102. Cotton to McAfee, December 1, 1932; McAfee to Cotton, December 5, 1932, PHS.

103. Xi, *Conversion*, 228.

104. Xi, *Conversion*, 208–214; McAfee, *Uncut Nerve of Missions*.

105. Barnhouse "Travel Notes," January 7, 1935, PHS.

Paul Eakin's Modernist Conceptions of Salvation and Christian Mission

Although several missionaries left the Thailand mission field as a result of religiously pluralistic views, not all missionaries with modernist tendencies did so. Paul Eakin, who was born in Thailand to missionary parents and worked there as a missionary himself from 1913 to 1949, held beliefs and promoted mission policies influenced by both his deep association with Thai society and his American educational training.[106] Eakin had modernist convictions on numerous points of doctrine and believed numerous Thai Buddhist emphases made a positive contribution to the practice of the Christian faith. These included an emphasis on character rather than creed, a non-proselytizing message, and the importance of one's personal life over concerns about the future.[107] Eakin spoke Thai extremely well and maintained personal friendships with Thai people throughout his life, even after returning to the United States in 1949. His long experience in Thailand surely contributed to his respect for Thai culture and his disdain for those who would view Thai people as inferior. He thought that any motive for missionary service based on pity for "the poor benighted heathen" was "most unsatisfactory" and obsolete.[108]

Though Eakin recoiled from viewing the Thai as "heathen" who needed to be saved from damnation, he nonetheless thought that Christianity had something to offer the Thai people. Eakin believed that Christianity had both a proselytizing and non-proselytizing message. On the one hand, Christians should be motivated to do good simply because it is good to do so and reflects how Christ treated people. When people are "touched and transformed" by Christ even without becoming "a member of the Christian church," then Christians should rejoice. However, Christians also needed to be witnesses because, as Eakin explained, "when we link up with God though Christ, we find released within us divine resources which are sufficient to transform our characters . . . We would not be truly Christian if we did not care enough for all others to make these facts known to them." The unique contribution of Christianity, Eakin believed, lay in its power to "create desire to do good and power to live up

---

106. Eakin's personal papers stored at the Payap University Archives contain occasional clippings from materials by Harry Emerson Fosdick and Henry Sloane Coffin, suggesting continuing interest in modernist teaching during his tenure in Thailand.

107. Eakin, "B. has made Xty," PUA; Swanson, "Paul A. Eakin," 257; Eakin, "My Reasonable Faith," PUA.

108. Eakin, "Fundamental Christian Convictions," PUA.

to it."[109] His convictions on the nature and purpose of Christianity were reflected in his preaching which focused on finding spiritual resources for successful living in today's world.[110]

The focus of Eakin's faith and missionary service was formed and informed by his long experience with Thai Buddhist society in combination with theological reflection on the Christian faith. His resulting convictions made for a this-worldly faith that sought this-worldly salvation for the Thai people. For Eakin, heaven and hell were not endless conditions after death, but hell was a sense of remorse and deprivation while heaven was "a new joy of fellowship with our fellow men." Though he acknowledged every metaphor of salvation had a kernel of truth, salvation did not consist in penal substitutionary atonement and he believed that "guilt [for sin] can not be transferred to another." Rather, Eakin wrote, "it is living together with Christ after having been drawn to the Cross that will save us from our sins."[111]

Eakin's modernist views are particularly notable because of his prominent position as Thailand mission executive secretary from 1930. Eakin's intra-mission correspondence indicates he did not talk about his modernist positions with other missionaries. Rather, he formally affirmed the conservative consensus of the mission, seeking to quell dissension among missionaries and finding ways for missionaries of divergent views to find places to work that would contribute to a broadly conceived goal of Christianizing Thailand. Eakin himself did not favor so-called "soul winning" evangelism that sought to save people from hell. Rather, he prioritized the mission schools as an essential ministry for evangelism. For Eakin, evangelism did not mean "multiplying adherents" in order to "defeat other religions," but rather using indirect methods of influence and providing examples of moral Christian living in order to help people find spiritual resources in Christianity to desire to do good and have the ability to live up to it.[112] His priority on the schools was shared by several APM Thailand educational missionaries who stressed the long-term impact of mission schools, emphasizing their ability to influence Thai society with Christian values even where there were few accessions to the church.[113]

109. Eakin, "Fundamental Christian Convictions"; Eakin, "New Approach," PUA.
110. Eakin, "Sermon Outlines," 1928 to 1931, PUA.
111. Eakin, "My Reasonable Faith," PUA.
112. Eakin, "New Approach," PUA.
113. Barnhouse, "Travel Notes," January 2–6, 1935, PHS; Eakin, "Meeting of Missionaries with Dr. Barnhouse in Bangkok, January 3, 1935," PUA.

This priority on institutional work over direct evangelistic work for modernist-leaning missionaries was not uncommon on Asian mission fields. Lian Xi has noted that in China, missionary appreciation for traditional indigenous religion sometimes led to a softening of the desire for conversion and a diversion of the impulse to "save" into institutional work and social services.[114] In Thailand, Eakin and others who favored this type of social salvation over evangelization as traditionally conceived did not go unchallenged. Intra-mission debate over the purposes and effectiveness of mission schools, which Eakin vigorously defended as essential to evangelism, will be discussed in chapter 9.

DIMENSION 4 ~ MODERNIZING CHRISTIANITY FOR AN EDUCATED ELITE

A fourth dimension of modernism in Thailand was the perceived need to make Christianity attractive to educated Buddhists. Traditional doctrines and methods of presenting them were seen as stumbling blocks to evangelism in the modern world but if those obstacles could be removed, then missionaries might have greater success in influencing the upper classes to embrace the Christian faith. Contrary to conservative criticisms, modernist updates to Christianity were intended to save Christianity for the current generation, not destroy it. William Hutchison pointed out it was widely believed by theological liberals that the "new theology in actual fact converted more souls to Christianity than the old."[115] This belief was evident on the foreign mission field as well. Lian Xi noted that in China the desire of missionaries to solve modern problems and achieve mission success led to greater religious inclusivity.[116] This desire for mission success also contributed to the pursuit of modernism among missionaries in Thailand.

Carl Elder and Modernist Books at the Seminary

In Thailand, the desire to make Christianity appealing to modern people was important to several missionaries, especially seminary director Carl Elder and APM Thailand mission executive secretary Paul Eakin. They believed that preaching traditional Christian beliefs might be effective among rural and uneducated people but evangelism among urbanites and

---

114. Xi, *Conversion*, 10–13.
115. Hutchison, *Modernist Impulse*, 154–55.
116. Xi, *Conversion*, 19.

the educated required a more modern, intelligent type of Christianity. Citing an article in the *International Review of Missions*, Carl Elder told Arthur Brown that Korean young people wanted modern and scientific books, and the same was true in Thailand. Elder believed that the Thailand mission would never reach the upper classes unless they became more modern in their mission standards and approach.[117] Desiring the modern did not always include theological modernism but Elder saw modernist approaches to the faith as an important component of propagating Christianity. This was revealed in Elder's responses to charges leveled against him in the wake of evangelist John Sung's visit to Thailand, which will be discussed in chapter 7. Loren Hanna, a fundamentalist-leaning missionary, wrote to Elder claiming he was so shocked at two of the books that were being assigned to seminary students that he felt he "ought to take an antiseptic bath after reading them." The books in question were Conrad Skinner's *Concerning the Bible: A Brief Sketch of Its Origin, Growth and Contents* and Edward Bosworth's *The Life and Teaching of Jesus According to the First Three Gospels*. Hanna urged Elder to "get right with God and accept the truth in His word," warning he was headed for tragedy if he did not renounce such "so-called" scholarship and education, and accept God's grace.[118] In a letter to Paul Eakin, Elder admitted that the books Hanna objected to did present "the modern viewpoint of the Bible," which he was "willing to defend." However, he explained they were only used in the higher classes at the seminary and were necessary because some of the students would meet people with a university education and needed to be able to "present the Bible intelligently." Hanna did not know, claimed Elder, that he also used books by R.A. Torrey and William Evans which presented viewpoints Hanna would agree with. Elder thought this was a fair and balanced approach.[119] In a conservative-majority mission, it would have been difficult for Elder to exclusively teach only those modernist views with which he agreed.

---

117. Elder to Brown, January 27, 1928, PHS. The article Elder cited was Paton and Underhill, "World Survey," 11–73.

118. Hanna to Elder, September 15, 1939, PUA.

119. Elder to Eakin, September 29, 1939, PUA.

Rev. Carl Elder, 1922
(Courtesy of the Presbyterian Historical Society, Philadelphia).

Keeping Fundamentalists Away from the Educated

The perceived need to modernize Christianity to evangelize the educated also manifested itself in the efforts of Eakin, Elder, and other APM Thailand missionaries to keep fundamentalist-leaning evangelists out of the cities and out of Thailand. Outdated messages and approaches to spreading the Christian faith would harm evangelization efforts among urban, educated classes even if they were fine for "making conversions among the demon and spirit worshipers of the jungle," as journalist Charles Selden put it in his article about mission work in Thailand. In a 1937 letter to Board secretary Charles Leber, Paul Eakin wrote against a proposal for missionary Kenneth Landon to move from the far southern province of Trang to Bangkok after his return from furlough. Eakin considered Landon, a graduate of both Wheaton College and Princeton Seminary

Dimensions of Modernism in the American Presbyterian Mission 137

who arrived in Thailand in 1927, to be too dogmatic and ill-suited to working with "students and more highly educated people" in Bangkok. He thought that Landon should remain in Trang working with the Chinese while ministry among the Thai in Trang, which Landon failed at, should be left to Thai evangelist Rev. Sook Pongsanoi, who had been doing well since Landon went on furlough.[120]

Kenneth Landon (center) and a Chinese Christian group in Satun, southern Thailand
(Courtesy of the Presbyterian Historical Society, Philadelphia)

120. Eakin to Leber, December 29, 1937, PUA.

138   Conservative in Theology, Liberal in Spirit

Congregation of Presbyterian Church in Trang, southern Thailand, 1938 (Courtesy of Buswell Library Archives & Special Collections, Wheaton College, IL).

The following year, Eakin wrote to Board secretary J.L. Hooper, explaining that the Thailand mission only needed certain types of evangelists. They must be broadminded evangelists, sympathetic to Buddhism and to students, and not dictatorial.[121] Eakin asserted that Thailand did

---

121. Ironically, Eakin himself was accused of dictatorial and authoritarian tendencies by some of his fellow missionaries. Landons to Board, October 9, 1940, WCSC; Edna Bulkley to Women of the Siam mission, November 3, 1932, PHS.

not need mass appeals or graduates from the fundamentalist institutions of Wheaton College, San Francisco Theological Seminary, or the Bible Institute of Los Angeles. Some of the mission's most fervent evangelists were "pushers and insisters on their own ways of presenting the Gospel [such] that they cannot get along either with their fellow-missionaries or their national workers whom they have trained."[122] Eakin did not specify which missionaries he was thinking of but it is probable that he had in mind Kenneth Landon, Loren Hanna, and Paul Fuller. In a letter to Cleland McAfee several years earlier, Eakin likewise urged the Board to be "very careful in selection of missionaries" whom they sent to Thailand. He wanted no one who would make "disparaging remarks about Buddhism" but only those who could have "backbone without bristles."[123] One of the bristles Eakin may have had in mind was the occasional jabs at modernism that fundamentalist-leaning missionaries engaged in. Carl Elder, for example, complained about Kenneth Landon's public opposition to modern biblical scholarship. Elder had heard Landon's preaching, most likely at the Sunday afternoon English-language worship service at Fourth Church in Bangkok, and said it was "very hard to hear a man speak of Biblical scholarship as 'bunk' and refer to those who accept the findings of scholars, even in part, as 'fools.' This Mr. Landon has done twice in that many sermons."[124] On another occasion, Paul Eakin's modernist sympathies were rankled by the preaching of another fundamentalist-leaning missionary, Paul Fuller. Fuller had spoken on "the Verbal Inspiration of the Bible," which Eakin thought "a rather belligerent topic."[125]

William Harris and Marion Palmer Refuse a Burmese Gospel Team Access to Their Students

In addition to Elder and Eakin, there were other APM Thailand missionaries who wanted to guard against evangelism that was not sufficiently modern. Between 1931 and 1933, the Thailand mission received gospel teams from Burma who held meetings in many locations, combining fun

---

122. Eakin to Hooper, October 5, 1938, PHS.

123. Eakin to McAfee, July 6, 1931, PHS.

124. After leaving the mission field in 1937, Landon eventually moved away from the Christian faith, specifically the Fundamentalist form of it. Elder to Brown, September 12, 1927, PHS; Kenneth Landon to Margaret Landon, April 1–2, 1942, WCSC; Hollinger, *Protestants Abroad*, 191–92.

125. Eakin to Brown, September 6, 1927, PHS.

activities with preaching and testimonies.[126] The first team that came in 1931 visited all the mission stations, including the major mission schools, reportedly leaving a positive impression on many Thai and missionaries, including Paul Eakin.[127] Eakin recalled that he was "especially pleased because they made it evident that religion and fun were not incompatible" and "the testimony and preaching was definitely based on scholarly interpretations of the Bible. There was nothing spectacular or grotesque."[128] Paul Fuller saw these teams as a great example of how Christian schools could be used well for evangelism and the gospel team strategy was adopted by numerous Thai Christians and missionaries in Thailand.[129]

However, the Burmese gospel teams were not universally praised. The *Laymen's Inquiry* was critical of the gospel teams they observed in Burma.[130] Board Secretary Cleland McAfee, however, guessed that the *Laymen's Inquiry* was thinking of the U.S. situation and wrongly imposed it on other places in the world, thus judging gospel teams unsuitable. Yet their criticism was unjustified, thought McAfee, because these gospel teams were "helpful for the primitive condition in Siam and Burma."[131] Nevertheless, a couple of APM Thailand educational missionaries in major cities still didn't care for the teams. In a conversation with Donald Barnhouse, Loren Hanna reported that Marion B. Palmer and William Harris, directors of Bangkok Christian College and Prince Royal's College (Chiang Mai), respectively, refused to allow a Burmese gospel team into the schools they oversaw. Since such a team previously visited their schools in 1930, it can be deduced that Palmer and Harris saw what a Burmese gospel team was like and did not care to have a subsequent team hold activities for their students. Barnhouse summarized Loren Hanna's comments, writing that "when the Burma Gospel team came over to Siam to work, Palmer refused to allow them to speak in the Bangkok Christian College, saying that the active propagation of Christianity would drive the non-Christians away from the school. Harris would not have them in Prince Royal [College] on the ground that their approach

---

126. For a summary of Burmese gospel team work in Thailand, see Son, "Christian Revival," 141–146.

127. "Burmese Gospel Team," 456–60.

128. Eakin, "Influence of Foreign Evangelists," PUA.

129. Fuller, "Siamo-Burmese-American Gospel Team in Siam"; Suriyakham, "Siamo-Burmese Gospel Team"; Fuller to McAfee, September 1931, PHS.

130. Hocking, *Re-Thinking Missions*, 141–42.

131. McAfee to Bachtell, November 7, 1932, PHS.

Dimensions of Modernism in the American Presbyterian Mission 141

was on too low a level, thus cheapening the Gospel."[132] In light of the fact Eakin thought the testimonies and preaching of the team were sufficiently scholarly, it is difficult to understand why Harris thought their evangelism was "too low of a level." Palmer's eschewment of "active propagation of Christianity" for the fear of driving students away from his school raises the question of what role he thought schools should be playing in the Christianization of Thailand. Had he abandoned conversion as a desirable goal and embraced ethical and social influence as benchmarks of mission success? Whatever their thinking was, Palmer and Harris's rejection of a gospel team visit stands witness to their concern that Christian witness needed to be sufficiently "modern" and intelligent, and perhaps modernist-leaning to some degree, in order to leave a positive impression of Christianity in the minds of students.

APM THAILAND MISSION'S CONSERVATIVE CONSENSUS AND THE LAYMEN'S INQUIRY, 1933

The four dimensions of modernism discussed above demonstrate the diverse ways in which the impact of modernism was being felt in the American Presbyterian mission in Thailand over the course of fifty years. Yet in spite of spreading modernism, the Thailand mission as a whole remained theologically conservative, or at least that is what they believed about themselves and wanted to convey to outsiders. As a way of examining the nature of this consensus in the face of spreading modernism, the final section of this chapter will look at the Thailand missionaries' reactions to the *Laymen's Inquiry*. As discussed in chapter 3, *Re-Thinking Missions: A Laymen's Inquiry After One Hundred Years* was a modernist assessment of missionary work in India, Burma, China, and Japan. The authors of the inquiry extrapolated from their survey of those countries to Protestant mission work more generally, concluding that high-quality social services and societal development should be prioritized over the antiquated goals of conversion and church growth. As news about the contents of the *Laymen's Inquiry* first started to circulate in November 1932, the PCUSA Board of Foreign Missions was generally unhappy with much of the criticism made by the report, as well as the harsh anti-mission comments of Presbyterian China missionary Pearl Buck who lavishly and uncritically praised the report.[133] However, they tried to show restraint and nuance

---

132. Barnhouse, "Travel Notes," January 11, 1935, PHS.
133. For detailed discussions of controversy over the Laymen's Report and Pearl

in their public responses because, according to Board secretary Cleland McAfee, "the number in our church who agree with the details are as many as those who disagree." McAfee thought the best strategy was to look for some unifying principle in the report that could help the whole church move forward in mission. To this end, he thought it would also be best to take a neutral position on Buck in order not to stir up controversy.[134] The approach expressed by McAfee characterized both the Board's responses to the report within and without the Presbyterian Church in the USA as well as the Board's communication with its overseas missions.

The mediating, nuanced response of the Board also characterized the response of the Thailand mission. A full published version of the *Laymen's Inquiry* arrived in Thailand in early 1933 and several APM Thailand missionaries read the report, finding themselves both concerned and challenged by its assertions.[135] The Executive Committee of the Thailand mission assigned sections of the Laymen's Report to members of their committee to read and review prior to a discussion of the report at their meeting in June 1933.[136] Following that meeting, missionary Lucy Starling wrote a summary of the committee's discussion for publication in the October 1933 issue of *Siam Outlook*, a quarterly journal published by the Thailand mission.[137] The summary was also sent to the Board.[138] The committee did not directly address the modernist theological viewpoint of the report aside from repeated affirmations of the importance of evangelism and the national church, both of which were legitimate goals of mission, contra the *Laymen's Inquiry*. Though the Thailand mission's executive committee agreed with the *Laymen's Inquiry* that social service was a legitimate form of evangelism, they wanted to clearly state the importance of verbal proclamation of the gospel alongside social service. They stood against a redefinition of evangelism that excluded the goal of conversion:

Buck, see Longfield, *Presbyterian Controversy*, 199–208; Hutchison, *Errand*, 158–75; Hollinger, *Protestants Abroad*, 33–46.

134. Cotton to McAfee, December 1, 1932; McAfee to Cotton, December 5, 1932, PHS.

135. Seigle to McAfee, January 25, 1933; M. Gillies to Friends, January 28, 1933; McDaniel to Speer, January 28, 1933; May Palmer to Friends, February 10, 1933, PHS.

136. G. Fuller to Station Secretaries, March 15, 1933, PUA.

137. G. Fuller to Station Secretaries, June 23, 1933, PUA; Starling, "Re-Thinking Missions and Siam," 120–27.

138. McAfee to G. Fuller, August 16, 1933, PUA.

> We feel that ministry to the secular needs of men in the spirit of Christ is evangelism in the right use of the word, and that all of the various forms of mission activity need the interpretation which the spoken Gospel message provides . . . Without this, there is a likelihood that we will be misunderstood by the Oriental mind, which is deeply imbued with the ideas of doing good works for the sake of acquiring merit.[139]

Beyond such affirmations of the unity of word and deed in evangelism, the published summary of the Executive Committee's discussion did not expand on any other objections to the theology of the report which the committee may have had. While the APM Thailand missionaries were not unconcerned with the boldly modernist theological conclusions of the report, they did not feel the need to make their own statement. They were largely satisfied with the re-affirmation of the evangelical basis of missions already given by the Board, and were encouraged by Robert Speer's article-length response to the *Laymen's Inquiry*, later published as a booklet entitled *Re-Thinking Missions Examined*.[140] The Thailand mission also reported their approval of a response to the *Laymen's Inquiry* issued by Christian leaders in Japan who re-affirmed the importance of evangelism and reacted against the report's rosy view of non-Christian faiths and negative view of older missionaries.[141]

Though the Executive Committee did not spend much ink addressing the theological underpinnings of the report, they did seriously consider the ways in which they could improve their social service ministries in light of the report's conclusions. Though not all of the report's observations and recommendations were relevant to the situation in Thailand, the committee acknowledged that the current "stage of world development calls for adjustment." The Thailand mission was trying to adapt and appreciated the "contribution that the report has made to our thinking."[142] The committee found the report helpful in thinking about how to improve in the areas of education, literature, agriculture, women's work and meeting the social needs of youth.

In the committee's evaluation, and other letters to the Board, APM Thailand missionaries did take umbrage, however, at the claim that most

---

139. Starling, "Re-Thinking Missions and Siam," 121.

140. Speer, *Re-Thinking Missions Examined*; G. Fuller to Station, June 23, 1933, PUA; Harris to Speer, February 17, 1933, PHS.

141. "Japanese Christian Leaders Appraise the Appraisal," 151–52.

142. Starling, "Re-Thinking Missions and Siam," 120.

missionaries were second-rate workers doing low-quality work.[143] The Thailand missionaries wanted to provide high-quality education and medical care to the Thai people but felt continually hampered by limitations of personnel and finance. "We have attempted," wrote Starling on behalf of the Executive Committee, "to meet pressing needs with such service as we are able to render with our present resources, even though it has not always been able to attain the highest standards of excellence which we desire."[144] On this point, missionary Charlotte Bachtell conceded that most of the missionaries in Thailand were mediocre but they were trying to meet the changes of the modern world without compromising the gospel of Jesus Christ. In defense of the "mediocre" missionary, she asserted that the Thailand missionaries cared for the sick and were concerned for the social life of the church.[145] While acknowledging their limitations, the APM Thailand missionaries and the Board nonetheless felt the pressure to strive for high standards, both for the sake of serving the Thai people and to retain the support of their home constituency. Board secretary Cleland McAfee reminded William Harris, principal of the Thailand mission's boys school in Chiang Mai, that since the *Laymen's Inquiry* "takes us to task for lowering our educational standards for the sake of larger evangelistic effort," the Thailand mission and Board would have to make greater efforts to show mission supporters more details of the purely educational work of their mission schools, not only the evangelistic aspects.[146] May Palmer, wife of Bangkok Christian College principal Marion B. Palmer, also felt the need to respond to the *Laymen's Inquiry* for the sake of maintaining relations with the couple's mission supporters. Without addressing any of the modernist theological conclusions of the report per se, Palmer wrote in a circular letter to supporters that the *Laymen's Inquiry* was undoubtedly prepared "in the best spirit of helpfulness" and "should arouse us all at home and abroad to concerted action with more wisdom and devotion that ever before."[147]

In assessing the influence of modernism among the American Presbyterian missionaries in Thailand, the reactions to the Laymen's Report reveal two things.[148] First, Thailand mission leaders were not prepared

---

143. Hocking, *Re-Thinking Missions*, 15–16.
144. Starling, "Re-Thinking Missions and Siam," 121.
145. Bachtell to McAfee, November 4, 1932, PHS.
146. McAfee to Harris, November 11, 1932, PHS.
147. Palmer to Friends, February 10, 1933, PHS.
148. For discussion of reaction to the Laymen's Report in the United States, see Hutchison, *Errand*, 158–75; Baker, "Reactions to The 'Laymen's Report,'" 379–98.

formally to abandon the traditional goal of Christian conversion as the primary and legitimate goal of evangelism and missions. In this respect, the Thailand mission, on the whole was resistant to any significant modernization of the primary theological aim of their missionary work. Liberal evangelicalism, such as that represented by Paul Eakin, was quietly permissible but the overt relativistic religious pluralism of the *Laymen's Inquiry* that put Christianity on a par with other religions was unacceptable. Secondly, aside from strictly theological and evangelistic concerns, the Thailand mission was open and willing to change with the times in improving and updating their social service work in light of modernizing changes then happening in the world. Their only regret in this later area was that they were not able to do more to bring the best and most modern advancements in education, medicine, and other areas to meet the needs of contemporary Thai society. The relativistic modernism of the *Laymen's Inquiry* was a bridge too far for the Thailand mission, but they did affirm the Inquiry's call to improve society and promote modern standards in education and medicine.

CONCLUSION

From the 1890s until the start of World War II, there were four primary dimensions of modernist influence among American Presbyterian missionaries in Thailand. These were 1) responses to modern biblical criticism, 2) the influence of theological revisionism in the west, 3) the encounter with Thai Buddhism and its implications for Christian uniqueness, and 4) the desire to modernize Christianity to appeal to Thailand's educated elite. Some APM Thailand missionaries who held modernist views left the mission field because of their views. Others, however, expressed modernist convictions in modified approaches to mission, especially modernizing the Christian message to appeal to the educated and prioritizing institutional work for the sake of spreading Christian influence in society at large. Paralleling developments in the PCUSA, from the 1920s, there was increasing tolerance for modernism within the Thailand mission and less tolerance for those who objected to those views. Throughout this time, the Thailand mission maintained a broadly conservative consensus in line with the former American Protestant missionary consensus that was breaking down elsewhere. The next chapter will build on this foundation by examining how selected foreign visitors interpreted what they found in Thailand though the lens of experience with modernism and fundamentalism in the United States and China.

7

Outsider Interactions with Modernism and Fundamentalism in Thailand

As SEEN IN CHAPTER 6, modernist views were not unknown among the APM Thailand missionaries yet not all who held modernist views remained on the mission field, especially in the period before 1920. However, during the following two decades, not a few APM Thailand missionaries held modernist positions on at least some issues. Nevertheless, the mission as a whole wanted to be united in their goals and work, and maintain a conservative consensus. Yet, there was an increasing diversity of theological views among them that threatened that unity. Not all missionaries shared the same understanding of the message and methods of evangelism, an important fact that some sensed but not all were consciously aware of. Because the missionaries were busy and spread out, communication was difficult and they were often not aware of the nature or depth of the differences between them. Half of the missionaries were located in the cities of Bangkok and Chiang Mai, largely engaged in educational work. The remainder were scattered across several rural provinces running the length of the country. The early twentieth century witnessed a massive growth in mission schools even while the overall number of missionaries declined. New personnel requests sent to the Board of Foreign Mission in New York often prioritized educational workers over evangelistic workers. There were growing divisions in the mission between those who favored direct evangelistic work and those who put their hopes for evangelization of Thailand in educational work. Underlying the tension between these two groups were theological differences, although such differences were often discussed in terms of methodology rather than theology. Sometimes it took the inquiries of outsiders to the APM Thailand mission to bring out into the open theological differences among the missionaries that existed but were not explicitly acknowledged. Questions and concerns arising from the modernist-fundamentalist debates in the United States and China served as a lightning rod to make more explicit the often unspoken theological commitments of APM Thailand missionaries.

This chapter will examine how three foreign visitors interpreted and interacted with what they found in Thailand though the lens of their experience with modernism and fundamentalism in the United States and China. Thailand did not receive nearly the degree of attention China did due to its smaller size and lesser prominence in the minds of the American public. However, foreign travelers occasionally passed through the country, especially the capital city of Bangkok, and it was a mission field to which American Presbyterians were committed. The visitors examined in this chapter have been selected for what their visits uniquely revealed about theological matters among the Thailand missionaries. The background of each visitor influenced what they noticed and how they reacted to it. The first visitor to be considered is Charles Selden, a modernist-leaning magazine reporter travelling through Asia to research a series of articles. The second was Donald Barnhouse, a fundamentalist-leaning American Presbyterian minister who sought to discover if modernism was infecting Presbyterian mission fields. The third visitor was Chinese evangelist John Sung who briefly studied at modernist-leaning Union Theological Seminary in New York City and subsequently associated himself with the fundamentalist movement upon return to China. Each visitor brought their own perspective and viewed what they found in Thailand through the lens of their own background and experience. As will be seen in the following pages, Selden and Barnhouse's visits revealed cracks in the Thailand mission's conservative theological consensus which Sung later broke wide open with his fiery and polarizing brand of revival preaching. Thailand mission leaders long sought to preserve mission unity and to avoid the modernist-fundamentalist controversies that plagued the church in the United States and China, but in the wake of Sung's revival meetings, unity was ultimately unsustainable.

CHARLES SELDEN: HAS THE FUNDAMENTALIST-MODERNIST CONTROVERSY COME TO SIAM? 1927

In 1927, journalist Charles Selden, a Unitarian, visited Bangkok as part of his tour of Asia to gather information for a series of articles on "Christianity in Asia" that he was writing. His report on Thailand was part of an article published in the June 1927 issue of *Ladies Home Journal* and solicited strong reactions from members of the American Presbyterian mission in Thailand as well as the Board of Foreign Mission in New York.[1]

Selden's Claim of Controversy and Missionary Responses

The most objectionable part of the article was the claim that the fundamentalist-modernist controversy was causing conflict within the American Presbyterian mission in Thailand. After commenting on the irony that many missionaries continued to preach a gospel of supernatural and miraculous beliefs while modern Thai Buddhists were moving away from such unscientific views, Selden wrote:

> In the face of all this Siamese equivalent for Western modernism in religion, the Presbyterian Mission in that country is now acquiring for itself a new difficulty by injecting into its own group the American controversy between Fundamentalism and Modernism. Young people have come out recently from the Fundamentalist schools for training in exhortation and evangelism based on literal interpretation of the whole Bible. So far as making conversions among the demon and spirit worshipers of the jungle is concerned they can do just as effective works as the moderns. But they are hopeless and helpless among the educated Buddhists of the ruling and professional groups of the Siamese. And these are the groups which must be reached by Christianity, if Siam is ever to be anything but a country the prevailing and official religion of which is Buddhism.[2]

Aside from this paragraph, the rest of the article was positive towards missionary work in Thailand. However, his claim that the fundamentalist-modernist controversy had come to Thailand solicited an immediate negative reaction from two missionaries on furlough when the article was published.

---

1. I am grateful to Herb Swanson for first making me aware of Selden's visit. Herbert Swanson, "Conservative in Theology, Liberal in Spirit."
2. Selden, "Christianity in Asia Today," 170, 189–90, 193.

In a letter to Board secretary Arthur Brown, missionary Faye Kilpatrick, a teacher at Wattana Wittaya Academy in Bangkok, rejected Selden's claim that the Thailand mission had "injected into its group the controversy between Fundamentalism and Modernism." She asserted that "any one at all acquainted with the facts would deny" this claim and was confident all the other missionaries in Thailand would agree with her. On the contrary, she wrote, "there has been a remarkable spirit of mutual tolerance." Her statement that her fellow missionaries were tolerant of each other was an implicit acknowledgement that divergent theological camps existed within the Thailand mission. There were theological differences among them, but just not controversy. She did agree with Selden, however, in his assertion that some missionaries were "hopeless and helpless among the educated Buddhists." It was true, she admitted, that some new missionaries came from so-called fundamentalist schools, but they had not brought "bitterness and bigotry" with them as Selden asserted.[3] Like Paul Eakin and Carl Elder, Kilpatrick believed traditional Christian beliefs needed to be modernized in order to reach the educated classes, a task for which Kilpatrick thought her fundamentalist-leaning fellow missionaries were unsuited. How Christian beliefs should be modernized, she did not specify.

Ray Bachtell, husband of Charlotte Bachtell who was mentioned earlier, wrote to Brown in a similar vein. A graduate of San Francisco Theological Seminary and a dedicated evangelist, Bachtell had worked in Thailand since 1911 as a teacher at the Boys School in the northern province of Chiang Rai.[4] On furlough when the article was published, he felt Selden's statement was unfair because it represented "only a very small minority of the young people who have come to the mission within the last ten years." Among the new missionaries in Thailand, Bachtell could only think of two who had shown any of the "bitterness and bigotry" Selden complained of, though he did not name them. Bachtell acknowledged the value of criticism from outsiders but was convinced that Selden's conclusion was based on insufficient knowledge of "the

---

3. Kilpatrick to Brown, June 22, 1927, PHS; Eakin, "Biographical Notes on Jennie Faye Kilpatrick Yoder," PUA.

4. The year after Bachtell graduated from San Francisco Theological Seminary, the school controversially removed one of its instructors, Thomas Day, due to modernist views on higher criticism. This may have had an impact on the formation of Bachtell's perspective on theological controversy. Anderson, "Modernization and Theological Conservatism," 76–91; Eakin, "Biographical Notes on Rev. and Mrs. Bachtell," 1949, PUA.

actual spirit that governs the conduct and work of the great majority of the missionaries in Siam."⁵

Selden's criticism concerned Arthur Brown sufficiently for him to address the matter in one of his regular letters to the Thailand mission. In his letter, Brown assumed that the APM Thailand missionaries were mostly already aware of Selden's article which was then being prepared for publication as part of a book titled, *Are Missions a Failure?: A Correspondent's Survey of Foreign Missions*.⁶ Brown had pre-publication proofs of the book and both he and the editor at the Fleming Revell Company tried to convince Selden to omit or modify the objectionable paragraph, but to no avail. In general agreement with both Kilpatrick and Bachtell, Brown was convinced if there was any ground for Selden's criticism, it was only a few individuals, and not representative of the whole. However, he continued, someone in Thailand must have given Selden the impression that the fundamentalist-modernist controversy had come to Siamese shores and it was unfortunate that it was published in a magazine with a circulation of two million and would now be perpetuated in a book. If a missionary has anything to criticize in a fellow missionary, warned Brown, he should talk to him personally or even bring it to the Board, but certainly not criticize their fellows in the presence of outsiders. In this case, the outsider had used this for the injury of the missionary cause as a whole. Brown's concern was not whether there were differing theologies among the missionaries in Thailand or if some missionaries were fundamentalists. The question, he said, was one of "disposition, not doctrine."⁷ As with Evander McGilvary, mission unity and the forward progress of the work was more important than theological conformity on all issues. Also, in the 1920s it was becoming increasingly dangerous to try to ferret out unorthodox doctrine in the American Presbyterian Church as happened in the inquiry of Henry Sloane Coffin to the Board in the wake of William Perkins' resignation in 1924, an event discussed in the previous chapter.

---

5. Bachtell to Brown, June 23, 1927, PHS.

6. The phrase "bitterness and bigotry" and a reference to William Jennings Bryan do not appear in the article version of Selden's report but are included in the book version which Arthur Brown may have shared with Kilpatrick and other missionaries on furlough.

7. Brown to Siam Mission, "Board Letter #293," July 6, 1927, PHS.

Sources of Selden's Impressions

Two months after Brown's letter to the whole Mission, APM Thailand executive secretary Paul A. Eakin became concerned that some fellow missionaries may have wrongly concluded he was the source of Selden's misperceptions. Eakin, who was identified by name in the article, wrote to Arthur Brown to explain his role in the affair.[8] After chatting with Selden at his hotel on a Saturday night, Eakin invited him to attend an English worship service on Sunday afternoon after his interview with Prince Damrong Rajanubhab in the morning. Though Eakin does not say so, it is likely that Prince Damrong was a primary source of Selden's impression that Thai Buddhists were modernizing and abandoning supernatural elements of traditional Buddhism. In his article, Selden apparently generalized about Thai Buddhism as a whole based on what he heard, but he may not have realized that Damrong's views were not representative of the common Thai Buddhist who did not share Damrong's status, education, or English fluency. At the English worship service that Selden attended with Eakin, it was regular practice for a different missionary to preach each week and Eakin did not know that this Sunday it was Paul Fuller's turn. Fuller, who attended both the Bible Institute of Los Angeles (currently Biola University) and Princeton Theological Seminary, came to Thailand as a new missionary in 1923 and was doing evangelistic work and part-time teaching at Bangkok Christian College, a mission secondary school for boys.[9] On the day of Selden's visit, Fuller preached on "the Verbal Inspiration of the Bible," which Eakin thought "a rather belligerent topic." In Eakin's view, Fuller preached "very passionately" and "some of his statements were strong" but the sermon wasn't bad and Fuller didn't do anything wrong. However, Eakin judged it unfortunate that Selden was there to hear it. The following day, as Eakin was taking Selden down river to visit Esther Pradipasena, the first Thai female convert, Eakin recalled

> Mr. Selden suddenly turned and said:—"Is that young man's preaching the type that represents the majority of this Mission? To be more clear, does the majority of this mission belong to the American Fundamentalist group?" I said, "Mr. Selden, I should say that almost all of our Mission, both old and young, are conservative in their Theology, and liberal in their spirit." He

---

8. Eakin to Brown, September 6, 1927, PHS.
9. Eakin, "Biographical Notes on Rev. & Mrs. Paul Fuller, PUA.

then said, "Well, it is too bad that the fight in America has to be brought in here." That was absolutely all that passed between us on that subject.

Paul Eakin claimed the interchange above "was absolutely all that passed between us on that subject," namely the fundamentalist-modernist controversy. However, if this was true, one must wonder where Selden got his other information about fundamentalists in Thailand, namely his claim that newly arrived missionaries from fundamentalist schools were "hopeless and helpless" when doing evangelism among educated Buddhists. Though some of his fellow missionaries suspected Selden got his information on fundamentalist-modernist controversy in Thailand from Fuller, the young preacher had no recollection of seeing Selden at the worship service and claimed that he never met him.[10]

---

10. Fuller to Brown, July 16, 1928, PHS.

Outsider Interactions with Modernism and Fundamentalism 153

Rev. Paul Fuller, 1923
(Courtesy of the Presbyterian Historical Society, Philadelphia).

Despite Eakin's mild defense of Fuller in his explanation to Brown, evidence presented in chapter 6 demonstrated that Eakin had a low view of missionaries like Fuller who had fundamentalist tendencies. As such, it is highly likely that Selden formed his conclusions not only from Fuller's sermon but also from opinions shared with him by Paul Eakin. It is probable that Eakin was the source for Selden's statement that fundamentalists were useless for evangelizing the educated because that is what Eakin believed, and sharing that view with Selden was in the best interest of promoting Eakin's vision of evangelism. As discussed previously, Eakin's theological convictions were strongly modernist, and he wanted to limit the influence of fundamentalist-leaning missionaries in Thailand for the sake of reaching the educated classes. This included not only limiting their evangelistic activities but also discouraging public criticism of both modernism and fellow missionaries with modernist views. Both Eakin and the Board of Foreign Missions wanted peace within the mission and did not appreciate those who would stir up trouble by objecting to the theology of their fellow missionaries. A certain amount of modernist theology could be tolerated on the mission field, but the agitations of fundamentalists could bring unwanted attention to the theological diversity that existed and cause a loss of support for mission work if American supporters lost confidence in their missionaries. The real danger of Selden's criticism was not that he believed it, but that he published it in a popular American magazine that supporters were likely to read. In order to give a good impression to American Presbyterian rank-and-file, Eakin's response to Selden's question was guarded and ambiguous in order to fend off potential criticism from both conservatives and liberals on the American homeside. The affirmation that the American Presbyterian mission in Thailand was "conservative in theology" was surely intended to quell suspicions that the missionaries were modernists, yet the follow-up affirmation that they were "liberal in spirit" was likely intended to reassure liberal Presbyterians who would have wondered if the Thailand mission was safe for those with modernist views. Eakin diplomatically sought to portray a moderate stance that was sufficiently conservative but also sufficiently tolerant to those with modernist views. Though Selden was a Unitarian and would have been sympathetic to modernism, Eakin did not want to reveal too much to this outsider, especially since he was in a position to misrepresent the Thailand mission to the American public, a fear that was unfortunately realized. When talking to Selden, Eakin tried to avoid a definitive theological label for either himself or the APM Thailand mission as a whole. When accused of being a modernist in the late 1940s, Eakin rebuffed the modernist label, preferring to be called a "liberal in spirit," a phrase he also used with Selden, and stated that his theology had not changed in 30 years.[11] In Eakin's

---

11. Eakin, "Executive Committee Letter of Sept., 17, 1949," PUA.

mind, mission success depended on publicly maintaining a conservative yet tolerant image that would not attract unwanted inquiries or attention in an increasingly divided American Presbyterian church.

Quenching Fires Before They Start: Board Responses to Outspoken Missionaries

While Eakin sought to uphold a neutral, yet positive public image for the Thailand mission, Carl Elder privately vented his frustrations to Board secretary Arthur J. Brown. In response to Brown's letter to the Thailand mission addressing Selden's article and book, Elder told Brown that Selden had "not over-stated the case" and he should not be surprised at Selden's report of controversy in the Thailand mission.[12] Elder asserted that a person with "any powers of observation could not long associate with our missionaries without feeling himself in the midst of a battle." Before coming to Thailand in 1926, he knew there would be differences of opinion among missionaries, but he was not "prepared to find the same controversy which has torn the Church at home already begun here." In an allusion to the fundamentalist schools mentioned in Selden's article, Elder specifically cited "Los Angles [sic] Bible Institute, Moody Institute and the present Princeton" whose "temper and teaching" are "known to the church," implying that these schools tended to produce fundamentalist-minded graduates who were "trained to be controversialists." Elder did not leave Brown to guess whom he meant and specifically named fellow missionaries Paul Fuller and Kenneth Landon. All the same, Elder claimed that it was the attitude of these men more than their beliefs which he found objectionable and he did not "mean to cast reflection on the men" to whom he referred. However, Elder's irritation with such men was palpable and Brown urged Elder to stay calm and not let fellow missionaries in another part of the country perturb him.[13] Elder, who lived in the city of Pitsanuloke more than 250 miles (400 km) north of Bangkok, previously wrote to Brown that he and his wife were happy in their work and had good relationships with their missionary colleagues in Pitsanuloke.[14] If that is the case, wondered Brown, then "why not continue the happy work to which you have consecrated yourself and in which you have so free a field?" If he was content in his

---

12. Elder to Brown, September 12, 1927, PHS.
13. Brown to Elder, March 23, 1928, PHS.
14. Elder to Brown, January 27, 1928, PHS.

local circumstances, Brown reasoned, then he should not let himself become embittered by news that the same differences dividing the church at home also existed in Thailand. Although Brown assured Elder that he was not unsympathetic to problems in Thailand and was planning to have a "frank conference" with Fuller when he came on furlough, he nonetheless thought that Elder should just focus on the work at hand and not worry about what other people were doing.[15]

It is curious that Elder was the sole voice among the missionaries affirming Selden's claim that modernist-fundamentalist conflict had come to Thailand. However, it may be that those with modernist-leanings, such as Elder and Selden, were more sensitive to expressions of what seemed to them like anti-modernism. Perhaps they saw conflict because they were more attuned to it, given their theologies and personalities. Conversely, perhaps Eakin and other Thailand missionaries disavowed the presence of theological conflict among them because they did not want it to be true. Theologically conservative missionaries would likely have been less alarmed by fundamentalist saber-rattling because they shared the same theological commitments. Eakin is an interesting case, however, because his personal convictions were strongly modernist yet he did not affirm the presence of modernist-fundamentalist controversy as Elder did. Eakin's response likely had its root in his personal disposition towards diplomacy and the suppression of conflict. The Thai cultural value for maintaining relational harmony and avoiding public confrontation may have also influenced Eakin's personal values given his long experience in Thailand, having been born and raised there. As the head of the Thailand mission, Eakin also had a greater responsibility to keep the mission united and moving forward, a position much different from that of Elder who was a new missionary at the time and had more leeway to rock the boat.

After Arthur Brown sought to quench the agitations of Elder against his fellow missionaries, he also endeavored to impress upon Fuller the importance of having the right attitude. When Fuller went on furlough in June 1928, Brown asked him if he was still able to work harmoniously with his fellow missionaries, and whether the question of his return to Bangkok was decided. Fuller was greatly unsettled by Brown's doubts about him and sought to reassure Brown that the Thailand mission's Executive Committee settled the question of his return before his departure from Bangkok. Despite rumors to the contrary, he had no issues

---

15. Brown to Elder, March 23, 1928, PHS.

in cooperating with colleagues in the right spirit. Brown was satisfied with this response and told Fuller to proceed with his furlough plans, including studies at San Francisco Theological Seminary, and to assume he would return to Thailand. However, Brown wanted Fuller to be aware that some of his fellow missionaries had suspicions about him and there could be problems in the future if he was not careful.[16]

An examination of the responses to Selden's article provides a helpful window into emerging tensions over modernism and fundamentalism among APM Thailand missionaries in the late 1920s and the ways in which they were navigating those tensions. Whereas thirty years previous, the modernist views of Evander McGilvary were a primary factor in his decision to resign, missionaries with modernist theological leanings such as Carl Elder, Paul Eakin, and Faye Kilpatrick apparently felt no such pressure in 1927. On the contrary, it was those who too boldly asserted traditional conservative positions whose suitability for ministry was called into question, albeit the question was raised in response to the criticism of an outsider to the mission. Brown's responses to the article and to the missionary reactions to the article, however, show an historical continuity in the Board's response to theological unorthodoxy. Brown was not concerned to investigate or assess the theological views of any of the Thailand missionaries. In correspondence with Fuller, Eakin, and Elder, Brown assumed whatever their views, they all fell within the accepted range of evangelical belief of the Presbyterian Church. Rather, he was primarily concerned with preserving the internal harmony of the mission and the external image of the American Presbyterian mission in the public eye, a concern paralleled in the responses of Eakin, Kilpatrick, and Bachtell. In order for the work of the mission to progress, unity among missionaries was necessary and it was a shared attitude of mutual forbearance, not homogenous theological views, that mattered most in securing that unity. Tensions did exist, however, and they would not be able to be suppressed indefinitely.

DONALD GREY BARNHOUSE'S THAILAND TOUR, 1935

While Charles Selden evaluated mission work in Thailand as one with modernist sympathies, the APM Thailand mission received a very

---

16. Fuller to Brown, June 19, 1928; Brown to Fuller, June 27, 1928; Fuller to Brown, July 6, 1928; Fuller to Brown, July 16, 1928; Brown to Fuller, July 25, 1928, PHS.

different kind of visitor in 1935, Donald Grey Barnhouse.[17] Barnhouse, an American Presbyterian minister, author, and radio host with strongly fundamentalist sympathies, had been urged by church members and radio listeners to make a tour of Presbyterian foreign missions to discover whether modernism existed on the mission field, as had been rumored.[18] Were Presbyterian missionaries loyal to Presbyterian doctrine and the great truths of the Christian faith or had they diverged? In the wake of controversy surrounding the Laymen's Report and the recent formation of the Independent Board for Presbyterian Foreign Missions, in 1934 Barnhouse commenced a tour of mission stations in Asia, a trip that took him over a year to complete. During that time, he visited a substantial majority of the Presbyterian mission stations and missionaries in Japan, Korea, China, the Philippines, Thailand, India, Mesopotamia, and Persia.[19]

Overview of Barnhouse's Visit: Expectations and Reality

Arriving in Bangkok on January 2, 1935, Barnhouse spent ten days in Thailand, visiting Presbyterian missionaries and mission stations, Presbyterian mission institutions (schools and hospitals), and Thai and Chinese churches. He began in Bangkok (January 2–6), then proceeded to visit Chiang Mai (January 7–8), Chiang Rai (January 9), and Lampang (January 10–11), before returning to Bangkok (January 12) for an onward train journey to Malaysia. During his visit to Thailand, as well as to other countries, Barnhouse kept copious notes of where he went, how he traveled, what he saw, whom he met, significant conversations, and occasional commentary and evaluation of the above as he saw fit.[20] The missionaries in each location welcomed him and assisted him by providing accommodation, tours of mission works, and ample opportunities for discussion of mission matters. To judge by Barnhouse's personal notes, he enjoyed generally good interactions with the missionaries, although there were times of awkwardness and uncertainty in response to some of his questions, which will be discussed below. In his notes,

17. For more on Barnhouse's life and ministry, see Margaret Barnhouse, *That Man Barnhouse*, Russell, "Donald Grey Barnhouse," 33–57.

18. Eakin, "Meeting of Missionaries with Dr. Barnhouse in Bangkok, Jan. 3, 1935," PUA.

19. Barnhouse, "Report of Dr. Barnhouse Concerning His Visit to Presbyterian Foreign Mission Stations in Asia," 1, 5–10.

20. Barnhouse, "Travel Notes," January 2–12, 1935, PHS.

Barnhouse recorded several indications of the presence of modernism in the Thailand mission, and an accompanying lack of priority on evangelism. However, the overall tenor of his notes was matter-of-the-fact reporting rather than critical analysis. This stands in contrast to the observations of Paul Eakin, APM Thailand executive secretary, who found Barnhouse to be too critical. Ironically, Eakin himself was very critical of Barnhouse in a letter to Board secretary Cleland McAfee. Eakin reported that Barnhouse's preaching was "fundamental" and "black and white," not giving regard to the reaction to his listeners. Eakin was also disappointed that Barnhouse did not suggest any helpful methods for mission work in Thailand. In his meeting with the missionaries of the Bangkok station, Eakin reported that Barnhouse made them feel tense and defensive. This feeling may have been the result of their own expectations that Barnhouse was on a modernist witch hunt more than it was due to anything that Barnhouse himself did or said. However, Eakin said that this feeling was somewhat reduced when Barnhouse stated that he opposed the formation of Machen's Independent Board and spoke approvingly of Cleland McAfee's fairness when the two men discussed Barnhouse's plan to visit Thailand. Nonetheless, Eakin's overall impression of Barnhouse was negative. "We are really sick over his visit," Eakin told McAfee, "and although we have done all we could to take him in with open arms and be fair to him, we see now he is plainly on a mission with his mind already made up."[21] Eakin was afraid of what Barnhouse would report about Thailand on his return to the United States and that he would "become a real menace to the cause of Christ." As such, he felt compelled to write to McAfee to tell his side of the story. It would be a "calamity," wrote Eakin, if men like Barnhouse became members of the Board. Eakin knew that there were missionaries with modernist views in Thailand and a heresy hunter like Barnhouse could bring unwanted scrutiny to the APM Thailand mission and hamper their work.

Eakin's fears, however, did not materialize. Barnhouse's subsequent published report of his tour was largely positive towards the work of the American Presbyterian mission. Summarizing his tour of mission stations in multiple countries, Barnhouse reported, "I found the theological situation on the field better than I had expected and the spiritual situation about what I had expected." He judged the claim of the Laymen's Report that many missionaries are of "low calibre" to be "entirely erroneous"

21. Eakin to McAfee, January 8, 1935, PUA.

and was pleased to discover that the vast majority of missionaries were theologically sound, personally devoted to Christ, and held to the historic truths of Christian faith. There were, however, an "unfaithful minority" of missionaries who were doctrinally adrift. He thought that the Board should address these individual cases as well as systemic issues within the Board's administration that allowed such people to go to, or remain on, the mission field. Nevertheless, despite the need for reformation of the Board, for which he gave specific, practical recommendations in his published report in *The Presbyterian*, Barnhouse concluded from his tour that the vast majority of missionaries were faithful and deserved the support of the American Presbyterian Church.[22] Despite his criticisms, the Board was overall pleased with Barnhouse's affirmation of the Board's missionaries and used this in their defense during the trials of ministers who supported the Independent Board. The Independent Board was understandably unhappy with some of Barnhouse's report, the conclusion of which called into question the *raison d'être* of the new Board.[23]

When considering Barnhouse's notes on the Thailand mission, a few things should be kept in mind. Barnhouse had a reputation for being a fundamentalist and it is likely that this reputation influenced the impressions and answers of Paul Eakin and other missionaries. Barnhouse himself, later in life, regretted his judgmental and condemnatory attitudes of his younger years, so it is possible that Barnhouse did exude a critical spirit during his Asian tour, as noted by Eakin, but at the time did not have the self-awareness to realize this. However, despite his penchant for criticism and his ostensible goal of exposing modernism on the mission field, his concluding report, as noted above, gave a largely charitable assessment of what he observed. The character of his report aligns well with the liberally-oriented *Christian Century*'s posthumous praise of Barnhouse as a journalist who was "responsible and honest [in] handling the truth."[24] As such, Barnhouse's notes on the Thailand mission should be regarded as largely accurate insofar as the information reported to him by his missionary interlocutors was accurate.

As Barnhouse visited the stations of the Thailand mission, his conversations and experiences varied but he asked similar questions

---

22. Barnhouse, "Report of Dr. Barnhouse Concerning His Visit to Presbyterian Foreign Mission Stations in Asia," 1, 5–10.

23. Bennet to Barnhouse, July 8, 1935; Editorial on Full Board Response to Executive Council Response to Barnhouse Report (unpublished draft), November 1935, PHS.

24. *The Christian Century* 77 (December 7, 1960), 1428 in Russell, "Barnhouse," 33.

in different locations, receiving a similar range of responses. He asked open-ended questions of the missionaries, wanting them to tell him their general impressions of mission work in Thailand, how churches were organized on this field, how leaders were trained, and what were the future prospects for mission work in the country. He also asked pointed questions about whether the investment of home churches in Thailand was justified, which methods produced the best results, and whether there was spiritual and theological unity among the missionaries. Unlike fundamentalist-leaning John Sung who would visit four years later, Barnhouse came primarily to learn the state of mission work in Thailand, not to directly influence what was actually happening on the ground. In terms of seeing action taken on curbing modernism on the mission field, Barnhouse's strategy was to find out if there was modernism and to make a report to the Board so that they could handle it. He shared the same concerns as people like J. Gresham Machen, but he believed in using established Presbyterian denominational channels to push for change rather than going outside those channels when changes were not happening fast enough.

In examining the information Barnhouse collected, his findings are most insightful in three areas vis-à-vis assessing modernism among APM missionaries in Thailand, namely 1) the question of theological and spiritual unity, 2) the question of the best methods, and 3) the question of the future of the Thailand mission.

Spiritual and Theological Unity

Firstly, Barnhouse asked the gathered missionaries in the Bangkok Station and the Chiang Mai Station at separate meetings in their respective cities whether there was theological and spiritual unity in the Thailand mission.[25] In both locations, the missionaries generally affirmed that there was spiritual unity within the mission although the Chiang Mai missionaries were more explicit in affirming theological unity.[26] William

---

25. Barnhouse and Eakin both made notes on Barnhouse's meeting with the Bangkok missionaries. The significant overlap between them provides confirmation of the discussion from men with divergent convictions. Barnhouse "Travel Notes," January 2–6, 1935, PHS; Eakin, "Meeting of Missionaries with Dr. Barnhouse in Bangkok, Jan. 3, 1935," PUA.

26. In neither Barnhouse nor Eakin's notes is there an attempt to define the difference between theological and spiritual unity, though discussion participants apparently thought the two were not synonymous.

Harris, director of Prince Royal's College, the Thailand mission's flagship school for boys in Chiang Mai, admitted that with any group the size of the Chiang Mai station there was some diversity of opinion. However, Harris affirmed, all members of the Chiang Mai Station "believed absolutely in the necessity of the death of Christ as atonement for sin." In the ensuing discussion, Chiang Mai station members agreed that there was unity on "the great essentials." As compared to the Chiang Mai station meeting, the missionaries at the Bangkok Station meeting showed little interest in theological unity, though they did affirm spiritual unity within the mission. Faye Kilpatrick, director of Wattana Wittaya Academy, the Thailand mission's flagship school for girls in Bangkok, thought the Thailand mission had spiritual unity, but theological unity was not necessary. On the latter, she was dismissive, claiming, "I care so little about it I haven't tried to figure it out." Marion Palmer, director of Bangkok Christian College, the Thailand's mission's flagship school for boys in Bangkok, thought "[t]he spirit is more important than theology." Paul Eakin tacitly admitted there was some theological diversity among the missionaries but not enough to affect the overall unity of the mission, telling Barnhouse that he did not think there was "tremendous cleavage even in theological lines." However, Eakin was likely playing down the existence of differences for the sake of Barnhouse. Only a few years earlier, Eakin wrote to Carl Elder that he feared there would be an explosion in the mission along theological lines that would lead to personal conflicts.[27] This prediction was partially fulfilled in the wake of John Sung's revival meetings in Thailand which will be discussed later in this chapter. At the Bangkok station meeting, Graham Fuller, elder brother of Paul Fuller, recalled a time when one of the missionaries presented a paper on the premillennial second coming of Christ and someone asked, "What do the Posts believe?," referring to missionaries Richard and Mame Post. Fuller's point was that APM Thailand missionaries were not actively concerned about whether everyone had exactly the same theological beliefs or not. Fuller concluded, "I don't think, therefore, that the theological problem here is a divisive one." Whereas the Chiang Mai group wanted to give Barnhouse some indication that they were solidly agreed on essential theological truths of the Christian faith, the Bangkok group tried to dismiss the question, preferring to affirm spiritual unity without getting into the specifics of theological beliefs that they affirmed. At the Bangkok station meeting,

---

27. Eakin to Elder, June 16, 1932, PUA.

Albert Seigle was the sole fundamentalist-leaning missionary present, though neither Barnhouse nor Eakin's notes indicate what Seigle thought on the question of theological and spiritual unity.

While the Bangkok missionaries did not want to address theological questions per se, the Bangkok station discussion revealed that there had been a missionary who left the field due to confusion in her beliefs. Margaret Neuber, who was discussed in chapter 6, left the mission in a state of religious confusion, believing Buddhism was better suited for Thai people than was Christianity. The Bangkok missionaries likely brought the case of Margaret Neuber to the attention of Barnhouse to assure him the Thailand mission did not have missionaries with unorthodox views. Those few who did hold such views left the mission. They wanted to convey that only those with orthodox beliefs and sufficient spiritual resources to sustain biblical faith remained. The Bangkok missionaries wished to present an orthodox face and a united front to Barnhouse. Though he likely did not tell them as much, Barnhouse was not convinced.

From the answers he received from the Bangkok and Chiang Mai missionaries to his question about theological and spiritual unity, Barnhouse noted that it was "very clear" that the mission was divided in their beliefs.[28] This was confirmed by a conversation he had on the train with Robert Franklin during Barnhouse's final day in Thailand.[29] Franklin and his wife were formerly members of the Thailand mission, teaching at Bangkok Christian College from 1903–1908, and again from 1913–1919. Then, following ten years back in the United States, the Franklins returned to Thailand in 1931 under the auspices of the American Bible Society, retaining an informal relationship with members of the American Presbyterian mission.[30] As a former insider who was now officially an outsider to the Thailand mission, Franklin thought that the APM Thailand missionaries were "pretty badly mixed in their beliefs." As an example of what he meant, Franklin told Barnhouse of a particular missionary who believed that Christ was raised from the dead only in a spiritual fashion and not in a bodily manner. Although Franklin knew this man was a "keen believer in evolution," he never heard "anything off" in his preaching. His modernist understanding of the resurrection of Christ only surfaced in the context of a prayer meeting. Barnhouse wrongly supposed the missionary in question was

28. Barnhouse, "Travel Notes," January 2–6, 1935, PHS.
29. Barnhouse, "Travel Notes," January 12, 1935, PHS.
30. Eakin, "Biographical Notes on Dr. & Mrs. Robert Franklin," PUA.

Paul Eakin, most likely because Barnhouse either had evidence of Eakin's modernistic beliefs, or suspected that such was the case. The missionary to whom Franklin referred, however, was in fact Allen Bassett. Arriving in Thailand in 1917, Bassett was a school teacher in Chiang Rai, Chiang Mai, and Bangkok where he taught at Bangkok Christian College from 1931, following completion of a Masters degree in Science in the United States.[31] Franklin summarized for Barnhouse his thoughts on the characteristics of various members of the Thailand mission and concluded that the mission was not like what it was thirty years previously when the mission had "giants" like John A. Eakin, Eugene Dunlap, Frank Snyder, William McClure, Daniel McGilvary, and Jonathan Wilson. In Franklin's estimation, these men were all "mighty men of God," the likes of whom did not currently exist in the Thailand mission.

---

31. Eakin, "Biographical Notes on Rev. and Mrs. Allen Bassett," PUA.

Allen Bassett, 1915
(Courtesy of the Presbyterian Historical Society, Philadelphia).

Best Methods of Mission Work in Thailand

Aside from asking directly about theological and spiritual unity, Barnhouse also sought to sound out modernist influences in the Thailand mission by asking about the best methods of work employed by the missionaries. The value of a method in this context was gauged by whether it furthered the APM's goal of bringing people to faith in Christ and growing the indigenous church in Thailand. The answers he received to the question of methods revealed conflicting views among the missionaries. Their divergent opinions on methodology are significant because they help reveal some of the underlying theological fault lines among the missionaries.

During Barnhouse's meeting with the missionaries in Bangkok, Paul Eakin gave a nuanced answer that sought to acknowledge the value of all the methods employed by the Thailand mission.[32] However, he clearly favored the schools. In times of epidemic, Eakin claimed, the hospitals brought many into the church. The Thai, however, according to Eakin, would say that schools have been the backbone of the church. Nonetheless, it was also true that at times definite evangelistic work had brought greatest results. In the north, the majority of Christians came primarily from direct evangelistic work, and secondarily medical work. In Bangkok, however, Eakin thought the influence of the schools was greater. He claimed that the long-term contact that schools had with students resulted in long-lasting results, meaning not only church members but especially church leaders. Albert Seigle, who did evangelistic work with Chinese churches in Bangkok, disputed Eakin's estimation of the effectiveness of the schools, citing statistics from the previous year showing that only a fraction of the people joining the church came through the schools:[33]

Location	Total	From Schools
Chiang Mai	221	21
Phrae	77	2 or 5
Lampang	45	17
Bangkok	36	6

Accessions to the Church of Christ in Thailand, 1934

Seigle also took umbrage at Eakin's claim that the best church leaders came as a result of mission schools. He asserted that the church had just as many strong and valuable leaders who came through evangelistic work as came through educational work. Mary Jane McClure and Allen Bassett, both long-time teachers in mission institutions, jumped to the defense of the schools and Eakin's statements. The majority of students, claimed McClure, were very young and most would become Christians,

---

32. Barnhouse, "Travel Notes," January 2–6, 1935, PHS; Eakin, "Meeting of Missionaries with Dr. Barnhouse in Bangkok, Jan. 3, 1935," PUA.

33. Barnhouse did not record the source of Seigle's statistics.

but their parents have not given permission. However, she had faith that the seed sown would one day bear fruit. Bassett pointed out that much of the evangelistic work done in the north was done by Christian leaders associated with the schools. Though willing to concede that schools can contribute to evangelism, Seigle replied that schools and hospitals are only evangelistic if they are used evangelistically. His implication was that the educational and medical work done by the Thailand mission was not always evangelistic. The other missionaries present agreed with Seigle's statement in principle, but some were convinced that all of the Thailand mission's institutions were functioning evangelistically.

The accuracy of this last assertion, that all of the Thailand mission's schools and hospitals functioned evangelistically, was called into question by information from Loren Hanna, Robert Franklin, and Lucy Starling. In Lampang, Loren Hanna told Barnhouse that his fellow missionaries were "fine personalities" but few had a real grasp of the great gospel message and there was little evangelism in the schools, even in chapel. Hanna believed that the schools were not very open to evangelism and some missionaries had no interest in evangelism. As an example, Hanna said that neither Marion Palmer, director of Bangkok Christian College, nor William Harris, director of Prince Royal's College in Chiang Mai, would allow gospel teams from Burma to evangelize in the schools, believing they would drive away non-Christians because their evangelism was on too low of a level.[34] This account is consistent with Robert Franklin's claim that evangelism did not have an important place in the schools. Franklin, who was principal of Bangkok Christian College (BCC) before returning to the U.S. for an extended period in 1919, told Barnhouse that Marion Palmer, then-current principal of BCC, was a good educationalist but he put his educational standards above the evangelization of the students. Franklin thought that an important factor in the deprecation of evangelism in mission schools was the desire for government recognition. In order to be a government-approved school, "no actual Bible teaching under that name could be included in the curriculum. It must be introduced as ethics."[35] Presbyterian mission schools on some other fields, including China and Iran, also saw Bible teaching squeezed out of the curriculum as a result of increasing government regulation.[36]

34. Barnhouse, "Travel Notes," January 10–11, 1935, PHS.
35. Barnhouse, "Travel Notes," January 12, 1935, PHS.
36. Bays, *New History*, 111; Rostam-Kolayi, "From Evangelizing to Modernizing Iranians," 213–39.

Rev. Loren Hanna, 1917
(Courtesy of the Presbyterian Historical Society, Philadelphia).

Information provided by Loren Hanna and Lucy Starling about Dr. William Beach also cast doubt whether Overbrook Hospital, a mission institution in Chiang Rai, was functioning evangelistically.[37] Dr. William Beach, the sole doctor at the hospital and member of the APM Thailand mission, reportedly said he was not a missionary, but rather a doctor. Overbrook Presbyterian Church in Philadelphia, which Hanna classified as "liberal," provided funding to Beach which was earmarked for the

---

37. Barnhouse, "Travel Notes," January 10–11, 1935, PHS; Brown, "Board Joint Mission Letter No. 229," December 19, 1923, PUA.

hospital alone, not to be used for other mission work. During the Great Depression, Dr. Beach and fellow Chiang Rai missionary Ray Bachtell clashed because Beach thought that the money Bachtell was spending on evangelism could be better spent on the hospital. From Beach's perspective, the money Bachtell spent on evangelism was wasted. Though neither Hanna nor Starling said anything to Barnhouse about Beach's theology per se, Hanna reported that the minutes of the Chiang Rai station included a "definite statement they don't want a fundamentalist missionary assigned to their station at any time." This was done, according to Hanna, in spite of the fact that Bachtell was conservative.[38] Though the evidence is not conclusive, it is possible that Dr. Beach embraced a modernist emphasis on mission as societal improvement through medicine and had deprecated the importance of evangelism as an essential goal of missionary work. If this was the case, the Overbook Hospital in Chiang Rai may not have been functioning evangelistically.

From the information he was able to gather, it was evident to Barnhouse that the Thailand mission was divided on both method and belief. As regards the mission schools in Thailand, Barnhouse concluded there was "a group of educationalists here who have no real knowledge of evangelism though they think they are doing a wonderful piece of work in carrying on their schools."[39]

The Future of Mission Work in Thailand

Though some missionaries in the Thailand mission thought that educational and medical work should be emphasized over direct evangelistic work, other missionaries believed that due to increasing government pressure, the days of educational and medical missions were numbered. As previously mentioned, government recognition was forcing a deprecation of Bible teaching in mission schools, rendering more difficult the case that the schools had an evangelistic purpose. Rising standards for school teachers were also making it more difficult for foreigners to teach in mission schools. Cornelia Harris, for example, was a daughter of Daniel McGilvary who spoke the Lao (Northern Thai) dialect since her youth but was denied a teaching license because she could not pass a government examination in Central (Bangkok) Thai, the national language of the increasingly integrated nation.

38. Barnhouse, "Travel Notes," January 10–11, 1935, PHS.
39. Barnhouse, "Travel Notes," January 2–6, 1935, PHS.

Schools were not the only mission institutions being pressed by the government. McCormick Hospital, the Thailand mission's hospital in Chiang Mai, was under threat of being either co-opted or made redundant by the government. Ray Bachtell told Barnhouse that the government had been giving 10,000 baht per year to McCormick Hospital on the condition that its free clinic work was extended. Along with this funding came continual pressure to do more and more free work. To do so, however, would necessarily curtail direct missionary activity to some extent. The latest development, however, was a proposal for the government to take over the mission hospital with missionary doctor Edwin Cort in charge in order to make McCormick into a second medical training school for class B doctors.[40] If the Mission refused, Bachtell thought it probable that the government would open up a rival hospital nearby and subsidize it so heavily that no one would come to the mission hospital anymore. This exodus of patients would occur, in part, because local people in Chiang Mai were already anxious about coming to the foreigners' hospital, and would prefer a Thai hospital.[41]

Though neither Ray Bachtell nor Robert Franklin opposed mission schools and hospitals, they both hoped that the tightening grip of inevitable government restrictions would have the unintended consequence of forcing the Thailand mission to return to an emphasis on direct evangelistic work. If the government made it impossible for the mission to continue their educational and medical work, the mission would be forced to redeploy more of their personnel in direct evangelism.[42] Both men thought a re-emphasis on evangelism to the exclusion of other lines of work would be most welcome, though Franklin thought that even evangelism might be difficult in the future given the government's efforts to emphasize the importance of Buddhism in Thai society.[43] As to when these changes would happen, Bachtell predicted that within ten years, the Thailand mission's medical and educational work would come to an end. "We can hope that this will be so," said Bachtell,

---

40. Thai medical law recognized first- and second-class doctors. First class doctors could practice every phase of medicine and surgery. Second-class (or class B) doctors could only perform minor surgery, sell accredited medicines, and give muscular injections. Landon, *Thailand in Transition*, 151–52.

41. Barnhouse, "Travel Notes," January 10, 1935, PHS.

42. In 1939, only 18.1 percent of Thai Christians hired by the Thailand mission were engaged in evangelistic work, while 61.5 percent did educational work and 19.5 percent did medical work. Son, "Christian Revival," 70.

43. Barnhouse, "Travel Notes," January 10–12, 1935, PHS.

"as it will turn missionary work back into the channel God meant it to be in, but once more that statement must be guarded by pointing out that it is all a question of personnel." As events turned out, all mission work in Thailand ended six years later when Japanese forces began their wartime occupation of the country in December 1941. The American Presbyterian missionaries did return after the war and continued with evangelistic, educational, and medical work, albeit in ways that Franklin and Bachtell could not have anticipated in 1935. These later developments, however, lie beyond the scope of this book.[44]

Summary of Barnhouse's Findings

Taken as a whole, the information gathered by Donald Barnhouse during his visit to Thailand is illuminating for taking the theological pulse of the Thailand mission. On the one hand, Barnhouse had very positive impressions of some of the work being done by Presbyterian missionaries. He greatly enjoyed, for example, visiting a village prayer meeting with Ray Bachtell and several rural stations with Howard Campbell.[45] Dedicated evangelists and Bible teachers like Ray Bachtell, Loren Hanna, and Albert Seigle were the kind of missionaries whom Barnhouse valued. He was impressed with Dr. Crooks's development of indigenous leadership at Lampang hospital. Many of the missionaries, such as those at the Chiang Mai station meeting, affirmed theological truths that he regarded as essential. However, Barnhouse also found several indicators of the influence of theological modernism. Margaret Neuber held a relativistic view of Buddhism and Christianity, though she had already left. Carl Elder was liberal, though reportedly less so than when he first arrived. Both Loren Hanna and Robert Franklin lamented the lack of evangelistic emphasis in the schools, and Hanna claimed that many of his missionary colleagues knew little of the gospel. Barnhouse noted that William Harris owned a "rankly modernistic book," *The Meaning of the Cross* by liberal Presbyterian minister Henry Sloane Coffin. Yet book ownership does not prove the theology of the possessor. APM Thailand missionary Harry Knox, however, wished that there were more ministers in Thailand like Coffin.[46] William Beach opposed the evangelism of Ray Bachtell and did

44. For post-war developments in the APM Thailand Mission, see Wells, *History*, 142–62; Kim, *Unfinished Mission*, 65–182; McLean, "Thai Protestant Christianity," 87–112; Dahlfred, "Bumpy Road," 42–45.

45. Barnhouse, "Travel Notes," January 8–9, 1935, PHS.

46. Barnhouse, "Travel Notes," January 7, 1935, PHS.

not even see himself as a missionary. None of the missionaries except former Thailand mission member Robert Franklin, admitted there were any significant theological problems within the mission. While it is possible that the missionaries did see theological diversity among them as problematic but did not want to admit as such to an outsider like Barnhouse, it is likely that only a minority of the missionaries cared to think about theological matters or the doctrinal positions of their fellow missionaries. This latter train of thought is succinctly epitomized by comments from Faye Kilpatrick and Lucy Starling. Kilpatrick said she cared so little about theological unity in the Thailand mission that she hadn't tried to figure it out, and Starling thought that "modernist" and "fundamentalist" were nothing more than Presbyterian swear words.[47]

Barnhouse's Thailand travel notes and Eakin's account of his visit reveal that theological differences did exist within the Thailand mission. But aside from privately shared comments on other missionaries, the mission as a whole was not interested in bringing such differences to light or discussing them. To judge by Barnhouse and Eakin's records of the visit, the missionaries attempted to keep a united front as a mission, perhaps especially when meeting with outsider inquirers. The missionaries themselves had limited personal and anecdotal knowledge of what their fellow Thailand-based missionaries were doing and what they believed, leading to favorable or unfavorable impressions of their colleagues.

Unlike fundamentalist-modernist controversies in the Presbyterian Church in the USA, theological differences among the missionaries in Thailand did not lead to protracted controversy over explicitly theological matters, though they did have consequences. Modernist and fundamentalist leanings influenced intra-mission debate over the role of educational and medical ministries vis-à-vis the mission's evangelistic purpose, as well as changing approaches to evangelism and Buddhism, which will be discussed in chapters 8 and 9. Underlying theological differences also found expression in the divisions among missionaries and Thai that resulted from the revival meetings of John Sung in the late 1930s.

---

47. Barnhouse, "Travel Notes," January 11, 1935, PHS; Eakin, "Meeting of Missionaries with Dr. Barnhouse in Bangkok, Jan. 3, 1935," PUA.

JOHN SUNG'S FUNDAMENTALISM CATALYZES CONFLICT IN THAILAND, 1938–1939

Both Charles Selden and Donald Barnhouse came to Thailand primarily as observers and chroniclers of mission work but Chinese evangelist John Sung came as a full participant in ministry with the aim of making converts, reviving nominal Christians, and establishing evangelistic bands. Sung's ministry in Thailand had an enduring and profound impact on the Thai church and a catalyzing effect upon existing theological and personal tensions among missionaries and Thai Christians. To appreciate how and why this occurred, it is necessary to understand Sung's background, especially the formation of his conversion narrative and his association with fundamentalism. Both of these influenced the ways in which he interpreted what he found in Thailand and interacted with missionaries and Thai Christians.

Sung's History with Modernism and Fundamentalism

According to Sung's own testimony as popularized in both his spiritual autobiography and Leslie Lyall's 1954 biography, Sung attended Union Theological Seminary in New York City following completion of a PhD in chemistry and experienced an intense conversion experience which was misinterpreted by the modernists at Union Seminary as insanity. Union committed Sung to an insane asylum where he read the Bible many times over and had visions which would form the foundation of his calling to itinerant revival ministry in China and Southeast Asia. When he was finally released from the asylum with the help of some friends, he returned to China to preach the gospel.[48] In this narrative, modernists such as those found at Union Theological Seminary were the opponents of the gospel and Sung was an earnest seeker after God who fell victim to their machinations. However, despite this opposition, God rescued him and gave him new life. This popular version of Sung's conversion, however, has been called into question by Daryl Ireland whose research has shown the timeline and circumstances of Sung's conversion were more ambiguous and his testimony only started to take its popular form through the collaboration of Sung with a fundamentalist-leaning Methodist missionary after his return to China.[49] In the midst of rising fundamentalist-modernist tensions among missionaries in China, Sung

---

48. Song, *Wode Jianzheng (My Testimony)*; Lyall, *John Sung*.
49. Ireland, *John Song*, 11–55.

found it useful to throw his lot in with the fundamentalists. In order to shake off the stigma of mental illness, Sung molded his testimony to depict his time at Union as the mighty work of God rescuing him and calling him to ministry in the face of opposition from godless liberals. In Sung's testimony, fundamentalists found an example of modernist opposition to true gospel preaching that fitted their perceptions of modernism. In fundamentalists, Sung found allies who supported and legitimized his ministry in order to further their goal of fighting modernism. Taking sides in the fundamentalist-modernist controversy helped Sung to gain a platform for speaking and the trust of listeners. The fundamentalist emphasis on the authority of the Bible alone also meshed well with Sung's own strongly Bible-centric message. Sung spoke on many themes as he taught and preached from the Bible during the course of his ministry during the 1930s and early 1940s, and he also attacked modernists who questioned the reliability and authority of the Bible, especially the books of Genesis and Revelation. For Sung, modernism was dangerous because it undermined the basis for his preaching. Sung believed that he had deep insights into the meaning and interpretation of the Bible and he confidently preached his understanding of the Bible, which was connected with his own intense spiritual experiences. In examining the impact of John Sung's ministry in Thailand, it is important to keep in mind that he wedded himself to fundamentalism in order to launch his ministry and believed that modernism, particularly modern biblical scholarship, was a threat that could undermine his revival preaching.

Sung's Revival Meetings in Thailand

John Sung visited Thailand twice, for about a month from September to October 1938 and again from May to August 1939. His first visit came through the personal invitation of Rev. Boon Mark Gittisarn, pastor of Second Church in Bangkok, after the executive committee of the CCT had voted against inviting him. Missionary Margaret McCord encouraged Boon Mark to invite Sung but several missionaries opposed inviting him because they heard Sung was divisive.[50] Because the American Presbyterian mission was nearly the sole mission and the Church of Christ was the sole Protestant denomination in Thailand, they were in a good position to keep out of the country the influences they did not want. But they were not able to control Boon Mark Gittisarn who

---

50. Son, "Christian Revival," 148; Eakin, "Mr. Hanna's Case," PUA.

invited Sung anyway. In the years to come, Boon Mark's relationship with the APM and the CCT would become increasingly polemical until he finally left the Church of Christ in Thailand, citing modernism and paternalistic mission control over Thai churches as the main reasons for his separation from them.[51]

Sung's 1938 meetings were held at Chinese churches in Bangkok, in Nakon Pathom, and in the southern province of Trang. Initially, he was not welcomed by the Church of Christ in Thailand but after many saw the positive impact of his preaching, he was formally invited by the Thai churches to return the following year. From May to August 1939, Sung preached in Chiang Mai, Lampang, Chiang Rai, Prae, Nan, Petchaburi, Nakon Sritamarat, and Trang. His preaching was eccentric and dramatic, but many were impressed by his messages and spirituality. At his meetings in Thailand, Sung stressed salvation in Jesus Christ alone, the need for repentance, the importance of evangelism, personal sanctification, and the authority of the Bible.[52] He also emphasized prayer for healing of the sick and the importance of the anointing of the Holy Spirit for ministry. Sung had a loud, direct style and was known to point a finger at his audience, walk around on the platform, and down aisles. His messages addressed traditional gospel themes of sin, repentance, redemption, and forgiveness, but did so in new and disconcerting ways. He read lists of specific sins and called people to repent, spoke against sin and hypocrisy, and spoke critically of pastors, missionaries, nominal Christians, and the seminary in Chiang Mai. According to Sung's own account and that of others, hundreds of conversions and recommitments of nominal Christians, as well as open weeping and repentance, took place as a result of Sung's meetings. Many witness bands, namely small groups for preaching and evangelism, were formed.[53]

---

51. Eakin, "Influence of Foreign Evangelists," PUA; McIntire and Gittisarn, *Modernism Takes Its Toll*.

52. Son, "Christian Revival," 158–59.

53. For a detailed account of Sung's Thailand campaigns, see Son, "Christian Revival"; Song, *Diary of John Sung*, 330–41; Gittisarn et al., "Excerpts from Letters," 114–18.

176 Conservative in Theology, Liberal in Spirit

John Sung and witness bands in Thailand, 1938
(Courtesy of the Presbyterian Historical Society, Philadelphia).

A chapel built as a result of the work of witness bands near Trang, 1940
(Courtesy of the Presbyterian Historical Society, Philadelphia).

Sung's Preaching Causes Division

Despite widespread enthusiasm for Sung, both the content and style of his preaching became the cause for divisive conflict. Pro-Sung and anti-Sung groups formed among both missionaries and Thai Christians. Those in favor of Sung loved his Bible messages and exhortations to evangelism and soul-winning. They felt Sung had brought revival and new spiritual vitality to Thailand. Even those opposed to Sung admitted that he had done much good for Thai churches and Sung's supporters had trouble understanding why anyone would criticize him. The anti-Sung group was the smaller of the two but included significant leaders from the missionary and Thai Christian community. They objected to Sung for several reasons, and existing tensions between fundamentalist-leaning and modernist-leaning missionaries came into play in the divisions between the pro-Sung and anti-Sung groups.

Dr. Edwin Cort reported that Sung's first contacts with the Thailand mission were Loren Hanna and Albert Seigle, both fundamentalist-leaning missionaries who were in theological agreement with Sung. Hanna and Seigle, who believed that seminary director Carl Elder was unorthodox and leading his students astray, likely told Sung about Elder. Cort reported that as a result, Sung viewed Elder with suspicion and even considered him a menace. Cort described Elder's personal encounter with Sung as "unfortunate" and that Sung's response to Elder was "rude and non-cooperative."[54]

The tenor of Sung's preaching was polarizing and either attracted or repelled people. As such, Sung served as a catalyst that drove a further wedge between theological opposites in the Thailand mission, such as Loren Hanna and Carl Elder. Sung's dichotomistic denunciations left little middle ground for listeners to partially agree and partially disagree with him. Sung's black-and-white, "for-me-or-against-me" attitude rubbed off on his Thai followers, as reflected in statements in a Thai-language magazine put out by the pro-Sung group in July 1939:

> The Devil uses our older Christian leaders to be his agents. Perhaps some that you admire will be against you. Beloved, they are just human beings. They are Satan's agents. Do not be fearful or doubting.
>
> Whoever speaks a word against the preaching of Dr. Sung, let us brand him as "Satan". Whoever opposes our preaching of the Gospel, he is the Devil.
>
> The missionaries have fought the coming of Dr. Sung because there is something rotten in their minds. Our churches do not

54. Cort to Hooper, Leber, and Ruland, April 19, 1940, PHS.

need these pastors because they are no use. They are learned but they use their learning at the Seminary to aid the work of Satan."[55]

Sung's divisive comments also took aim at other mission institutions besides the seminary. While visiting Pitsanuloke, Sung called non-Christians working at Christian institutions "devils" that were a "curse" to the work, to which Thai Buddhists working in the mission school and hospital took offense.[56]

In light of Sung's denunciations, it can be understood why opposition arose from some missionaries and Thai Christians, albeit only a minority. Banchop Bansiddhi and Prasert Intaphantu, teachers at the seminary in Chiang Mai, believed that some of Sung's teachings were unbiblical and his methods unethical.[57] Dr. Edwin Cort, who returned to Chiang Mai from furlough soon after Sung left, described the evangelist as a strong premillennialist, a literalist in biblical interpretation, and a militant "Fundamentalist" who "bitterly denounced Missionaries."[58] Paul Eakin objected to the emotionalism of Sung's meetings and his emphasis on "fulfillment and numerology."[59] Eakin also objected to the unloving spirit stirred up by Sung in his followers who reportedly said that anyone who didn't interpret the Bible like Sung did were heretics from the devil.[60] Carl Elder, whom Dr. Cort described as the "greatest and most aggressive opponent" of the Sung movement, claimed that he initially tried to be supportive when Sung came to Chiang Mai but it was "impossible to enter into the spirit of the meetings . . . His highly emotional methods, his self-boasting and his merciless and unfounded criticism of both national workers and missionaries, were utterly repugnant to one who was raised as a Scotch Covenanter."[61] Elder saw two major problems with Sung's teaching. Firstly, Sung conveyed the Holy Spirit by the laying on of hands and by anointing with oil. Elder reported that Sung's followers were taught that "once the Spirit had been received in

---

55. Eakin, "Influence of Foreign Evangelists," PUA.

56. Eakin, "Brief Review of Recent History of Pitsanuloke Project," February 17, 1940, PUA.

57. Bansiddhi and Intaphantu to Eakin, October 25, 1939, PUA.

58. Cort to Hooper et al., April 19, 1940, PHS.

59. Eakin to Elder, October 18, 1939; Eakin, "Brief Review of Recent History of Pitsanuloke Project," February 17, 1940, PUA.

60. Eakin, "Influence of Foreign Evangelists"; Eakin, "Mr. Hanna's Case," PUA.

61. Elder to Johnson, September 24, 1940, PHS.

this way that person was qualified to preach regardless of his knowledge either of the Bible or other branches of human knowledge." Secondly, Elder admitted that even though Sung did encourage Bible study, he did so only "after the method and content of his own teaching, and was the kind that decrys [sic] as destructive of religion all scientific learning and truth."[62] Elder objected to the witness bands formed by Sung because they preached without any connection to the authority of the church and had the audacity to claim that a person did not need any seminary training in order to preach. As such, Sung and the movement inspired by him were an affront to the *raison d'être* of the seminary that Elder led and threatened to deprecate the ordained ministry of the church. Elder's seminary colleagues Banchop and Prasert reported that John Sung and Boon Mark Gittisarn said the seminary was "no use and it was useless to study there." Elder asserted that Sung brought the ordained ministry of the church into low repute. To illustrate this point, Elder lamented that his seminary colleague Banchop, who graduated with honors from Union Theological Seminary in the Philippines, was leaving to go into government service. Also, Thai evangelist Sing Keo Suriyakham refused to take seminary studies because he thought his influence would be narrowed by becoming an ordained minister.[63]

The Bible Institute Controversy and On-Going Divisions After Sung's Departure

Conflict regarding Sung did not cease when the evangelist left Thailand in August 1939. Following his departure, a group of pro-Sung Thai Christians, together with APM missionaries Forrest Travaille and Margaret McCord, requested to use the facilities of the seminary in Chiang Mai to run a Bible institute for lay people along the lines of a twelve-day Bible school that Sung had conducted in Bangkok.[64] Loren Hanna and other pro-Sung missionaries backed this proposal but some, including Paul Eakin and Carl Elder, opposed it. On the one hand, they wanted to conserve the enthusiasm generated by Sung's meetings and support indigenous initiatives for Bible study. However, they feared that the type of Bible study that the pro-Sung group wanted would do more harm than

---

62. Cort to Hooper et al., April 19, 1940, PHS; Elder to Friends, July 10, 1940, PUA.

63. Elder to Johnson, September 24, 1940, PHS.

64. Attendees of Bangkok Bible Conference to Executive Committee of Siam Mission, August 2, 1939, PUA.

good. The request was submitted to the seminary's board of directors, which included Thai and missionary members, and various alternative ideas were proposed for solving the impasse between those who opposed and supported the Bible institute.[65] Carl Elder suggested making the new Bible institute part of the seminary, under the authority of the seminary's board of directors. But Dr. Chinda Singhanetra, leader of the pro-Sung group in Chiang Mai, rejected that solution. It wouldn't work, claimed Chinda, because Elder did not accept the pro-Sung group's interpretation of the Bible and they did not accept Elder's interpretation.[66] While a solution to the problem was still being considered, a group of Christians in Chiang Mai wrote to the Thailand mission requesting that Elder be removed from the seminary.[67] They claimed that Elder had failed to do his duties as a missionary by opposing Sung and the evangelistic bands. A missionary should be praising and backing up the preaching of the gospel, but instead Elder was proud and uncooperative. There would be no peace and harmony, they claimed, until Elder was removed. However, Thailand mission executive secretary Paul Eakin was hesitant to take action on this request, fearing some personal grievance was behind it.[68] Banchop Bansiddhi and Prasert Intaphantu, Elder's colleagues at the seminary, agreed with Eakin. They thought that the charges against Elder were baseless. Elder may have had different opinions on some matters of interpretation, they admitted, but that was common among preachers and such differences were minor and did not injure the faith of the students. Their conclusion was that any charges against him came from "impure motives rather than sincere knowledge, and for the most part come from those who have practically no knowledge of the Scriptures themselves." They suspected that the real reasons behind the request for Elder's removal were personal grudges and the desire of Boon Mark Gittisarn and the pro-Sung group to take control of the seminary.[69]

---

65. "Ideas of Board of Directors of Seminary on Bible School," PUA.
66. Singhanetra to Eakin, September 26, 1939, PUA.
67. Christians of Chiang Mai to Paul Eakin, September 25,1939, PUA.
68. Eakin to Singhanetra, September 30, 1939, PUA.
69. Bansiddhi and Intaphantu to Paul Eakin, October 25, 1939, PUA; Elder to Eakin, October 9,1939, PUA; Pongudom, *History*, 88.

Loren Hanna's Concerns about Modernism at the Seminary

Both Eakin and Elder hoped that the conflict over John Sung and the proposed Bible institute would not bring old modernist-fundamentalist controversies into the equation, but it seemed nearly impossible to avoid.[70] Loren Hanna saw the problem with Elder as theological and, as discussed in chapter 6, he urged Elder to abandon modernist biblical scholarship and to turn to God. Elder, however, believed the current controversy was not "a matter fundamentally of belief, but of ethical practice."[71] But it was much more than that. Elder and Eakin were naïve in thinking that modernist-fundamentalist tensions were external to the real issues at hand in the controversy over Sung and the proposed Bible institute. The type of intelligent, modern evangelism that they promoted in order to appeal to educated Buddhists was at the other end of the spectrum from the enthusiastic soul-winning practiced by Sung. The theology of Eakin and Elder led them to promote a particular type of evangelism and that of Sung and his followers led them to support another type of evangelism. The controversy over Sung and the Bible institute ostensibly revolved around Sung's methodology and style, but divergent theologies underlay the conflict. Even after the executive committee of the Thailand mission refused the request of the Thai Christians to use the seminary for a Sung-style Bible institute and instead proposed short-term Bible conferences at local churches, controversy did not die down.[72] Intra-mission and intra-church conflicts persisted.

Loren Hanna continued to oppose Elder and others whom he thought had unorthodox views. When Thai pastor Charoen Sakulkan was proposed for appointment to the seminary in 1940, Hanna objected on the basis of Charoen's life and doctrine. In a letter to Elder, Hanna stated "I approve of having NO ONE on the Seminary staff who can not take a 100 percent stand on the verities of the Bible, and who lives accordingly, and who makes the proclamation of the whole gospel of Christ his major interest in life."[73] In years previous, numerous accusations had been brought against Charoen when he was a pastor in Nakon Sritamarat province in Southern Thailand. After Kenneth Landon published

---

70. Eakin to Elder, August 26, 1939; Eakin to Elder, September 6, 1939; Eakin to Elder, October 18, 1939, PUA.

71. Elder to Eakin, December 19, 1939, PUA.

72. Paul Eakin to Chinda Singhanetra, November 24, 1939, PUA.

73. Elder to Eakin, January 3, 1940, PUA.

damning testimonial letters against Charoen from Thai Christians in his intra-mission publication *Mission Opinion*, Paul Eakin and CCT moderator Pluang Sudhikam visited Nakon to investigate. They found the charges to be largely unsubstantiated, many of them originating from one young man who had personal animosity against Charoen. Only the charge of drinking alcohol was substantiated, and this was only a charge of drinking, not drunkenness.[74] Nevertheless, missionaries who were close to the situation, namely Edwin and Agnes McDaniel, Lucius and Edna Bulkley, and Kenneth and Margaret Landon, thought that there were many problems with Charoen, in particular his failure to do evangelistic work. Edna Bulkley claimed that when Charoen came back from the International Missionary Council meetings in Jerusalem in 1928, where he had been sent as a delegate, he was joyous about God's answers to prayer. However, Paul Eakin "took him in hand" and by 1932, he had "no more sermons on Christ, gospels, [or] prayer." She claimed that this was real reason that the McDaniels did not want him to come to Nakon Sritamarat.[75] Kenneth Landon reported that when Charoen was pastoring Second Church in Bangkok and working at Margaret McCord's Bible school for girls, he admitted that "he had many doubts about the veracity of the scripture." McCord concluded he was "spiritually sick." Kenneth Landon claimed that the only reason Charoen was still in ministry was because he was a personal favorite of mission leaders, presumably Paul Eakin and Bertha McFarland. According to Landon, Eakin's philosophy was to transfer failures from one mission job to another in hopes that they would change.[76]

Ultimately Charoen Sakulkan did not take a post at the seminary, apparently hesitant to enter into a situation in Chiang Mai where there was so much division related to the seminary.[77] Although the Thailand mission denied the requests of the pro-Sung group to dismiss Elder from the seminary and to establish a lay Bible institute at the seminary, Elder eventually resigned from the seminary in protest. Already weary from conflicts related to Sung and the seminary, the final straw was the ordination of Boon Mee Rungreungwongse as pastor of First Church, Chiang

---

74. Landon, "Nationalization, Whither Bound?," 17–23, 56–58; Eakin and Sudhikam, "Report on Situation at Sritamarat with Reference to the Sakunals," January 1935, WCSC.

75. E. Bulkley to McAfee, October 1, 1932, PHS.

76. K. Landon to Cort, December 27, 1934, WCSC.

77. Elder to Eakin, February 15, 1940, PUA.

Mai. Boon Mee lacked formal theological training and Elder viewed his irregular ordination as a failure of the mission to support the value of an educated ministry, something to which he thought Thailand mission leadership only gave lip service.[78] After Elder's resignation from the seminary, the school closed and remained so until after the Second World War. Pre-war plans to re-open it never came to fruition.

A year after Elder resigned from the seminary and moved to Bangkok, Board secretary Charles Leber reported on-going divisions among the missionaries in Thailand. There were three main groups. He said the "liberal" group included Paul Eakin, Horace Ryburn, Mowbray Tate, Edwin Cort, and Kenneth Wells. The second group were those pushing for evangelistic training and included Jack and Gladys Holladay, Herbert and Margaret Stewart, and John Eakin, Paul's brother. Thirdly, Albert Seigle and Loren Hanna still wanted a Bible institute. Tensions related to modernism, fundamentalism, and evangelism existed in the mission before Sung's arrival but his visit catalyzed those tensions and caused them to erupt into division and controversy.[79] Issues in the controversy over John Sung and the proposed lay Bible institute at the Chiang Mai seminary were only sometimes framed in theological terms that bore resemblance to the fundamentalist-modernist controversies in the United States. Nevertheless, theological differences were intertwined with other factors including conflicting personalities, proper methods and emphases in evangelism, the qualifications and value of ordained ministry, and developing tensions in indigenization between the foreign missionaries and Thai Christian leaders. Paul Eakin and Carl Elder wanted to keep modernism and fundamentalism off the table in the controversy related to John Sung. But that was impossible. The modernist approaches to biblical scholarship and evangelism favored by Eakin and Elder came into conflict with the fundamentalist emphases and biases of Sung and missionaries such as Loren Hanna. Previously, theological tensions had been kept under control but when the whirlwind of John Sung blew through Thailand, it was too much to bear and the divisions that were created had still not healed by the time missionary work in Thailand ended when the Japanese began their occupation in December 1941.

78. Elder to Friends, July 10, 1940; Elder to Executive Committee, November 24, 1940; Eakin to Executive Committee, December 18, 1940, PUA; Elder to Johnson, September 24, 1940; Leber to Hooper, October 23, 1941, PHS.

79. Leber to Hooper, October 23, 1941, PHS.

CONCLUSION

In this chapter, the interactions of three foreign visitors with modernism and fundamentalism in Thailand have been examined. The background and biases of these visitors influenced how they interpreted what they found, and how they responded. In 1927, Charles Selden, a modernist-leaning Unitarian journalist, spoke derisively of what he saw as the injection of fundamentalism into the Thailand mission. His published comments caused a stir among the missionaries, all of whom except one vigorously denied the presence of controversy and instead affirmed that a spirit of mutual tolerance prevailed in the mission. Selden interpreted emerging tensions as controversy. However, there does not seem to have been any significant intra-mission conflict either before his visit or as a direct result of his published comments. Eakin's claim that conservative theology and a liberal attitude of tolerance prevailed would appear to have been an accurate description of the Thailand mission at that point of time. In 1935, fundamentalist minister Donald Barnhouse made a more extensive survey of mission work in Thailand than Selden, seeking to discover whether modernism had tainted Presbyterian mission work. What he found was a broadly conservative majority with several indicators of modernist influence among the missionaries, though some of these signs of modernism were ambiguous or submerged beneath intra-mission debate about the nature and methods of evangelism. Theological diversity existed and was influencing the evangelistic effectiveness of mission institutions, but there was not open warfare between missionaries along theological lines. However, in 1938 and 1939, when Chinese evangelist John Sung made two whirlwind evangelistic tours of Thailand, latent theological tensions mixed with divergent personalities and views on evangelism to produce open conflict among missionaries and Thai Christians.

The conflict resulting from Sung's visits did not look like modernist-fundamentalist conflicts in the United States and China because the issues being openly debated in Thailand were not explicitly about modernism, namely the application of social and scientific learning to the nature and interpretation of the Bible. The focus of debate was instead how to promote spiritual life and the Christian message in the modern world. For missionaries like Loren Hanna, American debates on fundamentalism and modernism contributed to his reasons for siding with Sung and against Elder, whose modernist theology Hanna saw as dangerous to true spiritual life. Some Thai Christians, however, framed the debate in dichotomous terms. In their eyes, one side was for spiritual life and evangelism and the other was against them. Their public and private correspondence and published articles do not reveal a desire to debate explicitly doctrinal issues. In Thailand, there was no on-going public controversy about the five fundamentals often cited in American debates, namely the inerrancy of Scripture, the reality of miracles, the Virgin Birth, the substitutionary atonement of Christ, and the bodily resurrection of Christ. Undoubtedly, there were APM Thailand missionaries who questioned or denied some of those points of belief. But those positions were quietly held, or only mentioned in private correspondence or conversation. The open debate that embroiled the APM missionaries and Thai Christians revolved around one man, the correctness of his particular interpretations of the Bible, and the legitimacy of preserving those teachings in a new layperson's Bible institute. Those missionaries most enthusiastically supporting Sung were fundamentalist-leaning and those most vigorously opposing him were modernist-leaning, and those sympathies played into the reasons for their support or opposition to Sung. But in the correspondence between missionaries and Thai Christians, the points of contention were not particular doctrines, but whether one was "for" or "against" Sung, and "for" or "against" the Bible institute.

For these reasons, it can be concluded that during the 1920s and 1930s, modernist and fundamentalist views were causing tensions between missionaries in Thailand but those tensions did not contribute to open conflict until John Sung's visit mobilized those tensions into a separate, but related conflict about spiritual life and evangelism. The doctrinal issues most commonly associated with fundamentalism and modernism were not front-and-center in the conflict among APM missionaries and Thai Christians but they were not unrelated to the way in which they divided into pro-Sung and anti-Sung groups. APM mission leadership, particularly the Board of Foreign Missions and Thailand executive secretary Paul Eakin, had long tried to diffuse and suppress theological tensions by maintaining a formally conservative consensus and an atmosphere of mutual toleration, but that was ultimately impossible.

While concerns about modernism and fundamentalism were a contributing factor to the controversy over John Sung, that conflict was not the only area in which modernist views impacted the American Presbyterian mission in Thailand. The next two chapters will examine the ways in which modernist leanings manifested themselves in changing missionary perspectives on inter-religious communication and intra-mission debate about the role of mission schools vis-à-vis the evangelistic purpose of the mission.

8

Changing Perceptions and Approaches to Non-Christian Religions and Evangelism

IN THE LATE NINETEENTH and early twentieth centuries, missionaries across the theological spectrum were experiencing and responding to developing trends in the church and the world. Modernist perspectives or some degree of sympathy to such views were one of multiple factors influencing these changes among missionaries, both in Thailand and other parts of the world. Some of the most significant theological changes within Protestantism were surveyed in chapter 2, and in the present chapter some trends particularly relevant in the mission context will be considered, namely changing perceptions of non-Christian religions and approaches to evangelism. Missionaries were on the frontlines of Western encounter with peoples of other faiths and thus were forced to think more deeply about how Christianity related to those faiths. While there were still many in the United States who knew few to none who did not identify as Christian, missionaries often lived in societies that were majority non-Christian. When most of your neighbors are Buddhists, Muslims, or Hindus, what are appropriate modes of speaking about their faiths? Must they trust in Christ for salvation? What are appropriate ways of making Christ known? Increasing familiarity with the faiths and societies of the world's non-Christian peoples, combined with evolutionary thought and decreasing confidence in the Bible and Western cultural normativity, led to changes in missionary perceptions of the eternal destiny of non-Christians, missionary motives, appropriate ways of speaking about non-Christian faiths, and how the evangelistic task should be carried out in relation to other priorities such as education. Missionaries responded to these trends in a variety of ways, due to personality, background, theological convictions, and local contexts. As changes and differences among APM Thailand missionaries are examined in this chapter, it should be noted not all missionary responses were influenced by theological convictions. However, theological leanings sometimes had an impact on the ways and extent to which missionaries responded to changes happening around them. Sometimes it is possible to uncover a connection between a missionary's theological convictions and his actions. Sometimes it is not. Not all smoke is evidence of fire, and ambiguity in the historical record must be acknowledged as theological leanings are considered as one of multiple factors in missionary thinking and actions. The role of theological convictions in the changes that occurred is sometimes difficult to discern because missionary discussions in Thailand were rarely framed in explicitly theological terms. Underlying differences were masked by use of a common theological and ecclesiastical vocabulary, and a common commitment to "evangelism" even where understandings of that term were divergent. Because most missionaries assumed their fellows shared the same evangelistic goals, accusations of ineffectiveness were more common than those of unorthodoxy. Nevertheless, there is sufficient data to conclude that even though the majority of APM Thailand missionaries were broadly conservative, and wished to be seen as such, modernist leanings contributed to the thinking and priorities of some.

CHANGING PERCEPTIONS OF NON-CHRISTIAN RELIGIONS

Influenced by the Puritans, Anglo-American Protestant mission efforts in the seventeenth and eighteenth centuries were largely propelled by millennial expectations of a time when the gospel would be universally proclaimed, and the glory of God fill the earth.[1] This Protestant vision for global recognition of the lordship of Christ over both church and society continued into the nineteenth century but was challenged and modified by the rising popularity of premillennialism. Premillennial pessimism about the prospect for societal transformation led some conservatives to focus on individual conversions over efforts for societal change. Many nineteenth-century Protestant missionaries, however, continued to hope for the conversion of individuals and the transformation of societies as

---

1. Jong, *As the Waters*; Murray, *Puritan Hope*.

complementary goals of a coming Christianized era in world history. Another change in nineteenth-century missions thinking was a growing anthropocentric motivation. The theocentric vision of the glory of God filling the earth that previously dominated Protestant missions thinking did not fade entirely but was being deprecated by an anthropocentric priority on compassion for fellow humans, particularly those in the non-Christian world, as it was conceived at the time.[2] As the nineteenth century rolled over into the twentieth, this increased anthropocentric focus, together with growing interest in the comparative study of religion, contributed to changing perceptions of non-Christian religions and so-called "heathen" beliefs and practices.

Whereas all spiritual beliefs and practices outside of Christianity, Judaism, and Islam were formerly thought of as "heathen," there was increasing awareness in the West of other belief systems that should be recognized as religions in their own right, such as Hinduism, Buddhism, Shintoism, and (perhaps) Confucianism. In many parts of Southeast Asia, however, these religions mixed easily with indigenous, or "heathen," spirit beliefs and practices such that missionary recognition and response to the practiced faith of indigenous people remained mixed. Non-Christian religions and "heathen" practices were widely regarded as false, and the customs of their adherents were seen as inextricably bound up with their false beliefs. As such, many thought the false religion and immoral customs of these peoples needed to be replaced with Christian faith and Christian civilization. Although American and European missionaries sometimes lamented the influence of sinful practices propagated by fellow westerners, spreading so-called "Christian civilization" was viewed as largely synonymous with spreading the values of Western civilization, the progress of which was seen as the fruit of Christianity. For many missionaries, it was difficult to see any inherent value in the beliefs or cultures of the peoples whom they were trying to save from damnation.[3] However, as the nineteenth century changed into the twentieth, attitudes began to change. As a burgeoning mission force, and Westerners more generally, came into greater contact with the peoples and religions of the world, perceptions shifted. Instead of being viewed as completely false, a certain amount of truth and light was recognized to be a part of non-Christian

---

2. van den Berg, *Constrained*, 174–76; Murray, *Puritan Hope*, 213–17; Walls, "Eschatology," 182–200.

3. Hutchison, *Errand*, 91–124; *Modernist Impulse*, 132–44; Stanley, "From 'The Poor Heathen,'" 3–10.

religions. Among missionaries, fulfillment theology was increasingly common, proposing that religions could be placed on a scale from lower to higher religions with Christ as the pinnacle to which all others were progressing. Popularized by the Scottish missionary to India John Nicol Farquhar and prominent at both the World Missionary Conference in Edinburgh in 1910 and the International Missionary Conference in Jerusalem in 1928, fulfillment theology signaled a shift in missionary attitudes toward other religions.[4] In some cases, fulfillment theology developed in a relativistic direction, such as reflected in the Laymen's Report.[5] For some Westerners who came to view religious faith primarily as a phenomenon of human consciousness and experience, there was a tendency to relativize the truth claims of Christianity in recognition of the religious experience of non-Christian peoples. Compassion for fellow human beings meant a retreat from assertion of the exclusivity of salvation in Christ. Yet the majority of Western conservatives and liberals still viewed Christianity as the superior religion, albeit differently. For conservatives, Christianity was superior because Christ was the ultimate and final revelation of truth, and the only hope for salvation from sin and separation from God. For liberals, however, the uniqueness of Christianity was increasingly expressed in terms of ethics and spiritual experience rather than certain doctrines. Doctrine was not wholly unimportant to liberals, but there was a shift in which doctrines and beliefs they found to be important. Biblical and theological interests were shifting from the Pauline epistles and dogmatic theology to the synoptic Gospels, the moral teachings of Jesus, and the moral example found in the life and death of Christ. Penal substitutionary atonement was falling out of favor even as the incarnation and the immanence of God were becoming more prominent. If God was present among all peoples, as implied in modern emphases on immanence and incarnation, then perhaps other religions had redeeming value and contained more truth than previously imagined. The sincerity and morality of adherents of non-Christian religions was increasingly being acknowledged. Some of these changes were happening to a greater or lesser extent across the theological spectrum, though they were most prominent among those with modernist sympathies as they were more open to modifications of traditional positions.

---

4. Sharpe, *Not to Destroy but to Fulfil*; Bosch, *Transforming Mission*, 490–93; Stanley, *World Missionary Conference*, 205–47.

5. Hocking, *Re-Thinking Missions*, 16, 29–32, 112, 326; Hutchison, *Errand*, 158–65.

Early twentieth-century changes in the perception of non-Christian religions are well illustrated in the writing of Cleland B. McAfee, a PCUSA Board of Foreign Missions secretary who visited the Thailand mission for six weeks in late 1924 and early 1925, and was the Thailand mission's main contact with the Board for many years.[6] In his 1932 book *The Uncut Nerve of Missions*, McAfee testified to the change in attitude toward other religions that had occurred in recent years. McAfee asserted that the view that there was one religion that was wholly true while other religions were wholly false had now given way to the idea that God left a witness to Himself "in all sincere faiths" and there was "the possibility of error in some forms of any religion," including Christianity. In light of this, McAfee wanted to answer the apologetic question as to whether or not this new attitude cut the nerve of missions, destroying the motivation for people to be missionaries.[7] On the way to his conclusion that this new attitude did not destroy the missionary motive, McAfee outlined four possible attitudes to other religions. The first was indifference. The missionary does not care what other religions teach or practice because they only need to be replaced, not studied. The second attitude was opposition, or intolerance. Other religions are false and satanic, and must be denounced as such. In its "milder form, this attitude produced a genuine fear that any real appreciation of other faiths must mean a lessened approval of the Christian faith." The third attitude was over-appreciation, or tolerance, which regarded all religions as equally true and little more than a matter of taste or preference. None of these three options were suitable, however. In McAfee's view, if a person had wrong beliefs about God, it was wrong for a Christian to denounce that person, but it was also wrong to accept those ideas as being equally true as the teaching of Christ. McAfee's preferred choice was a fourth option, namely intelligent appreciation, with discrimination. McAfee believed that God had not left himself without a witness in other faiths and that the true aspects of other faiths should be recognized as "part of the one Truth." Pressing his main point, McAfee affirmed

> Such an attitude does not cut the nerve of missions and yet it is the modern attitude. It appreciates all the good in other faiths; it recognizes the sincerity of adherents of those faiths; yet it maintains assurance of the uniqueness and necessity of Christ

---

6. Brown to Board, May 13, 1925, PHS; Eakin to McAfee, June 27, 1936, PUA.
7. McAfee, *Uncut Nerve*, 43–61.

and the Christian faith . . . Nothing of this sort cuts the nerve of missionary effort unless an attitude develops which reduces Christ to a level with other religious leaders.[8]

For McAfee, the missionary motive was preserved as long as one held on to "the uniqueness of Jesus Christ Himself and the incomparable significance of His cross and resurrection." An appreciation for Christ together with the desire to help other people who were experiencing "loss" of some type was enough to sustain the missionary motive. Personally, McAfee felt he could not escape from the logic that people would go to hell. But even if others could escape from the logic of eternal damnation for non-Christians, they might still reasonably be motivated to help non-Christian peoples escape from their "loss," however that was defined, and to experience Christ.[9] Although some, McAfee noted, believed saving people from hell was a fundamental motive for missions, he thought it was non-essential. The primary motive should be to share our "best," which must have something to do with Christ. Saving people from "loss," however conceived, and extending civilization were legitimate goals, but should only be collateral motivators.[10] Although he had his own personal convictions, McAfee was relatively unconcerned about theological differences among missionaries because there were differences among home constituencies. As expressed in his earlier book on *Changing Foreign Missions*, McAfee's pragmatic approach was that any theory about Christ that did not ignite missionary zeal on the mission field would die off eventually. Therefore, Christians should not worry about missionaries with beliefs or motivations that differed from their own.[11] The practical outworking of McAfee's convictions on proper missionary motivations has already been seen in the account of Cornelia Gillies in chapter 6. Even though Gillies confessed that she had "no evangelistic feeling" and didn't want to convert anyone, McAfee was content for her to become a missionary to Thailand after she affirmed that "her fundamental purpose in going to the field was the bringing of Christ to the people whom she touched."[12] Although McAfee displayed modernist leanings in his approach to theological differences among missionaries and their motives for serving, he

---

8. McAfee, *Uncut Nerve*, 56–57.
9. McAfee, *Uncut Nerve*, 29–30.
10. McAfee, *Uncut Nerve*, 23–33.
11. McAfee, *Changing Foreign Missions*, 158–59.
12. C. Gillies to McAfee, March 22, 1932; McAfee to R. Gillies, April 13, 1932, PHS.

remained conservative in his convictions on the reality of hell and the importance of the cross and resurrection of Christ. As such, it is difficult to place him along the theological spectrum. Indications that McAfee may have had modernist leanings did not appear among the letters of APM Thailand missionaries who wrote to him or about him, although the Presbyterian fundamentalist journal *Christianity Today* dismissed his book *The Uncut Nerve of Missions* in a brief article titled "Secretary McAfee's Book Hailed by Modernism."[13]

Within the Thailand mission, there were missionaries representing the range of attitudes toward other religions outlined by McAfee. However, before providing specific examples, a brief explanation should be given about the development of missionary understandings of religion in Thailand. As early as the seventeenth century, Roman Catholic missionaries recognized Buddhism as an identifiable religion in the kingdom of Siam.[14] By the early nineteenth century, Buddhism was more widely being recognized in the West as a religion in its own right but in the minds of some there was still confusion about the origin and extent of Buddhism. Among them was Thailand missionary pioneer Karl Gützlaff who was unsure whether or not "Sommona Kodom," whom he thought to be the founder of Buddhism in Southeast Asia, was a disciple of the Buddha himself.[15] Nevertheless, from the earliest days of Protestant missions in Thailand, Buddhism was acknowledged as the religion of the Thai people. Yet, Buddhism as practiced in Thailand incorporated a wide variety of indigenous spirit beliefs and practices that did not have their origin in Buddhist teaching. These indigenous beliefs and practices were often more important than Buddhism, especially in northern Thailand. Though Buddhist identity was strong in the kingdom of Siam centered in Bangkok, such identity was much weaker in the north where missionaries often dismissed local spirit practices as mere "superstition" or "demon" worship. As such, a summary picture of missionary attitudes towards non-Christian beliefs and practices in Thailand is complicated because of eclectic and multiple religious beliefs and practices that were evaluated differently by missionaries who saw more value in Buddhism than they did in the indigenous beliefs with which it was mixed. With this background in mind, we now turn to examples of the range of

---

13. "Secretary McAfee's Book Hailed by Modernism," 22–23.
14. Pascal, "Buddhist Monks and Christian Friars," 5–21.
15. Almond, *British Discovery of Buddhism*, 7–12.

developing missionary views toward Buddhism and other beliefs and practices which were often practiced alongside Buddhism.

During a furlough, Daniel McGilvary attended the World Parliament of Religions, held in Chicago from Sept 11-27, 1893, a multi-day convention bringing together representatives of various world religions, ostensibly for mutual learning and consultation. The parliament was severely criticized by numerous Protestants for putting Christianity on the same level as other religions, but John Henry Barrows, organizer of the conference, defended it as a missionary enterprise.[16] McGilvary, like many others, was initially shocked at the "boldness of the idea—as if Christianity were to be put on a par with other religions," though he eventually came to see the parliament's goals as "legitimate and proper." McGilvary thought the parliament was "merely doing on a large scale what we missionaries are called upon to do on a smaller scale every time that we hold an argument with Buddhists or other non-Christian people."[17] McGilvary's colleague and former co-worker in Petchaburi, Samuel G. McFarland, contributed a short paper on Buddhism in Thailand to volume 2 of the collected papers of the parliament, alternatively praising Buddhist ethics that paralleled Christian ethics and detailing the vices of Thai Buddhists who lived without light or hope.[18] William Briggs, however, a fellow APM Thailand missionary who had not attended the parliament but may have been aware of McFarland's article, was dismissive of the conference. In a letter to the Board, Briggs wrote

> What is Buddhism in Siam? a compound of Agnosticism, Demon worship and superstitious idolatry—The pastic [sic] sentimentalism palmed off on Chicago audiences last year no more resembles Siamese Buddhism than a dirty wallowing pig resembles a mastiff. Talk about Brotherhood. We believe in the Brotherhood of Man—that's why we are here—But we stand for the Name given *above* every name, whereby we *must* be saved. Let some . . . who have been devoting themselves so magnanimously to the subject of Brotherhood of Religions come out here and see some of their little brothers.[19]

In the 1890s, a range of views existed within the Siam and Laos missions though in the years that followed, entirely dismissive views such

16. Hutchison, *Errand*, 105-6; Goodpasture, "World's Parliament," 403-11.
17. McGilvary, *Half Century*, 370-71.
18. Barrows, *World's Parliament*, 2:1296-97.
19. Briggs to Board, March 27, 1894, PUA.

as that expressed by Briggs became less common as views similar to those of McGilvary and McFarland became more common. William Harris, the only Thailand-based respondent to questionnaires sent out by Commission IV of the 1910 World Missionary Conference in Edinburgh, gave a mixed report on Buddhism, not dissimilar to that of McFarland. Though Theravada Buddhism was largely neglected at Edinburgh due to insufficient responses from the field, the comments of Harris and missionaries to Burma and Ceylon appeared in an appendix to the Commission IV report. Harris wrote of numerous vices and corruptions of Buddhism though he admitted that missionaries should rejoice at every element of truth or goodness that can be found in the religion and practice of the people with whom the missionary works.[20] Some missionaries, such as Evander McGilvary and Margaret Neuber, whose views have been discussed in previous chapters, came to relativistic conclusions about the uniqueness of Christianity. However, many APM Thailand missionaries during the period being considered came to some degree of intelligent appreciation of Buddhism even as they continued to regard Christianity as the superior and ultimate religion. For conservatives, that superiority was connected to the exclusivity of salvation available in Christ. For modernist-leaning missionaries, the superiority of Christianity stemmed from its ethical and spiritual ability to improve the lives of people in modern society.

ETERNAL DESTINY AND THE MISSIONARY MOTIVE

Even as missionary appreciation for at least some aspects of other religions increased, the relative importance of the eternal destiny of non-Christians as a motivation for missionary service decreased in the minds of some missionaries, from the late nineteenth century onward.[21] For some missionaries, increasing appreciation of non-Christian religions and their adherents led to questioning or abandonment of the doctrine of eternal damnation for non-Christians. Other missionaries did not necessarily abandon the doctrine but, as compared with earlier Protestant missionary rhetoric, spoke of the "perishing heathen" less often, and with greater reluctance, than was formerly common in missionary circles. Among those who rarely, if ever, spoke of eternal damnation were both those who

---

20. World Missionary Conference, *Report of Commission IV*, xiii, 236, 81–87; Stanley, *World Missionary Conference*, 213–14.

21. Rabe, *Home Base,* 106–07.

abandoned the doctrine and those who believed it but did not wish to emphasize it. Still others, especially those of a fundamentalist bent, stressed explicit affirmation of this doctrine as essential for both maintaining conservative theology and motivating missionary service.

As mentioned in previous chapters, in the 1890s the American Board of Commissioners for Foreign Missions (ABCFM) overturned its policy of requiring candidates to affirm the doctrine of eternal punishment for non-Christians. Among those in favor of overturning the policy were missionaries who argued against reprobation of the "heathen" due to their experience with intelligent Chinese and Hindus.[22] Although the PCUSA and its missions did not debate the doctrine of reprobation as ABCFM Congregationalists did, similar changes in thinking happened among some Presbyterian missionaries. Pearl Buck, who has been discussed in earlier chapters, was a Presbyterian missionary to China who abandoned the proselytizing goal of missions in favor of social service as she came to appreciate Chinese culture. As shown in the research of Lian Xi, her experience was not unique among China missionaries.[23] In Thailand, as discussed in earlier chapters, Evander McGilvary came to the conviction that Buddhists might not be eternally condemned, and the absence of a desire to convert anyone was an important factor in Cornelia Gillies's decision to decline her appointment to the Thailand mission. Yet even among missionaries who did not leave the Thailand mission due, at least in part, to divergence from traditional views on the eternal destiny of non-Christians, the issue was less prominent in their thinking than it was among their nineteenth-century predecessors.

In 1933, the Board of Foreign Missions held a conference among APM Thailand missionaries and representatives of the Board to discuss and assess mission work in Thailand. In his notes on that conference, Paul Eakin summarized discussion on the changing nature of the Thailand mission.[24] Eakin noted that there was a change in the ideas of motive and scope of missions everywhere and those differences were manifesting themselves among the Thailand missionaries. In contrast to the older generation of missionaries, younger missionaries did not feel it was as important for Thai Christians to make a complete break with their former lives as Buddhists. Even some older missionaries had difficulty believing that "fine Buddhists" would go to hell. There had been

22. Hutchison, *Modernist Impulse*, 134; Xi, *Conversion*, 208–11.
23. Xi, *Conversion*, 7–10; Hutchison, *Errand*, 166–69.
24. Eakin, Notes on Siam Conference, 1933, PUA.

a change in the type of missionaries coming to the field. Eakin noted that Thailand no longer had the "old flaming evangelists" of a previous generation and even those who felt a call to rescue the lost changed their actions when they met some of those "lost." Eakin thought that the Thailand mission was in a period of transition. On the question of whether or not the Thailand mission was justified in pursuing continued evangelistic expansion, the answer depended in part on one's view on the salvation of non-Christians. For those who lost the conviction that Thai people would go to hell unless they joined the church, expansion could not be so easily justified, especially in light of the increasing responsibility assumed by the national church. However, for those who were convinced that all Thai people needed to confess Christ for salvation, there was a strong case for ongoing expansion. Eakin believed that there had been a change in motives for mission work among some and while the Thailand mission was in this period of change, he thought there would be some "confusion" among the missionaries.

The confusion that Eakin refered to was evident in the diversity of motives that brought missionaries to Thailand. In his 1927 application to the Board, Kenneth Landon stated that the thought of people "perishing without even hearing of a way of escape makes me want to go and tell them of Christ."[25] However, after leaving the mission field in 1937, Landon began to move away from his life as a fundamentalist soul-winning evangelist.[26] In a 1940 sermon in the United States, Landon argued that social services should be viewed as a legitimate purpose of missions as much as saving souls. Landon claimed that earlier generations of missionaries went to save people from hell and would have felt insulted if told they were going for some other purpose. Although he may have been misreading the scope of nineteenth-century missions and their postmillennial vision for the transformation of both individuals and societies, Landon asserted that preaching the gospel was formerly seen as the primary product of missions and social services were merely the by-product. However, Landon queried, should we judge missions solely by their product and not their by-product? Missionary work is usually judged by its primary product but in the same way that differentiation

---

25. K. Landon, "My Motives for Seeking Missionary Appointment," 1927, PHS.

26. In letters to his wife, Landon expressed regret that his fundamentalism had caused a rift in their marriage. However, his highest priority was preserving their marriage, and this contributed to a progressive softening of his theological position. K. Landon to M. Landon, April 1–2, and April n.d., 1942, WCSC.

between product and by-product in the industrial world was fading, the differentiation between saving souls and social service in missions was dying out as well.[27] Though he started his missionary career with a focus on saving people from hell, by 1940 Ken Landon came to see societal development as an equally legitimate aim of missions. Although Landon was an ordained Presbyterian, his eschatology was premillennial, a fact that was reflected in his focus on the conversion of individuals for the duration of his time as a missionary in Thailand. After resigning from missionary service, his understanding of the purpose of missions shifted, coming closer to the postmillennialism that was more common among Presbyterians. However, it is likely that his revised convictions were influenced by modern notions of progress and his doctoral studies at the University of Chicago more than they were by any reconsideration of theological positions on the millennium per se.[28]

For other APM Thailand missionaries, it is uncertain whether a concern for the eternal destiny of non-Christians was ever a part of their motivation for missionary service. In a 1987 interview, former APM Thailand missionaries William Harding Kneedler and Christina Kneedler shared why they became missionaries.[29] Christina Kneedler, a granddaughter of Daniel McGilvary, was born in Chiang Mai and returned to Thailand as a missionary alongside her husband, a medical doctor, in 1931.[30] For Mrs. Kneedler, she wanted to go back to Thailand because she was born there and it felt like home to her. Dr. Kneedler, who was born and raised in the U.S., said he wanted to invest his life in helping other people. "And that seemed to be the best way that I knew," explained Dr. Kneedler. What the Kneedlers thought about the eternal destiny of non-Christians is uncertain, but apparently a desire to go "home" and to help society were more important motivators for them than the conversion of individuals or the transformation of society to the glory of God. It is possible they may have agreed with these aims if asked, but neither were uppermost in their minds when asked why they became missionaries.

27. Kenneth Landon, "The By-Products of Christian Missions," Sermon, Cambridge City, June 9, 1940, WCSC.

28. Though his dissertation was on Siam's recent political history, Landon studied philosophy and was influenced by his supervisor Albert Eustace Haydon, a humanist who challenged Landon's religious convictions. Hollinger, *Protestants Abroad*, 191–93.

29. William and Christina Kneedler, "Oral History Transcript," interview by Herbert Swanson, May 8, 1987, PUA.

30. Eakin, "Biographical Notes on Dr. & Mrs. Kneedler," 1956, PUA.

Paul Eakin, who was born in Thailand, recalled that he returned to Thailand as a missionary in 1913 out of pity and carried with him a superiority complex. However, as he made Thai friends, his pity for Thai people changed to respect. Eakin considered several motivations for missions to be ineffective and obsolete. These included rescuing the "heathen" from the wrath of God and a literal hell, proselytizing in order to report numbers of conversions, and spreading democracy and Western civilization as a panacea for the problems of the world. For Eakin, effective motivators for missions in the modern era included Jesus' command to "go into all the world" and helping solve the world's problems, such as the need for Christian unity and the relationship between church and state. Beyond these, however, Eakin thought the true motive of the missionary was "to share Jesus Christ, who alone is able to meet the real needs of the world, both East and West." Though Eakin had a deep respect for Thai people and appreciation of their culture and accomplishments, he believed Buddhism lacked "power to live" and the "joyous sense of having found God." Though saving Thai people from hell was not a concern for Eakin, he was nevertheless convinced that Thai people needed God in order to meet the challenges of modern living.[31] Though both Eakin and more conservative missionary colleagues shared a desire for Thai people to profess faith in Christ, Eakin held a modernist conception of the gospel. For Eakin, the uniqueness of the Christian faith consisted in ethics and experience rather than salvation from God's judgement through the substitutionary atonement of Christ on the cross.

In 1928, on the eve of a grand celebration of the centenary of Protestant missions in Thailand, Albert Seigle seems to have sensed a diversity of purpose within the mission. Unlike Eakin, he did not appear to view this diversity as a necessary time of transition, but rather a drift away from what should be the unquestioned highest goal of missions, namely, to lead people to faith in Jesus Christ. In an address to the annual meeting of the Thailand mission, Seigle recalled the evangelistic passion of previous generations of missionaries in Thailand and challenged his listeners to stay focused, or return their focus, to evangelism.

> Their ambition was to set a beacon of hope on every frontier of Siam; to plant the word of God in every province; reap the harvest of a kingdom for Christ. What is our ambition? What is our determination? What are we here for? Is it merely to heal

31. Eakin, "Being Realistic"; "Motive and End of Missions," n.d; Eakin, "Talk on Siam"; "Are Missions Worthwhile?"; "Why Am I a Missionary?," n.d., PUA.

the sick, and alleviate the suffering? Is it merely to educate this kingdom to the way of western civilization? Is it merely to direct the church, or get the names of men and women on the church roll? Or, is it to sow that seed, which if sown abideth not alone, and to reap a mighty harvest of God for Christ in Siam?[32]

In issuing this summons to lay down their lives for this highest missionary purpose, Seigle may have been indirectly questioning whether some of his fellow missionaries had diverted their focus from saving souls to providing medical care, teaching in order to promote Western civilization, or merely developing the institutional church. Had his fellows lost their purpose? Were they motivated by the same desire to "reap a mighty harvest" of conversions as Seigle was? It is likely not all of them were. Nevertheless, the broadly conservative goal of the mission was to see Thailand Christianized, a purpose which the Executive Committee of the Thailand mission made explicit five years later in their response to the *Laymen's Inquiry*. As discussed in chapter 6, the Thailand mission agreed with the *Laymen's Inquiry* that social service was a legitimate form of evangelism but reaffirmed verbal proclamation of the gospel was necessary in Thailand. Good works needed to be explained by the good news of Jesus Christ, otherwise Thai Buddhists would incorrectly conclude that Christians were doing good works in order to attain merit for themselves.[33] In practice, the missionaries did not always emphasize verbal proclamation of the gospel, especially in mission schools, which will be discussed in the next chapter.

THE ETERNAL DESTINY OF CIVILIZED THAI BUDDHISTS

Despite the seeming clarity of the Thailand mission's purpose vis-à-vis the goal of proclaiming Christ to Thai Buddhists, some missionaries experienced cognitive dissonance when they encountered intelligent, modern Buddhists whose lives appeared to reflect the fruits of Christian civilization, yet without profession of faith in Christ. This dissonance played a part in the resignation of Dr. John and Mrs. Julia Horst from the Thailand mission in 1932 after they were unable "to answer the questions of intelligent Siamese" Buddhists.[34] The identity of the

32. Seigle, "Life Laid Down," 322.

33. G. Fuller to Station Secretaries, June 23, 1933, PUA; Starling, "Re-Thinking Missions," 120–27.

34. Cotton to McAfee, December 1, 1932, PHS; McAfee to Cotton, December 5, 1932, PHS.

Buddhists who put challenging questions to the Horsts is unknown but in other cases, members of the Thai royal family presented the greatest challenge to the perception that Christian profession and Western civilization necessarily hung together.

Dr. John Horst, 1927
(Courtesy of the Presbyterian Historical Society, Philadelphia).

Thai royals were perhaps the most modern and progressive members of Thai society and were well respected by members of the American missionary community in Thailand. When King Prajadhipok visited the United States, he left a deep impression upon representatives of the PCUSA Board of Foreign Missions who held a grand reception for him in New York City on May 2, 1931. Charles R. Erdman and Cleland B. McAfee of the Board welcomed him, praising Thailand's modern development led by an "enlightened and progressive Royal House" and expressing gratitude for a liberal policy toward religious liberty. They reminded the king of the massive financial investment that the Board made in medical, educational, and evangelistic work in Thailand for which the "Board neither expects nor desires any return whatever for itself or its constituents. It is animated solely by the conviction that the people of Siam are our brother men." On his part, the king expressed appreciation for the Board's "high words of praise" and "substantial contribution to the happiness and the advancement of my people" that American missionaries made. These sacrificial contributions were made, according to the king, "for a noble and unselfish purpose—the improvement and betterment of mankind."[35] Paul Eakin later reported that Prince Damrong Rajanubhab, one of the most senior princes of the Thai royal family, was pleased with the Board's message to the King because it was "definitely Christian and put us on the right ground" and "at the same time it did not attack Buddhism, regarding which he seems to be rather sensitive."[36] A few months later, McAfee reflected on the king's visit in a letter to Edna Cole, an educational missionary in Bangkok, writing that the king "is himself a delightful man, and I believe the Lord has him in his love." While the phrase "has him in his love" could be interpreted in various ways, the context of the letter lends itself to the interpretation that McAfee thought King Prajadhipok would ultimately be saved. McAfee had this impression in spite of a very Buddhist greeting that the king sent back to Thailand following a medical procedure which he received during his 1931 visit to the United States. The king reported that "by the grace of Buddha and my own meritorious works the operation was successful." McAfee admitted that it was hardly surprising that a Buddhist ruler would send a Buddhist message to his nation any more than it would be surprising for a Christian ruler to send a Christian message to his nation. Nonetheless, McAfee remarked on what "a sharp contrast his message [was] to anything that a Christian would send." These facts notwithstanding, McAfee believed "the Lord has him in his love," apparently based on McAfee's observation that the king was "a delightful man" and the claim of APM Thailand missionary Mary Jane McClure that the king and queen were interested in Christianity.[37] In the same letter to Cole, McAfee brought up another Thai Buddhist royal whom he thought might be in heaven, Prince Mahidol Adulyadej of Songkla. The prince,

35. PCUSA Board of Foreign Missions, "Honor to Whom Honor is Due," May 2, 1931, PUA.

36. McAfee to Hanna, September 11, 1931, PHS.

37. McAfee to Cole, September 11, 1931; M. J. McClure to McAfee, December 22, 1930, PHS.

who trained as a medical doctor in the United States and had a close connection with the American Presbyterian mission, passed away at only 37 years old in 1929.[38] Mary Jane McClure, a long-time educational missionary who arrived in Thailand in 1886, wrote to McAfee saying that she expected to "meet Prince Songkla in Heaven." McAfee recounted

> [s]he says that some of her friends call her a Modernist for saying so, but she had talked with him enough to believe that he really had turned to God in humble penitence and trust in His mercy which he had expressed in our Lord Jesus. I suspect we will be surprised when we get to Heaven to find some people there whose going we had not realized. Certainly, Prince Songkla is one of whom I would think.[39]

This letter is the only evidence my research has uncovered indicating Prince Mahidol may have believed in Christ. In McAfee's letter, it is unclear whether McClure heard a verbal indication of such faith from the prince or if McClure and McAfee merely interpreted Mahidol's penitence and piety as evidence God would justify him through the work of Christ, even though he did not publicly affirm faith in Christ. Official records and histories agree that he was a life-long Buddhist. If Mary Jane McClure did hear a verbal indication of Christian faith from the prince, it is possible that he privately believed the Christian faith was true but declined to profess that faith publicly due to his prominent position. In the Thai Buddhist context, it would not have been unusual for someone to add belief in Christ to their existing Buddhist identity without viewing such dual allegiance as problematic, though this would be contrary to the exclusivism of conservative Christian theology. In other letters to McAfee, McClure recounted numerous conversations she had with members of the royal family and Thai nobles who expressed interest in Christianity. McClure thought some of these may have believed in Christ but did not profess Christ publicly because of the social ramifications it would have for them.[40] Given the paucity of data, it is difficult to say with certainty whether or not Thai Buddhists who never openly professed faith in Christ believed, to some extent, the Christian message. It may be that given their queries about Christianity and their modern, civilized

---

38. Cort, "Beloved Prince," 142–49.

39. McAfee to Cole, September 11, 1931, PHS; "Mrs. W. G. McClure," December 1935, PUA.

40. M. J. McClure to McAfee, December 22, 1930; M. J. McClure to friends, October 20, 1932, PHS.

disposition, McClure read too much into her interactions with Prince Mahidol and other Thai royals and nobles because she desired them to be saved. Both McClure and McAfee seemed to have found difficulty in believing that modern, intelligent Buddhists like the royals they encountered might not go to heaven. In the case of McClure, she likely believed the work of Christ was necessary to go to heaven, but the suggestion that public profession of Christ was unnecessary for salvation prompted accusations of modernism from her friends. The possibility of salvation outside formal church structures was not necessarily a modernist idea though it apparently reminded McClure's friends of the religious relativism that was associated with modernism. The ponderings of McClure and McAfee, however, do seem to foreshadow later twentieth-century developments in fulfillment theology, namely an inclusivist theory that adherents of other religions were saved through the work of Christ but were unaware that it was Christ who was saving them.[41] As the modernization gap between so-called "civilized" and "heathen" nations was rapidly closing in the early twentieth century, perceptions of the boundaries of the company of the saved were blurring, calling into question the assumed eternal destiny of non-Western adherents of other religions who increasingly looked, thought, and acted like modern Westerners, except they did not identify as Christian.

CHANGING APPROACHES TO EVANGELISM AND SPEAKING ABOUT BUDDHISM

In addition to modification to thinking about eternal destiny and missionary motivations, changes in the perception of non-Christian religions also impacted the way in which missionaries in Thailand spoke about Buddhism and conducted evangelism. In the late nineteenth and early twentieth centuries, non-Western peoples were increasingly aware of how they were being perceived in the West and they were not always happy with Western depictions of them. In Thailand, as discussed in chapter 4, elite Thai were consciously trying to cultivate a modern, civilized image of themselves in order to garner respect, both internationally and among their own people. With the rise of nationalistic feeling at the start of the twentieth century, Buddhism was promoted as a mark of Thai identity and Thai Buddhists became more sensitive to criticisms of their

---

41. Race, *Christians and Religious Pluralism*, 38–69; Bosch, *Transforming Mission*, 490–93.

religion. During this time period, missionary modes of speaking about Buddhism and Buddhists underwent changes and both conservatives and liberals became increasingly conscious of the need to speak respectfully about, and with, non-Christians among whom they ministered. Though theological convictions influenced the ways and extent to which the content of the Christian message was proclaimed, there was a general trend among missionaries towards greater respect and consideration in communication with those of other faiths.

A helpful window into changing missionary approaches to evangelism in Thailand is found in the viewpoint of Prince Damrong Rajanubhab. Born in 1862 to King Mongkut (r. 1851-1868), Damrong held many high government positions under successive kings and played a key role in modernizing educational and administrative reforms.[42] Damrong kept himself apprised of the work of the American Presbyterian mission and maintained a correspondence with mission leaders, both in Thailand and at the Board of Foreign Missions in New York. Owing to the good relationship he had with the American missionaries, Damrong was invited to write an introductory chapter to an edited volume commemorating the centenary of Protestant missions in Thailand in 1928.[43] As the only non-missionary and only non-Christian contributor to the book, Damrong appreciated the opportunity to publish his thoughts on missionary work in his country. A self-described "staunch Buddhist," Damrong used his chapter to express appreciation for the contributions to education and medicine that missionaries made to his country, to recall clever Thai Buddhist answers to missionary apologetics, and to detail the changes in missionary evangelistic approaches to Buddhism that he observed over the years. Damrong recalled his first encounter with an American missionary as a ten-year-old boy studying at a royally established "English school" within the palace grounds. The missionary, a "tall spare man with a beard similar to the traditional Uncle Sam himself" occasionally preached outside the school near the playground, distributing books and pamphlets, and talking with those who would engage him. Damrong remembered that he would say something to the effect of "Do you not know that your religion is wrong, and can only lead to hell?" This question alternatively disgusted and attracted listeners, some of whom mockingly retorted, "What have we to do to avoid hell?" Despite

---

42. Diskul, "Damrong Rajanubhab."
43. See Damrong, "Introductory Chapter," 1-15.

such an aggressive approach, Damrong and his friends were intrigued by this man and eventually worked up the courage to talk to him. Unusual though he was, Damrong recalled,

> I was impressed by the manner and the words with which he argued his points on religious matters, and the absence of anger when his arguments were sharply questioned. It was thus that at ten years of age, I first made friends with a missionary.

Over the years, Damrong came to know many missionaries and thought that, compared to the early pioneers, the current generation of missionaries had progressed in learning how to talk about Buddhism in relation to Christianity. Though mission schools were popular and well-respected by the late 1920s, Damrong attributed low attendance at the first missionary schools to their attitude toward Buddhism:

> If truth be told, the early missionaries were not well advised in picking out and criticizing severely what they thought were the faults of Buddhism. They took pains to show contempt for the religion of the land, and thus created the natural impression that their schools were opened for the ultimate purpose of teaching the youths of the country to despise the faith of their fathers. It was in consequence of such attitude on their part that the early missionary schools did not thrive to the extent that they do to-day.

Nevertheless, Damrong did not want to be too critical of the missionaries and attributed their aggressive attitude to generational difference. He judged that in the past "the attitude of men in Siam, be they Buddhists or Christians, was less liberal than it has since become." The previous generation were more "apt to indulge in fault-finding and other forms of malice against all faiths which were not their own" and overlooked the good points of other religions. Yet somehow that did not prevent their friendship and general good will towards each other.

In considering the progress of mission work in 1928, Damrong attributed its success, especially in educational and medical work, to a change in attitude among the missionaries:

> The reason appears to me to be this: that the missionaries, having lived long enough in Siam, have come to appreciate the character of her inhabitants, and have changed their methods to suit such character. Thus, instead of abusing Buddhism as a first step to the extolling of Christianity, they set about to exhibit

> Christian virtue, and thus inspire faith in a religion which possesses such good points. Aggressive works have been abandoned in favour of a gentler method, and the results must surely be more satisfactory from the missionary view-point.

Damrong's chapter in the centenary volume on Protestant missions presents an overall positive and appreciatory view of missionary work in Thailand and gives the impression that objectionable missionary engagement with Buddhism was a thing of the past. However, tensions still existed between Thai Buddhists and missionaries, and between missionaries of different convictions, over the proper approach to inter-religious communication in the modern era.

A few years after Damrong penned his magnanimous assessment of missionary work in Thailand, he summoned mission leaders to account for an evangelistic tract that he felt insulted Buddhism.[44] The tract in question was one of the pieces of literature that missionary Paul Fuller and his Thai co-workers Boon Mark Gittisarn and Nai Kitch were using to evangelize in the city streets of Bangkok. Fuller and associates distributed in great quantities a Scripture portion that included the books of Genesis and Luke. Tucked inside this Scripture portion was a tract about salvation penned thirty years previously by the late APM Thailand missionary John A. Eakin, father of Paul Eakin. This tract had been approved for publication by the Literature Committee of the APM Thailand mission and used extensively for many years. Despite decades of use without incident, in 1931 the Literature Committee decided to not republish this title and discarded it along with other older materials, at least some of which were retired due to "objectionable parts." Paul Fuller, however, was not aware of any potential problems with the tract and took it upon himself to reprint it for use in his own evangelism.[45]

In a letter to Cleland McAfee, Fuller told the Board secretary about the unfortunate incident with Damrong and quoted in translation the objectionable part of the tract, underlining the phrase that the prince found most distasteful:

> God (before the ten commandments were given) was pleased to teach the hearts of men and exhorted them to give up their sins. After that He came down to earth and gave the ten

---

44. A version of this account of Prince Damrong's objection to a tract appears in Dahlfred, "Missionary Communication," 45–54.

45. Eakin to McAfee, July 6, 1931, PHS.

commandments which were to warn the hearts of men to know good and evil, but mankind did not obey the commandments of God. Several hundreds of years afterwards Somenakodom, that is the Lord Buddha came and proclaimed a new way of salvation: that man should make merit and accumulate merit for himself in order to be able to escape from sin; but God in Heaven observed and beheld that Buddhists were tempted into wrong and fell into perishing just the same (likewise). Then God was greatly distressed and <u>could not endure it</u> (this phrase underlined by me, the offensive phrase in particular.) and He determined in his heart to come to this earth and provide the way of salvation for mankind according to the promise which He had proclaimed many hundreds of years before. Accordingly, He came to earth and was born as a man in the village of Bethlehem.[46]

Though Fuller underlined the part of the tract Damrong found objectionable, he did not specify why he objected to it. It is possible Damrong interpreted the tract to mean God could not endure Buddhists; or maybe Damrong was upset that the tract implied a weakness in Buddhism. The precise nature of the offense is unclear. Whatever the case may have been, the missionaries first became aware of Prince Damrong's objection to this tract when he summoned Dr. George B. McFarland to the palace and asked whom he should deal with as a representative of the mission "concerning the matter and method of propagating the Christian religion both in print and by word of mouth." McFarland in turn took the matter to Paul Eakin, executive secretary of the mission. Eakin immediately realized the seriousness of the matter and prepared a written statement of explanation and apology, with the assistance of Mrs. Bertha Blount McFarland and Mrs. Geraldine Fuller, sister-in-law of Paul Fuller. Eakin, together with Dr. McFarland, then secured an audience with Prince Damrong and presented the letter to him. Eakin wanted to reassure the prince that it was the "clear intention" of the mission "to do nothing that could be construed in any way as unfair to the Government or people of Siam."[47] Strictly speaking, the tract spoke of Buddhism, and not the government or people of Siam, but due to the intimate connection between Buddhism and Siamese identity, Eakin and McFarland may have been concerned Damrong would interpret an offense against Buddhism as an affront to the Siamese people and government as well.

46. Fuller to McAfee, September 1931, PHS.
47. Eakin to Mission, July 16, 1931, PUA.

Eakin reported that the prince was "very kind and gracious in his response" and was glad that the mission's policy had not changed. However, Damrong took the opportunity to lecture the missionaries concerning the attitude of King Prajadhipok and the government of Thailand towards other religions and religious communication. The objectionable content in the tract reprinted by Fuller was not an isolated incident and the prince "cited several cases which had come to his attention, where there had been ground for the charge of unfairness and misrepresentation."[48] The prince made clear that Thailand's policy of religious toleration did not allow for what he termed "free-thinkers," namely people who tear down other religions in order to win adherents to their own. "The King," explained Damrong, "is interested in other religions because He realizes that many of His subjects get real comfort from their own faiths" but would "grow very intolerant toward any attempt to defame or belittle Buddhism." Eakin reported that the Prince thus recommended that a "code should be prepared and submitted to each missionary who comes and every national worker in our Mission, making clear our message and a method of presenting that message that absolutely omits odious comparisons and misrepresentations." Furthermore, he asked that "special care be taken in the selection of missionaries that are sent to Siam to ensure that they will be willing to see this view point and respect it in their preaching and work in the schools and hospitals."[49] Eakin apparently took this admonition to heart and wrote to McAfee, recommending that

> the Candidate department should be warned to be very careful in selection of missionaries that come to Siam. There is certainly no place for any missionary that so feels the superiority of Christianity that disparaging remarks about Buddhism are natural to him in his presenting of the Gospel. As someone has said, "One can have back-bone without bristles."[50]

While the Candidate department of the Board may have been able to act on Eakin's recommendation, there was little they could do about missionaries and Thai Christians already in Thailand. Although Eakin's letter to his fellow APM Thailand missionaries did not reveal anything about the "other cases" that Damrong cited, it is possible that at least one of them involved Paul Fuller's co-worker Boon Mark Gittisarn. As

---

48. Eakin to Mission, July 16, 1931, PUA.
49. Eakin to McAfee, July 6, 1931, PHS.
50. Eakin to McAfee, July 6, 1931, PHS.

a fundamentalist-leaning missionary evangelist, Fuller took a liking to the bold and passionate Boon Mark and encouraged him to study at the seminary in Chiang Mai. Speaking of Boon Mark, Paul Eakin recalled many years later that

> While there [in Chiang Mai], he got into trouble with the local Buddhists, because of his unjust criticisms, and the matter was reported to Prince Damrong, who appealed to me to stop the lad, in the interest of good relations between the Mission and Government. I did my best to reason with the boy, but did not get far. He continued his tactics, saying that he must "obey God rather than man."[51]

In terms of their approach to evangelism, Boon Mark and Fuller had compatible outlooks. Boon Mark returned to Bangkok after completing his seminary studies and resumed working with Fuller. Their approach to talking about Buddhism was bolder and less concerned with Thai Buddhist sensitivities than that of Paul Eakin and some other APM Thailand missionaries. In 1935, educational missionary Kenneth Wells in Chiang Mai sent Paul Eakin a clipping from some Sunday school material that Boon Mark had prepared. The clipping that Wells found objectionable, and assumed Eakin would too, was a strongly worded admonition to dispose of idols, namely Buddhist statues or amulets, which could not give life, and instead to turn to Jesus Christ. Those who worshiped such statues would become like them, having no life, soul, love, or mercy. Wells asked Eakin, "Is there no way of censoring S.S. stuff like the enclosed? Every once in a while, some wild statement which weakens the cause creeps in. In this respect Kru [Boon] Mark and Paul Fuller are a bad combination. Surely it is not necessary to anger those whom we would win."[52]

---

51. Eakin, "Influence of Foreign Evangelists," PUA.

52. "Kru" means "teacher" and was a common title for Thai pastors and full-time Christian workers. Wells to Eakin, March 4, 1935, PUA.

210 Conservative in Theology, Liberal in Spirit

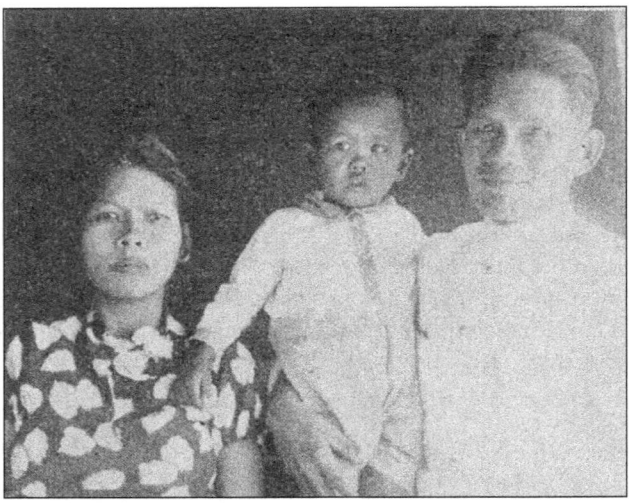

Boon Mark Gittisarn with wife Muan and child, 1938
(Courtesy of the Presbyterian Historical Society, Philadelphia)

CONCLUSION

In this chapter, several aspects of APM Thailand missionary attitudes toward evangelism and the Christian relationship to Buddhism in Thailand have been examined. As Paul Eakin indicated in his comments at the 1933 Siam Conference, the APM Thailand mission in the early twentieth century was in transition. Though a conservative theological majority prevailed in the mission, perceptions of the Christian relationship to Buddhism were changing and there was reconsideration of the priority and prominence of formerly assumed beliefs. Though attitudes and approaches to non-Christian religions were changing among missionaries of all theological persuasions, the ways and extent to which they were changing were not identical. There was a spectrum of convictions and approaches to evangelism. Though few seem to have abandoned it entirely, for some missionaries the eternal destiny of non-Christians had less importance in the missionary motive. As the modernization gap between so-called "civilized" and "heathen" countries was rapidly closing, it became more difficult for some missionaries to believe Thai Buddhists who increasingly dressed and acted like Westerners would really be eternally separated from God. Missionaries were adjusting the ways that they spoke about Buddhism and presented the

Christian message even as Thai Buddhists, especially those who were part of the elite, became more concerned about how they were being presented in the public square. These sensitivities, as well as developing cultural, political, and theological trends, contributed to divergent understandings of the nature and methods of evangelism in mission schools, a topic that will be examined in the next chapter.

9

Contested Approaches to Evangelism in Mission Schools

THE APM THAILAND MISSION, as discussed previously, rejected the Laymen's Report deprecation of verbal proclamation of the gospel and reaffirmed the need to tell people the gospel alongside social service work intended to display the love of Christ. The missionaries in Thailand went on record in affirming the need for both word and deed in faithful evangelism. However, when it came to the actual practice of evangelism, especially in mission schools, not all APM missionaries prioritized verbal proclamation of the gospel nearly as much as they did social service ministry. Though Lucy Starling did not say so in her published account of the mission's executive committee's discussion of the Laymen's Report, there was more diversity of views and approaches to evangelism among APM Thailand missionaries than would have been evident to a casual reader of *Siam Outlook*.[1] This chapter will examine varied ideas about the purposes, content, and methods of evangelism in the APM Thailand mission in relation to the role of mission schools in evangelism. As part of this analysis, modernist leanings will be highlighted where they may have contributed to the missionaries' views on the connection between evangelistic and educational ministries.

---

1. Starling, "Re-Thinking Missions," 120–27.

THE PURPOSES OF MISSION EDUCATION

The foundation of schools by Protestant missionaries was common throughout the nineteenth and twentieth centuries though the purposes for which they were founded were multiple. At the 1910 World Missionary Conference in Edinburgh, Commission III reported on the state of mission education in the Protestant mission world, based in part on responses they received from field missionaries in numerous countries. Summarizing the results of their investigation, the Commission found there were three primary purposes of mission education then current. The first was the use of education for direct evangelization of students, and sometimes parents and relatives of students. Missionary instructors hoped students would profess faith in Christ as a result of hearing the gospel at mission schools. The second purpose was developing and training leaders for indigenous churches. A third purpose was diffusion of Christian values through society even if there were few to no conversions as a result. The Commission referred to these three purposes as the evangelistic, edificatory, and leavening purposes of mission education. A fourth purpose was also included in the report although all but a minority regarded it as merely a supplementary purpose. This fourth aim was a philanthropic or humanitarian desire to "promote the general welfare of the people" apart from any promotion of the Christian faith. Prioritization of this fourth purpose was rare in 1910 but not unheard of, especially among those of a theologically liberal orientation. Regarding the effectiveness of mission schools in achieving these purposes, the results were mixed. While some missionaries reported splendid results from mission schools in achieving one or more of the three primary purposes listed by the Commission, others could not yet report success. In some cases, their hopes were greatly disappointed.[2]

Largely paralleling the findings of the 1910 World Missionary Conference, APM Thailand missionary discussion of mission education also focused on the relative priority of the evangelistic, edificatory, and leavening purposes of mission schools. In addition to these three, a fourth purpose featured prominently in discussion of mission schools and evangelism in Thailand, namely the education of Christian children. In order to conserve the biological growth that came through existing converts, some missionaries prioritized the education of children from Christian families, lest they be lost to the surrounding Buddhist society. The APM

---

2. Stanley, *World Missionary Conference*, 167–204.

Thailand missionaries, however, did not see disinterested benevolence or mere humanitarianism as a primary purpose of their schools. Nevertheless, this purpose was uppermost in the minds of elite Thai who lent verbal and financial support to mission institutions. In 1922, Prince Damrong Rajanubhab expressed gratitude to the APM Thailand mission for the "great service" they rendered to his country through their educational and medical work which he understood to have been "impelled by a desire to render a disinterested service to the Siamese people."[3] Similarly, at the 1928 gala celebration of the centenary of Protestant missions in Thailand, King Prajadhipok explained why Christian missionaries were allowed in his Buddhist nation. Citing their pioneering work in women's education and introduction of modern medicine, the king said the missionaries had done a lot to help the country.[4]

FINANCIAL AND STAFFING CHALLENGES FOR MISSIONS SCHOOLS IN THAILAND

In Thailand, intra-mission discussion of the purpose of mission schools was necessarily connected to discussion of evangelism because the schools absorbed a significant amount of the mission's limited personnel and funding. Since the APM Thailand's official main purpose was "to make the Lord Jesus Christ known to all men as their Divine Savior and to persuade them to become His disciples," diversion of resources away from direct evangelistic work and towards the schools had to be justified in light of that main purpose.[5] As discussed in the survey of Thailand mission work in chapter 5, schools of various types were a part of the APM Thailand missionaries' work since its early days in the mid-nineteenth century. However, following the turn of the century, there was a marked increase in the mission's educational emphasis. In a 1938 statistical survey of world missions, APM Thailand missionary John L. Eakin, brother of Paul, provided the following statistics on mission school growth.[6]

---

3. McClure to Brown, November 15, 1922, PHS.
4. "Protestant Missions Centenary."
5. PCUSA, *Manual 1922*, 5.
6. See Eakin, "Siam," 286–87.

Year	No. of Schools	No. of Students
1911	37	800
1925	53	3000
1938	65	5569

Growth of APM Thailand Mission Schools

The majority of these schools were primary schools though a handful included some high school coursework. None were at the university level although a couple bore the name "college." If there had been a steady increase of personnel and funding during this period to all departments of APM Thailand mission work, namely evangelistic, educational, and medical, there may have been little discussion about the relative priority of schools. However, due to the Great Depression, the APM Thailand mission and APM missions in other countries saw reductions of funding and personnel provided to them by the Board of Foreign Missions. Compared to more industrialized nations, the Great Depression had less of an impact on Thai society due to its largely agrarian, locally based economy. The APM Thailand mission, however, was hit hard because it received its funding from the United States.[7] Economic austerity meant not only reduced funding for mission institutions, but also reduced personnel. Some missionaries were not returned to Thailand after their furloughs, and the Board sent fewer new missionaries to the field. For various reasons, among which economics was not the least, the Thailand mission experienced a decline in missionary personnel from 102 in 1929 to only 68 in 1939, an overall loss of 33 percent of their entire missionary force.[8] With these realities at play, APM Thailand leaders had to decide where to allocate their limited personnel and funding. Missionaries varyingly committed to direct evangelistic work, to educational work, and to medical work all sought more funds and personnel to strengthen their own ministries and those of the mission stations where they worked. In this context, decisions were made by APM Thailand leaders to favor mission schools as the best places to invest limited resources for the evangelization of Thailand. Though the financial crisis ought to have logically led away from an emphasis on resource-intensive institutional work, APM Thailand leaders continued and strengthened their commitment to mission schools in the 1930s. As seen in the chart

7. Andrews, *Siam—Second Rural Economic Survey*, 2:1–2; Smith, *Siamese*, 178–80.
8. Wells, *History*, 142.

on the "Growth of APM Thailand Mission Schools," the overall number of schools increased over the period from 1911 to 1938, the rate of increase only slowing slightly in the wake of the Great Depression. Missionary personnel and indigenous Thai workers paid by the mission were increasingly channeled into the school work in order to maintain mission institutions. Numerous missionaries, Thai Christian ministers, and other Thai staff assigned to evangelistic ministries were reassigned to school work or obligated to use at least part of their time to fill in at understaffed schools.[9] An analysis of the Thailand mission's annual "force list," or personnel requests to the Board, from 1928 to 1940 shows requests for educational personnel regularly topped the list.[10] Each year's force list included 10 to 12 requests for particular types of missionaries, sometimes with specific locations and institutions listed. In 1932, APM Thailand missionary Richard W. Post remarked with disapproval on the situation, noting that "we rarely get more than 5 [new] missionaries per year and evangelistic workers are rarely in the top 5 requests. From 1927-1932, there were no evangelistic workers in the top 5. And when the requests higher up the list are supplied, the [requests for] evangelistic workers down the bottom are not moved up."

Although a desire to maintain and grow the schools seems to have been the main factor in prioritization of requests for educational missionaries, Paul Eakin's dissatisfaction with the evangelistic missionaries the Board previously sent may have also been a factor.[11] Evangelistic missionaries Paul Fuller, arriving in 1923, and Kenneth Landon, arriving in 1927, were among those workers with whom Eakin had substantial differences. Post, however, attributed this prioritization of educational over evangelistic personnel requests to the belief that "the school must have a missionary, [but] the evangelistic work can be carried on, without." In Post's view, the evangelistic work had not carried on very well at all because a disproportionate amount of funding and personnel were dedicated to mission schools. In a document prepared for the Board's 1933 conference to discuss APM mission work in Thailand, Post provided

9. Smith, *Siamese*, 160.
10. "Meeting of Exec. Cmte.," June 2, 1928; Brown to Siam Mission, "Board Letter #325," June 18, 1929; Eakin to Exec. Cmte., June 6, 1931; Eakin to Exec. Cmte., June 4, 1932; Eakin to Exec. Cmte, June 15, 1935; "Actions Taken By The Exec. Cmte. in Bangkok, June 23-26, 1937"; Eakin to Exec. Cmte., June 29, 1940, PUA; Geraldine Fuller to Exec. Cmte., July 4, 1938, WCSC.
11. Eakin, "Notes on Siam Conference, 1933," PUA.

statistics for distribution of APM Thailand missionaries among different categories of work for the year 1932, as represented in the pie-chart below.[12] Post's numbers differed somewhat from those cited elsewhere by Paul Eakin and Bertha McFarland and it was admitted by all that an accurate assessment of distribution of workers was hard to obtain because of missionary arrivals and departures, as well as missionaries designated to evangelism who also taught part-time in schools.[13]

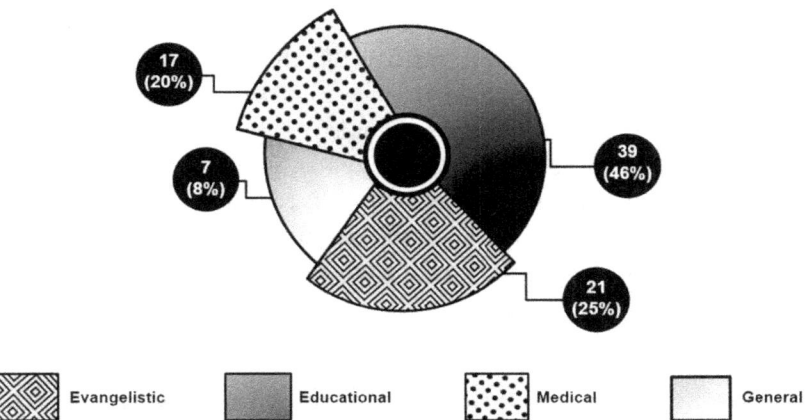

Distribution of APM Thailand Missionaries, 1932

- Evangelistic
- Educational
- Medical
- General

Distribution of personnel was a point of tension in intra-mission discussion because it was connected with how missionaries thought evangelism should be pursued. A number of missionaries in direct evangelistic work, including Post, interpreted the channeling of money and personnel to the schools as the channeling of money away from evangelism. Thus, a key point of discussion was the contribution of mission schools to achieving the evangelistic purpose of the APM Thailand mission. An examination of the educational policy of the mission will both provide context for understanding tensions over the disbursement of personnel and frame subsequent discussion of whether mission schools were fulfilling their evangelistic purpose.

---

12. Post, "Views Regarding Mission Work in Siam," July 28, 1932, PUA.

13. Eakin, "Notes on Siam Conference, 1933," PUA; McFarland, "Evangelism—Extensive or Intensive?," 8–9.

EDUCATIONAL POLICY OF THE APM THAILAND MISSION

Among the APM Thailand missionaries, there were none who denied the value of mission schools yet there was a divergence between stated policy and its implementation. The missionaries were optimistic and ambitious in what they hoped to accomplish with their schools, but they could not do it all, and different missionaries weighted the value of the stated goals of mission schools differently. There were differences in educational and evangelistic philosophy between individual missionaries, and also between the Laos mission in northern Thailand and the Siam mission in southern Thailand.[14] As mentioned in chapter 5, the two missions were administratively joined together under the name of the Siam mission in 1921, and were eventually rebranded as the Thailand mission in 1939.[15] However, formal unification of the two missions did not erase longstanding differences in philosophy of ministry between them. In 1928, for an edited volume to commemorate the centennial of Protestant missions in Thailand, APM missionary Kenneth Wells reiterated a 1912 summary statement on the educational goals of the Thailand mission which papered over the diversity that existed on the ground. He stated:

> The purpose of our mission schools should be recognized as four-fold:
>
> 1. to provide Christian education for the Christian youth;
>
> 2. To win non-Christian boys and girls to Christ through education in a strongly Christian atmosphere and by direct Christian instruction;
>
> 3. To permeate society with Christian ideals and standards, recognizing that there may be many students in our schools who will not be prepared to profess themselves Christian but will carry from their school experience the Christian viewpoint and an understanding and sympathetic attitude toward Christianity; and
>
> 4. To discover and to train Christian leaders—not only for the churches, but for positions in the government, business and professional life.[16]

---

14. In this context, "southern Thailand" included central Thailand and Bangkok.

15. Brown to North and South Siam Missions, March 9, 1920, PHS; Eakin to Exec. Cmte., September 23, 1939, PUA.

16. McFarland, *Historical Sketch*, 209.

These publicly stated goals of the American Presbyterian mission's educational work in Thailand were very similar to the purposes of mission education cited in the Commission III report at the 1910 World Missionary Conference in Edinburgh, referenced earlier. However, the practical prioritization of these goals differed. Views and practices of individual missionaries will be discussed momentarily, but it is first helpful to recognize the broad differences of educational philosophy between north and south Thailand.

From its foundation in 1867, the Laos mission in northern Thailand was heavily influenced by Daniel McGilvary who emphasized itinerant evangelism and believed the main purpose of mission schools was the education of the children of converts in order to conserve the biological growth of the church.[17] From 1902, there was a concerted effort in northern Thailand to found schools in all the locations where there were churches. In addition to older mission schools in Chiang Mai, by 1906 there were schools in the northern cities of Lampang, Phrae, Chiang Rai and Nan. These schools were founded in conjunction with Presbyterian mission stations in each of those locations.[18] Additionally, a number of small rural schools were partially managed and funded by the churches themselves and did not have a missionary present. The best students from these small schools might be sent to Prince Royal's College (for boys) or Dara Wittaya Academy (for girls) in Chiang Mai for further training so they might return home again and become school teachers themselves. By and large, these schools in the north were for the children of Thai Christians. Tuition fees for mission schools in the north were heavily subsidized by the American Presbyterian mission and any Christian child whose parents wanted him to go to a mission school could go. Fees were paid according to the family's means and many children studied for free. There were a small number of Buddhist students in the mission schools in the north, but they paid full price.[19] The mission schools in the north made considerable strides in accomplishing the first goal of mission schools cited above by Wells, namely "to provide Christian education for the Christian youth." However, as the northern mission schools had few Buddhist students, they were less effective in winning non-Christian youth to Christ or spreading Christian

---

17. Swanson, *Krischak*, 126–27; Bassett, "Evangelism—Extensive or Intensive?," 18–19.

18. McFarland, *Historical Sketch*, 214–15.

19. Taylor, "Missionary in Siam," 164, 76–77.

values through the broader society through the lives of non-Christian students who were influenced by their schooling. In meeting the fourth goal, "discovering and training Christian leaders," the northern schools were more successful in supplying schools and government with well-educated young people than they were at producing leaders for church and evangelistic ministry. However, many church leaders in the north benefitted from time spent at mission schools.

In contrast, the Siam mission (later South Siam mission) centered in Bangkok had a long-standing commitment to emphasizing mission schools in pursuing evangelization.[20] Though the first mission schools provided free education to students, the southern mission eventually shifted its policy to emphasize self-support for both churches and mission institutions. Bangkok Christian College and other schools became self-supporting through charging tuition fees to all students. However, because many Christians did not have the ability to pay school fees, the vast majority of students were Buddhists.[21] APM missionary Hugh Taylor, who worked in north Thailand, noted that mission schools attracted young people who wanted jobs that would require reading, writing, and speaking English. He said that they took what they wanted from their schooling in order to get white-collar jobs and left behind what they didn't want, namely Bible training that they were compelled to take. Though the schools in the south were successful in achieving self-support, the number of converts that came from the schools was very small. Though the missionaries in the south did not see their investment in the schools translate into church membership, Taylor remarked with dismay that "the Mission held to its policy in Hope" that the students who passed through the schools without converting would someday become Christians.[22] Allen Bassett, who worked both in the north and the south, summarized the positive and negative outcomes of the policies of the two missions as follows. The south had few Christians, but they were relatively stable. They were leaders in the Church of Christ in Thailand and among its chief supporters. However, they were not conspicuous for their evangelistic fervor and had an inferiority complex that came with their small numbers. The north had the

---

20. Hugh Taylor said this emphasis was already in place when he arrived as a new missionary in 1888. Taylor, "Missionary in Siam," 163.

21. B. McFarland to McAfee, April 12, 1932; May Palmer to Friends, February 10, 1933, PHS.

22. Taylor, "Missionary in Siam," 162–77.

majority of Christians in the country, though they were less developed in faith and practice. They were still dominated by a desire to please the missionary and provided almost no financial support to the movement. That notwithstanding, they had an evangelistic spirit that was winning their neighbors to Christ in much larger numbers as compared to the south.[23] Even after the northern and southern missions were joined in 1921, the distinct educational and evangelistic policies persisted and contributed to tensions over funding and personnel assignments in the wake of budget tightening due to the Great Depression. Some in the south thought there were too many free pupils in the schools, thus hampering efforts at self-support and fostering undue dependency on mission funds.[24] However, although northern missionaries acknowledged the lack of financial independence was a problem, hefty subsidies to schools and churches seemed justified to some missionaries in light of the evangelistic results that had been achieved.

With a broad overview of north-south differences in educational policy in mind, the spectrum of views among APM Thailand missionaries towards the purposes of mission schools, in particular their evangelistic purpose, can now be examined. The value of educating Christian children and training Christian leaders through mission schools was widely acknowledged among the missionaries. Both conservative and modernist-leaning missionaries recognized these two purposes as legitimate, and these purposes thus require little comment. The areas in which modernist leanings had their greatest impact was on the concept and practice of evangelism in schools and the relative importance of the schools as centers of diffusion of Christian values in Thai society. As such, the following section focuses on competing concepts of evangelism in the schools and diffusion of Christian values as an alternative metric of mission success in lieu of conversions.

COMPETING VISIONS OF EVANGELISM IN MISSION SCHOOLS

APM Thailand missionaries all agreed that mission schools should function evangelistically and they wanted to see Buddhist students come to faith in Christ as a result of their exposure to Christianity at

---

23. Bassett, "Evangelism—Extensive or Intensive?," 18–19.
24. "Report of Bangkok Station Meeting," November 18, 1931; Eakin et al., "Report of the Survey Committee," October 1934, PUA.

mission schools. However, there were divergent views among the missionaries about how students should be evangelized in the schools and what exactly constituted evangelism. On the one hand, some missionaries believed it was essential that verbal teaching of the gospel message inside and outside of school hours and invitations to put faith in Christ should be an explicit part of the mission school experience. Other missionaries, however, favored a more indirect method that pinned its evangelistic hope on students being impressed with the Christian living of their teachers and with more generalized moral and religious exhortations during chapel times.

Those in favor of direct evangelization wanted this to happen in Bible classes, regular chapel times, special events with visiting speakers, and through regular personal contact with missionary and Thai Christian members of the school staff. Ideally, staff contact with students would also provide opportunities to share the gospel message with parents of students. In practice, this was difficult to achieve. Lucy Niblock, who taught at Dara Wittaya Academy in Chiang Mai from 1920 to 1941, confessed that she was often too busy with school duties to seek evangelistic opportunities with students. "So much time," wrote Niblock, "must be spent on all school subjects, as well as on teachers, coolies, and accounts, that there is little left for even intensive evangelism."[25] Although she did try to make her weekly chapel talks "distinctly religious and not merely moral and entertaining," she admitted that she could not control what other teaching staff said in their chapel talks. Hinting that the messages given by other teachers fell short evangelistically, Niblock said, "I can do little more than suggest the proper way and make known my own determination to show forth Christ. They must make their own chapel talks."[26] Johanne Christensen, who ran a mission training school for nurses in Bangkok, thought a lot more should be done in terms of following up evangelistically in mission institutions. Faye Kilpatrick, long-time teacher at Wattana Wittaya Academy, confessed that most of the missionaries, including herself, were "guilty of using some of our time for activities that are non-productive evangelistically." Kilpatrick believed in doing personal evangelism with

---

25. In APM Thailand mission discussions, intensive evangelism was defined as evangelism that focused on a small group of people over an extended period of time. Extensive evangelism was evangelism that proclaimed the gospel broadly to many people, often over a large geographic area.

26. Niblock, "Evangelism—Extensive or Intensive?," 17–18; Eakin, "Biographical Notes on Lucy Niblock," 1956, PUA.

her students but admitted a disjunction between "the pattern of our present behavior" and what she and other missionaries said they believed. In other words, she thought that the missionaries all believed in doing evangelism in the schools, but they were not all doing it. At the very least, they were not doing it very well.[27]

Paul Fuller believed that the schools could be used effectively for evangelism but his own efforts to do so at Bangkok Christian College (BCC) were met with opposition. Fuller rented a house close to the school and taught some classes at BCC but did not want to become full-time faculty because he wanted to have time for itinerant evangelistic work in greater Bangkok. Marion B. Palmer, missionary principal of the school, gave Fuller permission to teach only a few hours per week so he could have the rest of the time free for outside evangelistic work. Palmer's approval notwithstanding, Fuller was accused of trying to avoid the routine duties of teachers at BCC and only wanting to teach Bible. Some said he taught too much Bible, a claim which Fuller answered with the rhetorical question, "Can anyone know too much Bible?" It is probable that Fuller thought that some of the opposition to his evangelism and Bible teaching at BCC came from fellow missionaries with modernist sympathies. As such, Fuller affirmed in his defense, "As to doctrine I am open-minded yet conservative. No one has asked a question yet about evolution. We are too busy learning what is in the Book."[28] Fuller claimed that he followed the prescribed curriculum and if anyone had doubts, he welcomed them to come sit in on his classes.[29] Though Fuller heartily endorsed the value of mission schools for evangelism and training church leaders, some claimed he was against the schools and wanted to follow the policy of faith missions that had no educational or medical work. This accusation apparently came from a misunderstanding of Fuller's assertion there was an imbalance between educational and evangelistic work within the Thailand mission. Because of this belief, Fuller spoke against a proposed expansion of BCC until there was greater equality between resources devoted to evangelistic and educational work. Ultimately, due to these accusations and friction with the school's principal, Fuller agreed to withdraw from his work with BCC and devote himself to full-time

---

27. Kilpatrick, "Evangelism—Extensive or Intensive?," 29–30; Christensen, "Evangelism—Extensive or Intensive?," 4–35; Eakin, "Biographical Notes on Johanne Christensen," 1939; Eakin, "Biographical Notes on Jennie Faye Kilpatrick Yoder," 1962, PUA.

28. Fuller's reference to "the Book" likely means the Bible.

29. P. Fuller to Friends, July 16, 1927, PUA.

evangelistic work in Bangkok upon return from his upcoming furlough.[30] While it is possible that those who opposed Fuller were not against direct evangelism in schools per se, but merely against the way Fuller evangelized, Fuller was not the only APM missionary who felt that his desire to evangelize in the mission schools was frustrated by other missionaries. William McClure, husband of Mary Jane McClure, taught at BCC after many years of doing itinerant evangelism and felt he was wasting his time teaching algebra to Buddhist boys who did not listen. There were so few Christian students in the school that there was not a sufficiently Christian environment to influence them, a marked difference from the approach of schools in the north. As such, he resigned from the school and returned to direct evangelistic work.[31] Fuller reported that Margaret McCord did educational work for many years until she got frustrated with the lack of results in evangelizing students and "struck out on her own" to start a Women's Bible training school. She felt unsupported by fellow missionaries in her evangelistic efforts and, Fuller reported with chagrin, she was laughed at for leaving her teaching post to start a Bible training school for women. The Bangkok station eventually sold the property she was using for her women's Bible training school without providing alternative provision. Nevertheless, she continued on with the school which bore fruit evangelistically and only then earned the praise of other missionaries for her evangelistic success.[32] At the Trang station in southern Thailand, missionary Edna Bulkley complained that government exams at the Trang mission school were more important than evangelism because teachers feared that the disapproval of parents would lead to fewer students.[33] As discussed in chapter 7, William Harris of Prince Royal's College in Chiang Mai and Marion Palmer of Bangkok Christian College refused a Burmese gospel team access to their students, which Loren Hanna saw as evidence of hostility to evangelism in mission schools.

Though there is no evidence that any APM Thailand missionaries directly repudiated the use of mission schools for evangelistic purposes, the difficulties Lucy Niblock, Faye Kilpatrick, Paul Fuller and others had in doing evangelism in mission schools highlight several challenges. First, even for those who sought to do direct evangelism in schools, it

30. P. Fuller to friends, July 12, 1927, PUA; Fuller to Mrs. Roys, January 16, 1927; Fuller to Brown, May 2, 1927; Marion Palmer to Brown, June 21, 1927, PHS.

31. Taylor, "Missionary in Siam," 174–76.

32. P. Fuller to Mrs. Roys, January 16, 1927, PHS.

33. Pongudom, "Apologetic and Missionary Proclamation," 43.

was difficult for full-time teachers to find the time to do so and to receive needed support from other staff. Secondly, even though a majority Buddhist student body meant opportunities to present the gospel to non-Christians it also impeded the creation of a school environment that would reflect Christian values. Thirdly, missionaries and Thai staff had various, sometimes divergent, ideas about how to best evangelize students and were influenced by concerns such as governmental and parental approval. These concerns, and perhaps modernist sympathies, contributed to the conviction among some missionaries that a more subtle, long-term, and indirect approach to evangelization of students was both more appropriate and more feasible.

In the nineteenth century, missionaries in Thailand pioneered modern education and were largely free to do as they liked in their schools without government interference. However, in the early twentieth century, the government of Thailand, like governments in other Asian countries, took an increased interest in the education of its people and made concerted efforts at universal education and the establishment of government schools.[34] Along with this rise of educational interest and effort on the part of the government came a desire to have a say in what happened with Buddhist students in Christian schools in Thailand. The government sought to establish quality standards for teachers and curriculum. This made it more difficult to find foreign teachers for the schools because of the Thai language test that they had to pass. It also meant that mission schools must be registered with the government and use the government's curriculum, a development paralleled in China where the government also sought to exert greater control over mission schools.[35] Initially, while the government was in the process of rolling out its curriculum for nationwide usage, mission schools were allowed to continue to use their own curriculum due to their long history and good reputation with the government. However, that was only a transitionary period. By 1936, Kenneth Wells, head of the Thailand mission's educational committee, reported that the government curriculum had now "crystalized into permanent form."[36] In 1941, Mowbray Tate, who

---

34. For more on government pressure on mission schools in other Asian countries, see Stanley, *World Missionary Conference*, 182–83; Hocking, *Re-Thinking Missions*, 140–41; Rostam-Kolayi, "From Evangelizing to Modernizing Iranians," 213–40.

35. Paton and Underhill, "A Survey of the Year 1937—Southeast Asia," 26; Bays, *New History*, 111.

36. Wells, Actions Taken by Exec. Cmte., December 15–21, 1936, PUA.

taught at Bangkok Christian College, reported that the curriculum was the same for all schools in Thailand, both government and private.[37] Mission schools fell under the category of private schools. Though the Thailand mission sought to preserve their schools as Christian schools, they also strove to cooperate with the government as much as possible. In practice, as Donald G. Barnhouse learned on his January 1935 trip to Thailand, discussed in chapter 7, the government curriculum was effectively squeezing Bible teaching out of the school day. Some Bible content could still be taught under the heading of "ethics" but any more than that must be taught outside of school hours.[38] In government schools, the teaching of Buddhism was part of the regular curriculum but this was not required for mission schools, for which the Thailand mission was grateful.[39] Although missionaries sometimes claimed mission schools were not in competition with government schools, the increase of government schools of all levels put pressure on the Thailand mission to re-examine their schools's *raison d'être*.[40] In regions where there were not yet government schools, it was easy to justify mission schools. But in larger towns and cities, government schools with more financial resources and higher teacher salaries called into question the purpose of mission schools. Were they merely replicating what the government was already doing? In order to avoid redundancy, Thailand mission leaders sought to make their educational work contribute something distinctive to Thailand. Firstly, they strove to develop programs for teacher training, a need felt by the Thai government who required ever more qualified teachers for their schools. Secondly, and more importantly in terms of the Thailand mission's stated evangelistic purpose and justifying itself to financial supporters in American churches, the Thailand mission sought to make their schools distinctively Christian. The "Christianness" of the schools might be evaluated in two ways. Firstly, did the schools lead Buddhists to profess the Christian faith and join the church? Secondly, did the schools leaven Thai society with Christian values? The latter will be discussed momentarily but the first was a difficult subject because very few students who entered the schools as Buddhists graduated as Christians. This issue was less relevant in northern schools where most

37. Tate, "Educational Progress," 163.
38. Barnhouse, "Travel Notes," January 12, 1935, PHS.
39. McFarland, *Historical Sketch*, 220.
40. McFarland, *Historical Sketch*, 218–20; Tate, "Educational Progress," 160–68; Hooper to Geraldine Fuller, June 26, 1939, PUA.

students were Christians when they began their studies. Mission schools with majority Christian student bodies fulfilled their evangelistic purpose if students did not wander away from the Christian faith. In the south, the question of the schools' effectiveness in evangelism was more pressing because the majority of students in mission schools were Buddhists. It has already been seen that some missionaries wanted to change this by direct evangelistic activities in the schools but others, including Paul Eakin and Kenneth Wells, preferred a more indirect approach.

Paul Eakin, who wielded significant influence as executive secretary of the Thailand mission from 1930 to the outbreak of the war, was convinced that in areas "where Buddhism is strongly entrenched and organized . . . our best method of extending the Kingdom of God will be the quiet but constant personal contact through our schools." Though Eakin diplomatically acknowledged that direct evangelistic approaches were useful among rural people "under the control of superstition or evil spirits," he firmly believed that "our most successful method here has been the evangelism in our schools, rather than the direct itinerating work."[41] The type of evangelism Eakin seemed to prefer was Christian living and moral example that would impress non-Christians and invite questions rather than making direct appeals to profess faith in Christ. Eakin, whose theological convictions have been discussed previously, thought saving people from hell was an obsolete and antiquated motivation for missions, and did not believe in penal substitutionary atonement, or the transference of guilt for sin from an individual to Christ. As such, he likely lacked the same type of urgency that compelled some of his fellow missionaries who emphasized conversion and favored more direct evangelistic methods.[42] For Eakin, it was not the exclusivity of salvation in Christ that made Christianity unique, but rather the power to enable moral living which would save people from their sins.[43] The way that Eakin conceived of Christianity spreading was through the witness of Christian living. Commenting on the spread of Christianity in the early church, Eakin noted that the church "spread rapidly underground by

---

41. Eakin, "Evangelism—Extensive or Intensive?," 5–7; Smith, *Siamese*, 168; Eakin, *Buddhism*, 62.

42. In his research on missionary candidates in the early twentieth century, Valentin Rabe noted that doing "good was not an imperative for haste or sacrifice in the sense that irrevocable damnation had been." Rabe, *Home Base*, 107.

43. Eakin, "Fundamental Christian Convictions," n.d; Eakin, "My Reasonable Faith," n.d; Eakin, "Sermon Outlines," 1928 to 1931; Eakin, "New Approach," n.d., PUA.

contagion from person to person—by radiance and dynamic. Till pagans asked the secret and wanted it too. Same today. While Christians differ in creeds, there is an underlying life that unites. Church is an extension of the Incarnation." Eakin's thinking on evangelism reflected modernist emphases in theology, previously mentioned, that prioritized incarnation over atonement and religious experience over creeds. While Eakin wanted to talk to Buddhists about Christianity, he seems to have preferred for Buddhists to ask rather than Christians proactively trying to convince them to believe.[44] Though Eakin did not openly reject the evangelistic emphases and methods that some of his more conservative fellow missionaries preferred, his personal convictions were modernist. As such, in his position as the Thailand mission executive secretary Eakin preferred approaches to evangelism in mission schools that sought to influence students towards the Christian faith through the example of Christian living and exaltation of Christian morals rather than potentially offensive direct proclamation of the gospel message of the substitutionary sacrifice of Christ and calls to convert. Kenneth Wells, an educational missionary in Chiang Mai and head of the Thailand mission's educational committee, also seems to have preferred an indirect evangelism of moral example. "Our schools are not bait to bring pupils near enough to hear the Gospel," affirmed Wells, "but a powerful method of presenting the realities and the practical results of the Gospel in human terms and by normal psychological processes to the consciousness of all their students." Wells believed that the largest contribution of the mission to education in Thailand was in "intangible, but indispensable values," namely "the silent contagion of spirit, the desire to serve, concern for character, the spirit of fair play."[45] The language of evangelism as contagion that appeared in both Eakin and Wells's comments also featured in the Laymen's Report. In its summary conclusions, the Laymen's Report affirmed that "the Christian way of life is capable of transmitting itself by quiet personal contact and contagion, and there are circumstances in which this is the perfect mode of speech. Ministry to the secular needs of men in the spirit of Christ, moreover, is evangelism, in the right sense of the word."[46] Though Wells' comments were made prior to its publication, his thinking seems to have paralleled the Laymen's Report in this regard, as he believed that "enlightenment of the mind and enlargement of the spirit" was "included in the

44. Eakin, "For Such a Time," 1945, PUA.
45. McFarland, *Historical Sketch*, 209, 220.
46. Hocking, *Re-Thinking Missions*, 326.

command of Christ, 'Go ye and make disciples of all nations, teaching them.'"[47] Though it would be going beyond the evidence to conclude that Wells was a modernist, the preference of Wells and Eakin for indirect evangelism by moral example over direct proclamation and invitation to believe was consistent with modernist modes of thought such as those expressed in the Laymen's Report.

In contrast to Eakin and Wells, APM Thailand missionaries committed to direct evangelistic methods were distinctly unimpressed with indirect, moral-influence approaches to evangelism in mission schools. In fact, they did not think such an approach even qualified as evangelism. Loren Hanna, a fundamentalist-leaning missionary who worked in Lampang province, rejected the notion that teaching English or chemistry was evangelistic even though no mention was made of Christ, an idea suggested to him by a member of the Laymen's Commission whom he met at a missions conference sponsored by the Board. Hanna agreed that teaching those subjects can provide evangelistic opportunities but they themselves were not evangelism. Hanna claimed that in "certain mission schools . . . teachers and leaders consistently avoid the gospel message" in chapel and Bible classes and "give instead lectures on good behavior." Hanna asserted that even when a missionary from outside the school was a guest speaker for chapel time, the gospel was not presented. Instead, the "text is some old legend and the theme 'bravery' or 'patience' but not a word of Jesus Christ and His message of life." Hanna claimed to have heard "much teaching and many [school] chapel talks that might as well have been given by a Buddhist priest as a Christian missionary." In other words, the chapel messages he heard had an ethical focus which was not distinctively Christian. He thought that missionaries were neglecting to proclaim the gospel because they were afraid of offending the students. However, it is also possible that some of his fellow missionaries did not engage in evangelism with students as Hanna envisioned it because they had different ideas of the nature of the gospel and what needed to be communicated to non-Christians. This would seem to have been the case for Paul Eakin, and perhaps also for others with modernist leanings. Modernist tendencies did not always express themselves in explicit rejection of traditional doctrines. More often, they found expression in a focus on the moral and ethical aspects of Christianity to the near or total exclusion of traditional emphases on a gospel of sin, repentance,

---

47. McFarland, *Historical Sketch*, 210.

and conversion. Summarizing his thoughts on the subject, Hanna concluded that the schools were useless for evangelism unless missionaries "aggressively make every possible effort to witness in distinct terms for Christ." He believed that there was great "danger that the simple message may be so covered up with pious phrases and exhortations of an ethical and aesthetic nature that pupils who have gone through our entire course will not know the actual character of the gospel message itself."[48] Hanna's concern was shared by fellow missionary Margaret Landon (wife of Kenneth) who was certain that many students graduated from mission schools "without ever having a missionary show the slightest interest in their spiritual welfare." To illustrate her point, Landon said she recently met a "young man who had attended a Mission school for years, but had never been invited by any individual, Siamese or foreign, to become a Christian, although he had a deep interest in the matter."[49] The assessments of Hanna and Landon that there was a lack of evangelism happening in the schools matched Donald Barnhouse's conclusion that there was "a group of educationalists here [in Thailand] who have no real knowledge of evangelism though they think they are doing a wonderful piece of work in carrying on their schools."[50]

Despite the views of Hanna, Landon, and Barnhouse, it would be saying too much to claim that their assessments held true for all APM mission schools in Thailand. Missionaries like Lucy Niblock and Faye Kilpatrick, mentioned earlier, expressed the desire to do personal evangelism with their students in a way that seemed consistent with traditional concepts of evangelism voiced by Paul Fuller, Loren Hanna, and others. The educational philosophy popular in northern Thailand fostered high numbers of children from Christian families enrolling in their schools, which would have facilitated a school environment less prone to teachers and chapel speakers avoiding direct Bible teaching for fear of parental disapproval. Because of paucity of data, it is impossible to do a proper assessment of the nature and extent of evangelism that occurred in all the APM Thailand mission schools. However, from the material that is extant, it is clear that among APM Thailand missionaries, there were divergent and competing ideas of what it meant for mission schools to function evangelistically. In addition to concerns for governmental and

---

48. Hanna, "Evangelism—Extensive or Intensive?," 34–36; Barnhouse, "Travel Notes," January 10–11, 1935, PHS.

49. Landon, "There Were Giants," 22.

50. Barnhouse, "Travel Notes," January 2–6, 1935, PHS.

parental approval, it is likely that modernist preferences for an ethical and societal conception of Christianity played a role in the lack of evangelism as traditionally conceived in mission schools.

SOCIETAL INFLUENCE: AN ALTERNATIVE METRIC OF MISSION SUCCESS

Yet no matter how evangelism was defined, it was producing meager results. Few Buddhists were openly professing the Christian faith and joining the church. In lieu of failing to achieve that metric of mission success, missionaries looked elsewhere to assess the value of their work. For missionaries engaged in forms of direct evangelism, the fact that they were proclaiming the gospel was often enough to justify their work and thus continued support from American churches. However, for missionaries who were not engaging in direct evangelistic activities as traditionally conceived, either through lack of opportunity or due to personal convictions on how evangelism should be done, another metric was often cited in justification of their work. Numerous missionaries, particularly those connected with mission schools, pointed to the positive influence the schools were having upon Thai society. Even though few Buddhists were converting, it was thought that they were being formed and influenced by Christian morals. It was claimed that society was being leavened by Christian ideas and values, and graduates from mission schools were making notable contributions to the developing Thai nation.

Writing in the 1928 centenary volume on Protestant missions on the value of mission schools, Kenneth Wells claimed that many non-Christian students who graduated from mission schools took with them "the Christian viewpoint and an understanding and sympathetic attitude toward Christianity." This, in turn, would help "permeate society with Christian ideals and standards."[51] Whether or not students converted during their studies, Paul Eakin asserted that "[a]ll over Siam the chief contribution [of mission schools] . . . has been the building of Christian character. The products of our schools—men and women who put their jobs before their personal interests—are in demand all over Siam."[52] Mowbray Tate, who taught at Bangkok Christian College, spoke glowingly of the progress of mission schools in an article published only a couple months before the start of Japanese wartime occupation of Thailand. In

---

51. McFarland, *Historical Sketch*, 209.
52. Eakin to Mack, June 25, 1936, PUA.

answer to the imagined query of readers, Tate wrote no one should assume APM Thailand mission schools were not distinctly Christian because they had few Christian students. On the contrary, asserted Tate, due to the influence of Christian teachers, "thousands who have passed through our schools" have "gone out to their life work with stronger characters and a better understanding of the Way." He admitted that the progress of the schools was not always spectacular, but he had high hopes for the future. He did not mention any hope that mission school graduates or future students would profess faith in Christ in greater numbers than the past. Rather, his confidence in the future of the schools was based on the positive influence upon society that mission schools were already having through "their graduates serving in places of leadership throughout the land."[53] Although all of the APM Thailand missionaries would have been pleased for more students to become Christians, this was an uncommon occurrence and numerous missionaries cheered themselves with a functional substitute for converts, namely non-Christian graduates who were contributing members of Thai society and spoke well of the mission schools. Wells, Eakin, Tate, and other missionaries were pleased to see the lives of former students reflect Christian moral values such as honesty, a strong work ethic, and dedication to the good of society, but whether they were truly content with the diffusion of such values in lieu of conversions is an open question. Faye Kilpatrick, for example, who sought to do personal evangelism with the girls at Wattana Wittaya Academy, did not seem content with the lack of converts but nonetheless comforted herself with the thought that her students' lives were being shaped by Christian values even though most did not profess faith.[54] For missionaries whose thinking had modernist tendencies, as in the case of Eakin, it is probable that Christian influence in society brought greater satisfaction than it did for more conservative missionaries like Fuller, Hanna, and the Landons who focused their efforts on urging people to profess faith in Christ and join the church. For this latter group of missionaries, if the schools were not leading students to faith in Christ, they were not effective evangelistically, even though they admittedly had value in educating Christian children and training church leaders.

Those with modernist leanings would have been particularly prone to be satisfied with the social impact that the schools seemed to be making. In their view, evidence of the positive ethical impact that Christianity was having upon society simultaneously demonstrated the worth of

53. Tate, "Educational Progress," 160–68.
54. Kilpatrick, "Her Future," 113–15.

missions work in the eyes of skeptics and proved that eschewment of traditional doctrines did not cut the nerve of mission work. Christianity was changing the world even though, or perhaps because, it was no longer tethered to traditional doctrines. Though it is difficult to draw a straight line between modernist views and missionaries who took pride in the social impact of mission schools, there appear to have been at least some missionaries who were more satisfied in the diffusion of Christian values than the proclamation of the gospel message of salvation from sin and death through the substitutionary atonement of Christ on the cross. That said, missionaries of all theological stripes were pleased to see the adoption of Christian moral values among Thai Buddhists. Both the regeneration of individuals emphasized by conservatives and the moral transformation of society emphasized by liberals fit within the postmillennial expectations of Presbyterian theology.[55]

CONCLUSION

In this chapter, we have seen that all of the APM Thailand missionaries supported evangelism in principle. Though they desired Thai people to become Christians, the missionaries sometimes differed markedly on how evangelism should be pursued. Some favored direct proclamation of the gospel and calling for professions of faith both inside and outside mission schools. Others believed that the best hope for pointing Thai Buddhists to Christ was indirect evangelism in the schools that focused on generalized moral and religious exhortation combined with the example of Christian living. This latter approach was likely influenced by modernist tendencies in the minds of at least some missionaries, though even conservative missionaries would have felt the pressure to curb direct evangelistic activity in schools in order to avoid offending students and parents and meeting government expectations.

In many instances, it has been difficult to find evidence of direct connections between modernist tendencies in the thinking of APM Thailand missionaries and the shape of the changes happening among them. However, when the overall picture of evangelism in the mission is considered, modernist tendencies do appear to have been one influential factor among several affecting the trajectory of evangelistic change within the mission.

---

55. Kenneth Wells noted if Presbyterian missionaries in Thailand had not established schools, they would have been untrue to Presbyterianism. McFarland, *Historical Sketch*, 209–10.

Conclusion

Six Reasons the American Presbyterian Mission in Thailand Experienced Little Modernist-Fundamentalist Controversy

IN THE NINE PREVIOUS chapters, we have examined various ways in which theological modernism and modernizing changes in American and Thai society affected the American Presbyterian mission in Thailand between 1891 and 1941. During this fifty-year span, liberalization in theology led to conflicts between modernists and fundamentalists in the Presbyterian Church USA and among missionaries on some foreign mission fields, notably in China. The leaders of the American Presbyterian mission in Thailand were aware of growing theological diversity and polarization in the United States and elsewhere yet sought to maintain the former Protestant missionary consensus that upheld the value of both evangelistic and social service ministry. In Thailand, some missionaries evidenced modernist tendencies while others exhibited fundamentalist tendencies, yet APM Thailand executive secretary Paul Eakin maintained that the American Presbyterian missionaries in Thailand were both conservative in theology and liberal in their attitudes towards others. These tendencies, or the perception of such tendencies, caused a degree of tension among missionaries and were one of multiple contributing factors in APM Thailand missionary resignations, and shifting approaches and priorities in evangelism and education. On the whole, however, leanings in a modernist or fundamentalist direction among missionaries in

Thailand did not produce the same level of conflict and polarization as that experienced in either China or the United States. Why not? In this final chapter, the answer to this question will be considered as a way of reviewing key findings of previous chapters and analyzing the internal and external dynamics of the American Presbyterian mission in Thailand that enabled it to evade much of the theological controversy that rocked churches and missionaries elsewhere.

As Kevin Yao has pointed out in relation to fundamentalism in China, each mission field had its own unique social and mission context that influenced the ways and extents to which theological concerns were weighted and expressed.[1] The issues that divided or united in one context cannot be assumed to be the same in another context. To that end, we will consider six interwoven factors that shaped the contours of the impact of modernism in the American Presbyterian mission in Thailand in the fifty-year period prior to World War II. As a way of understanding the situation in Thailand, reference to the Chinese and American contexts will be drawn at appropriate points.

1. SOCIAL AND MISSION CONTEXT

The first factor in the apparent lack of theological conflict in Thailand was the contrast in the ways that theological differences manifested themselves due to social context. In the United States, fundamentalist-modernist conflicts were animated by a sense of cultural crisis. Conservatives felt the culture was moving away from the traditional Christian beliefs of its past and embracing a secular, scientific worldview that found theological expression in denials of inerrancy, the virgin birth, miracles, penal substitutionary atonement, and belief in the bodily resurrection of Christ. Fundamentalists saw departure from these beliefs as a sign of cultural decline whereas modernists saw the modernization of these beliefs as precisely what was needed to save and retain Christian influence in the culture.[2] The concern of missionaries and indigenous Christians in Thailand, however, was not to preserve an existing Christian culture under threat. Thailand was a Buddhist country that never had a Christian majority. From the missionary point of view, the people of Thailand needed to be introduced to Christianity for the first time. As such, the

---

1. Yao, *Fundamentalist Movement*, 284–85.

2. Hutchison, *Modernist Impulse*, 145–84; Marsden, *Fundamentalism and American Culture*, 2–3.

most pressing matter was dissemination of the Christian message. What methods of influence would have the greatest effect in making the essence of the Christian faith attractive to Thai people?

In chapter 7, Donald Barnhouse's discussion with the Bangkok station missionaries revealed that the question of best methods was controversial. APM Thailand executive secretary Paul Eakin and educationalist missionaries defended the strategic role of mission schools in influencing Thai culture with Christian values even if they produced few public conversions. Though all the missionaries affirmed the desire for Thai people to profess Christ, seeking conversions was not given equal priority in the minds of all. For Eakin, strongly modernist in his theological convictions, mission success was not about number of conversions as much as it was about living a Christian life that influenced others by example. In contrast, Albert Seigle, Paul Fuller, Loren Hanna, Robert Franklin and other missionaries lamented the lack of gospel proclamation in the schools and longed for a return of an evangelistic emphasis in the mission. In their minds, the type of indirect evangelism through moral example and exhortation that was practiced in some mission schools did not qualify as genuine evangelism. The type of evangelism that some missionaries saw as essential was deemed by others as ill-suited for modern, educated Buddhists. As William Hutchison has observed, the need to consciously adapt Christian theology to modern culture was one of the hallmarks of modernism, and the perceived need to make such an adaptation was felt by Paul Eakin and seminary director Carl Elder who wanted to make Christianity appealing to an educated Buddhist elite, as discussed in chapter 6.[3] All the APM Thailand missionaries officially had the same evangelistic goal though their allocation of time, money, and personnel differed and caused some to doubt the value or effectiveness of their fellow missionaries.

Theological matters that took center stage in American Modernist-Fundamentalist debates only occasionally presented themselves in intra-mission tensions. Examples were the divergence over inerrancy and higher critical theory evidenced in the case of Evander McGilvary, and in Loren Hanna's objection to the books Carl Elder assigned to seminary students. However, underlying theological differences among the missionaries in Thailand mostly expressed themselves in tensions centered around the goal and methods of evangelism, especially evangelism in

---

3. Hutchison, *Modernist Impulse*, 2.

mission schools as those institutions absorbed an increasing portion of limited mission personnel and funds.

The crucial issues of debate in Thailand were not dissimilar to those in other Asian mission fields. In the Chinese context, Lian Xi noted that liberal emphases among China missionaries expressed themselves in a departure from some traditional doctrines and literalistic readings of Bible, and a preoccupation with regeneration of society instead of individual souls. Differing in their emphasis from modernists in the United States who wanted to reshape Christianity in the light of evolution and higher criticism, modernists in China sought a religious and cultural synthesis between Christianity and religions of the East.[4] Fundamentalists in China, however, were outraged at this advocacy for collaboration with non-Christian religions, which they saw as a challenge to Christian uniqueness and an attack on the legitimacy of mission.[5] Compared to Thailand, Korea experienced more theological conflict around issues similar to the United States, though in Korea a strongly conservative consensus prevailed and the most important controversies related to the challenge of socialism, communism, and the Japanese occupation of Korea.[6] In Japan, there was greater theological diversity than in either Thailand or Korea, representing the influence of both conservative and liberal Western theologies, yet there was a strong indigenous push for the "Japanization" of Christianity, an emphasis that grappled with how Christianity related to Japanese culture and history. This self-theologizing impulse among Japanese theologians is another example of the prioritization of the relationship between Christianity and non-Christian religions over American doctrinal concerns in an Asian mission context.[7]

2. LACK OF WESTERN INTELLECTUAL INFLUENCE

A second reason why there was little recognizable modernist-fundamentalist conflict was the paucity of Western education and modern cultural assumptions in Thailand during the period under consideration. Modern ideas about the progressive nature of history, the ability of humans to control their destiny through the use of rational principles and scientific laws, and the value of the new over the old were ubiquitous in Western societies

---

4. Xi, *Conversion*, 14.
5. Yao, *Fundamentalist Movement*, 284–85.
6. Yim, *Unity Lost*, 29–52; Yim, "Korea," 300–301.
7. Jennings, "Theology in Japan," 145–56.

during the nineteenth and early twentieth centuries, and led to the questioning of the supernatural presuppositions of traditional Christianity.[8] Modernist theological ideas grew from the encounter between modern scientific worldview assumptions and traditional Christian beliefs, and represented a synthesis between two worldviews that appeared to be in conflict.[9] In Thailand, where these modern assumptions did not exist in society at large, and were not propagated through higher educational institutions, especially universities, people did not ask the same questions of religion as did those formed by Western learning.

As discussed in chapter 4, from the mid-nineteenth century Thai royalty and other Thai elite were rapidly acquiring Western learning and seeking to modernize themselves and their country in order to retain power and status in a changing world, and they were adapting Buddhism accordingly. But this education which influenced their decision to pursue an ethically-oriented, rather than a supernatural, modern Buddhism was initially limited to Thai royalty and other elites. Universal education in Thailand, even at the primary level, only became more common in the 1930s and tertiary education was slow to be established when compared with China, Japan, and Korea which had multiple universities and colleges, many of them founded by American missions, by the late nineteenth or early twentieth century. In contrast, the first university in Thailand was Chulalongkorn University, founded in 1917, and the second was Thammasat University, founded in 1934. The educational emphasis of these universities, and many others established in Thailand following the war, was oriented towards practical and technical skills, not philosophical concerns.[10] The developing tension between religion and science evident both in the Western world and in other parts of Asia, notably China, was not replicated in Thailand. As recently as 1990, Suntaree Komin found no significant difference in religious attitudes among Thai people of varying educational levels. Her research showed that "the highly educated sought out fortune-telling as often as the uneducated" and "even Western educated Thai Ph.D. scientists refused to fathom the scientific and religious conflict, and would behaviorally never forget to wear their charms and amulets when traveling."[11] Given the educational options available to them in the late nineteenth and early twentieth

8. See Lauzon, "Modernity," 2–5; cf. Van Der Veer, "Global History," 285.
9. Hutchison, *Modernist Impulse*, 204.
10. Bovornsiri and Fry, "Higher Education," 30–35.
11. Komin, "Culture and Work-Related Values," 692–93.

centuries, and the cultural assumptions and values which they brought to the Christian faith, Thai Christians were not asking the questions of the Christian faith that Western Christians were forced to deal with. As a result, they were not compelled to reconcile traditional Christian beliefs with scientific learning and assumptions, and modernist theological ideas thus did not develop. Where such ideas did appear in Thailand, they originated with foreign missionaries or Thai who were directly influenced by Western learning, either by Thailand-based missionaries or by studying abroad. For example, the doubts that led Dr. William Perkins to resign, as discussed in chapter 6, originated in questions being asked in American society, not Thai society. Also, when Carl Elder was accused of unorthodox theology, one of the few Thai Christians who defended Elder was Banchop Bansiddhi who completed his theological education in the Philippines. Evidence indicates that sympathy towards modernist ideas may have developed only among those who were influenced by non-Thai sources. Nevertheless, the interaction of Thai Christians with theologically liberal ideas deserves further study, both in the interwar period and especially in the thirty years following World War II when Thai Christians were studying abroad in greater numbers and there was evidence of theological liberalism among APM Thailand missionaries teaching at McGilvary seminary in Chiang Mai.[12]

3. LACK OF COMMITTED FIGHTERS

A third reason for a lack of modernist-fundamentalist conflict in Thailand was a lack of committed "fighters." As noted in chapter 3, George Marsden lists militancy as one of the defining characteristics of fundamentalism, a characteristic that made fundamentalists distinct from other anti-modernist theological conservatives.[13] In the China context, Kevin Yao observed that modernist-fundamentalist conflict only occurred when fundamentalists stood up and fought.[14] In the absence of people willing to pick a fight, there was no conflict. Theologically modernist ideas may have been present among some APM Thailand missionaries but in the absence of anyone to press the issue with them, there were tensions and rumors, but little public conflict.

12. Post-war theological trajectories in the APM Thailand and CCT are addressed in McLean, "Thai Protestant Christianity," 87–112; Kim, *Unfinished Mission*, 45–75, 118–32; Dahlfred, "Bumpy Road," 35–47.
13. Marsden, *Fundamentalism and American Culture*, 4.
14. Yao, *Fundamentalist Movement*, 12.

APM Thailand missionaries did not often discuss theology or declare their own theological views. They were practically oriented and more concerned with the everyday matters of life and ministry than they were with explicitly theological concerns. However, questions of theology did come to the fore from time to time. Sometimes doctrinal issues arose among themselves in connection with other issues, as seen in the controversy in the wake of John Sung's revival meetings. Tensions over modernism and fundamentalism in the Thailand mission, as in other mission contexts, were interwoven with personal relationships, intra-mission and intra-church politics, budget and personnel limitations, and concerns for the progress of the mission work at hand. Sometimes, as seen in chapter 7, explicitly theological matters came to the fore in response to the questioning of outsiders to the missionary enterprise. Also, modernist sympathies among the missionaries in Thailand did not always manifest themselves in explicitly doctrinal terms and often did not call attention to themselves. Paul Eakin, the most clearly modernist member of the APM Thailand mission, did not own the modernist label and sought to suppress theological debate. He valued keeping the peace within the mission and avoiding open conflict even while using his position as executive secretary to push for his own vision of appropriate evangelism in the modern world. Yet, even in the absence of public conflict, modernist leanings concerning the nature and purpose of the Christian faith were sometimes hinted at in the emphasis of some missionaries on educational or medical work over direct evangelism.

Among the Thailand missionaries, there were some missionaries who were outspoken and concerned themselves at various times with modernist influences in the mission. The most prominent among these were Loren Hanna, Paul Fuller, and Kenneth Landon. However, at the end of the day, they were not willing to pursue theological issues to the point of trying to force theological opponents out of the mission. Like Clarence Macartney or Donald Barnhouse in the American Presbyterian context, they made critiques and pushed for change but ultimately remained committed to the denominational mission which they believed was essentially sound.[15] Internal critics of the Thailand mission were not willing to press their case to the point of division, probably due to a combination of needing friends in a small mission field, a lack of sufficient numbers of co-belligerents, a lack of institutional foci to mobilize fundamentalist

---

15. Russell, "Barnhouse," 48; Longfield, *Presbyterian Controversy*, 204–5.

action, a prioritization of their local ministries in Thailand over ecclesiastical wrangling, and the prospect of not being invited back to Thailand after furlough if they were seen to be divisive. This last point bears special mention as a motivating factor in suppressing conflict on the mission field. In the Presbyterian Church in the United States of America, it was necessary to follow a lengthy procedure at the congregational and presbytery level in order to remove a minister who was seen as problematic. On the mission field, it was much easier to get rid of a missionary. All it took was a simple vote of the executive committee of the mission to not welcome back the missionary after furlough. On several occasions the Thailand mission relieved itself of missionaries who were deemed problematic, a fact that potential troublemakers would have been aware of. In 1920, the Thailand mission declined to return Arthur McMullin and Dr. William Lyon to the field because they were "unsuited" to the field and "temperamental." Dr. Lyon's "chief pernicious characteristic was his habit of faultfinding in circles outside of the Mission."[16] In 1932, missionary Edna Bulkley accused mission executive secretary Paul Eakin of being a dictator, named several missionaries and Thai Christian leaders who were negatively influenced by his modernist theology, and claimed Eakin opposed the "aggressive preaching" of Kenneth Landon.[17] When she went on early furlough in 1934 to attend to her children's needs, her husband Dr. Lucius C. Bulkley stayed behind. He remained alone in Thailand until the war broke in 1941 because the Thailand mission leaders valued his work as a doctor but did not want Mrs. Bulkley back, privately citing her difficult personality as a primary reason.[18]

---

16. Taylor and McKean to Brown, December 29, 1920, PHS.

17. Edna Bulkley to McAfee, October 1, 1932; Edna Bulkley to Women of the Siam Mission, November 3, 1932, PHS.

18. In 1939, Mrs. Bulkley was given provisional approval to return after apologizing to Eakin but was unable to do so before the war. Eakin to Board, December 1935; Eakin to Exec. Cmte., October 1, 1935; Edna Bulkley to Eakin, August 7, 1939, PUA; K. Landon to McAfee, February 17, 1933, PHS.

Dr. Lucius C. Bulkley and Trang Hospital Staff, 1940
(Courtesy of the Presbyterian Historical Society, Philadelphia).

The possibility of such removal from the Thailand mission likely served to keep other missionaries in check. Following Paul Fuller's agreement to withdraw from Bangkok Christian College and the suggestion that Fuller's sermon was the source of journalist Charles Selden's impression that the APM Thailand mission was fundamentalist, Board secretary Arthur Brown questioned Paul Fuller's attitude. Specifically, as discussed in chapter 7, Brown queried whether Fuller had approval to go back to Thailand after his furlough. Fuller became anxious at the possibility of being denied the opportunity to return, which may have chastened his future willingness to speak out.

Among the Thai, there were also few fighters, though we find a notable exception in Boon Mark Gittisarn whom Edwin Cort compared unfavorably to J. Gresham Machen.[19] Though the divisions over John Sung and the proposed Bible institute revealed that both Thais and missionaries were willing to fight in certain instances, East Asian cultures in general, and Thai culture in particular, place a high importance on saving face and avoidance of public conflict. In her study of

---

19. Cort to Hooper et al., April 19, 1940, PHS.

Thai cultural values, Komin concluded that a combination of factors lead Thai to prioritize "smooth, kind, pleasant, conflict-free interpersonal interactions."[20] Larry Persons's research shows that Thai leaders are afraid of appearing to make mistakes and losing face, lest they lose the respect of their followers, a distinct possibility in situations of public conflict.[21] For these reasons, public controversy in Thailand today is shunned where possible. This cultural value would likely have been even more important in the early twentieth century when communities were smaller and the influence of Western cultural values less. The militancy necessary for fundamentalist-modernist controversy was often lacking among the Thai for cultural reasons, and among the foreign missionaries for reasons of organizational and ministry context.

In comparison to a large mission field like China, Thailand had relatively few missionaries and received little attention in the American press. China's vastly greater size and prominence in American foreign policy attracted more missionaries and more attention, which led to much larger overall numbers of missionaries of all theological stripes, thus enabling a critical mass of militant missionaries to establish a fundamentalist organization like the Bible Union of China.[22] In China, the Bible Union and the North China Theological Seminary served as institutional foci that mobilized fundamentalists in their fight against modernists.[23] In contrast, though there were individual missionaries in Thailand with fundamentalist tendencies, they never united for concerted action nor developed any formal institutional structures to move against those whom they suspected of modernism. Unlike China, there could be no gathering of fundamentalist-leaning individuals from various missions and churches because the American Presbyterian mission constituted the overwhelming majority of the Protestant missionary community in Thailand. With a single organization virtually dominating the Thailand field, there was less opportunity for diversity and more organizational ability to keep missionaries in line. When compared to China, the situation in Thailand suggests that modernist-fundamentalist polarization only occurred in mission contexts where there were both sufficient numbers of militant co-belligerents and organizational or institutional foci

20. Komin, "Culture and Work-Related Values," 692; Bhana, "Saying 'No.'"

21. Persons, *Way Thais Lead*, 75.

22. By 1890, China surpassed India as the mission field of greatest interest. Xi, *Conversion*, 4–5.

23. See chapter 3 and 5 in Yao, *Fundamentalist Movement*.

to polarize theological opposites into opposing camps. In the absence of such structures, individuals with modernist or fundamentalist sympathies never coalesced into discernable movements. Further research would greatly aid in confirming whether or not this generalization about modernist-fundamentalist tension among missionaries provides a satisfactory explanation for the absence of conspicuous theological conflict on early twentieth century mission fields other than Thailand.

4. AMERICAN PRESBYTERIAN DOMINANCE IN THAILAND

After the ABCFM and American Baptist missions ceased their work in Thailand in the mid-nineteenth century, American Presbyterians dominated the Protestant missionary community in Thailand through the Second World War.[24] A handful of missions from other denominations entered Thailand during this time but only maintained a token presence consisting of not more than a few stations and missionary families each.[25] This meant that the vast majority of missionaries and Thai Christians were associated with a single denomination and were exposed to little more theological diversity than that present in their own churches. APM leaders were effectively gatekeepers for theological diversity in the Thailand missionary community and missionaries whose views or actions were seen as problematic could be dealt with internally. China and many other mission fields, in contrast, had more significant ecclesiastical diversity, and thus missions that were more modernist- or fundamentalist-leaning could exist on the same mission field. In Thailand, however, groups other than the American Presbyterians were statistically insignificant in the Protestant missionary community and thus lacked the ability to fan any flames of controversy that did not already exist within APM Thailand.

APM dominance in Thailand also meant that the American Presbyterians were able to maintain the former Protestant missionary consensus in Thailand long after it lost its unifying power in countries such as China, thus heading off open warfare between modernists and fundamentalists. In China, where there was great ecclesiastical diversity and a rising fundamentalist voice in the form of the Bible Union of China,

---

24. Because of their *de facto* monopoly in Thailand Protestant missions, the American Presbyterians felt they were uniquely responsible for Christianization of the country. Eakin, "Siam, A Presbyterian Responsibility," February 1939, PHS; Hooper, "Enlarged Program."

25. McFarland, *Historical Sketch*, 249–69; Ford, "History of the CMA"; "Thailand," 789–93.

several conservative groups refused to join the Church of Christ in China, claiming it was infected by modernism, thus creating deep divisions within the Protestant missionary community in China.[26] In Thailand, however, the statistical insignificance of other Protestant groups meant the American Presbyterian mission did not have to take seriously voices other than its own. The denominational homogeneity and the centralized administrative and ecclesiastical control this monopoly enabled meant the American Presbyterians were able to maintain the former Protestant missionary consensus in Thailand long after it broke down elsewhere. Though tensions existed between some evangelistic and educational missionaries in Thailand, and modernist sympathies contributed to the shaping of mission priorities, the consensus among Thailand missionaries that both evangelism and social service were important meant that those with modernist views could find a place to work as long as they also professed to value evangelism, however they understood that term. The APM's maintenance of the Protestant missionary consensus in Thailand after it ceased to have unifying power elsewhere effectively kept in check the degree to which modernism could flourish in Thailand.

5. MISSIONARY PRIORITY ON UNITY

A fifth reason for little fundamentalist-modernist controversy in Thailand was the priority which the missionaries placed upon unity and harmony within the mission. This prioritization was largely due to the necessities of the mission context, though the personal convictions of Board secretaries and the specter of losing financial support from the American Presbyterian public also played a role.

As discussed in chapter 9, the APM Thailand mission was always asking for additional workers and never received as many as they requested from the Board. Their already small mission force was depleted by more than 30 percent between 1925 and 1936, dropping from 95 to 65 missionaries.[27] Before the war, this number only recovered slightly, rising to 72 missionaries by 1939.[28] Due to the large institutional build-up of mission schools in the early twentieth century, Bangkok and Chiang Mai had more than 50 percent of APM Thailand missionary personnel and a

---

26. Bays, *New History*, 110–11.

27. Wells, Actions Taken by Exec. Cmte., December 15–21, 1936, PUA.

28. Board of Foreign Mission, "Summary of Mission Force," September 19, 1939, WCSC.

still larger proportion of Thai Christian workers.[29] Given the small overall numbers of missionaries in Thailand, and the fact that many smaller stations had only a handful of missionaries, the necessity of getting along was elevated when compared to the United States or China where larger numbers and greater diversity of churches and organizations meant that controversies and divisions could sometimes occur with fewer adverse effects. Because missionaries were few, it was difficult to keep stations supplied with necessary personnel, and any internal conflicts would be less tolerable in situations where the number of foreign Christian friends in one's immediate area might be counted on one hand.

The fear of disunity harming mission work was a recurring theme for APM Thailand mission leadership as well as Board secretaries. As discussed in chapter 6, many of Evander McGilvary's fellow missionaries thought that retaining him on the field would lead to a loss of harmony among missionaries and confusion among Northern Thai Christians. It was thought that the forward progress of the fledging Christian movement in Thailand would be hindered. In 1919, there was apparently sufficient disagreement among APM Thailand missionaries to warrant a letter from Arthur Brown warning them to not condemn fellow missionaries with different millennial views.[30] Previous to the establishment of the Church of Christ in Thailand in 1934, Paul Eakin expressed concern that educated Thai Christians were reading church newspapers from the United States and were "beginning to feel the tragedy of divisions in the home base when we need so must [sic] an example of a united front."[31] If the mission was divided, or perceived to be divided, uniting Thai Christians to form a national church would be more difficult.

APM Thailand missionaries, as well as the Board, were also aware that news of divisions within the mission could result in loss of support from home. As discussed in chapter 7, this was one of Arthur Brown's primary concerns in his admonition to the Thailand missionaries to maintain unity and refrain from criticizing each other in the wake of Charles Selden's unflattering published comments.[32] Concern that the missionary cause would be harmed was also a driving factor in the caution displayed by Paul Eakin and others in answering Donald Barnhouse's questions

29. Rodgers to Cooper, October 29, 1929, PHS.
30. Brown to North and South Siam Missions, January 3, 1919, PUA; cf. Xi, *Conversion*, 4; Treloar, *Disruption*, 52–54.
31. Eakin to Friends, May 13, 1924, PHS.
32. Brown to Siam Mission, "Board Letter #293," July 6, 1927, PHS.

about the state of the Thailand mission. If Barnhouse gave a negative report to the American Presbyterian public, churches might stop giving and the missionaries might come under unwanted scrutiny.

The desire for unity in the name of preserving and advancing mission work, both in Thailand and elsewhere, also came from the very top of the Board of Foreign Missions. Robert E. Speer, who led the Board until 1937, believed that the time to fight for doctrinal truth was past, and unity was a prerequisite to evangelization of the world. For Speer, rivalry was disloyalty to Christ and the world because it was a waste of time and resources that diminished the ability to spread the gospel.[33] Speer's concern for unity was shared by Board secretaries Arthur Brown and Cleland McAfee, who were primary corresponding secretaries with the Thailand mission for many years.

In the Chinese context, many missionaries and Chinese Christians also valued unity for the sake of ministry, though it was ultimately difficult to maintain. As Kevin Yao points out, the National Christian Council in China avoided questions of doctrine and polity because of their potential for division. Chinese Christians valued unity with one another as minorities in a majority non-Christian context more than they did furthering doctrinal differences from the West.[34] Compared to Thailand, China was a much larger mission field with greater denominational and doctrinal diversity to which Chinese Christians were exposed. In Thailand, however, overtly modernist theology was rare, and most Thai Christians associated with the American Presbyterians would have been largely unaware of the nature or severity of Western doctrinal differences since there were few non-Presbyterian missionaries in the country prior to the Second World War. Such differences did not seem relevant in their context. Thai Christians, however, would have felt a desire for Christian unity living in the midst of a majority Buddhist culture which viewed Christianity as a foreign religion incompatible with Thai identity.

Though unity in Thailand lasted longer than in China, it was ultimately difficult to maintain. Although the APM Thailand leadership and the Board secretaries strove to keep together an increasingly diverse mission force, simmering tensions boiled over in Thailand through the catalyst of John Sung. APM Thailand leadership may have been able to rein in divisive missionaries but when factions developed among Thai

---

33. Longfield, *Presbyterian Controversy*, 194–95.
34. Yao, *Fundamentalist Movement*, 188, 202.

Christians over Sung's brand of Bible teaching, missionaries took sides with Thai Christians who shared their points of view and the mission entered into a time of conflict greater than it had previously experienced. Sung aligned himself with fundamentalists and against modernists in China and the conflict which he prompted in Thailand reflects a spilling over of theological conflict from China into the Thai context.[35] APM Thailand was largely able to avoid controversy over modernism when such views were largely confined to the missionaries themselves, but when theological concerns were bundled into other issues important to Thai Christians, it was extremely difficult to maintain peace and unity within the mission and within Thai churches. As seen in the case of the Bible institute controversy following John Sung's Thailand campaigns, the Thai preference to avoid conflict did not mean that Thai never engage in conflict.

6. THE TYPE OF PEOPLE THAILAND ATTRACTED

A sixth reason for the general absence of fundamentalist-modernist controversy was the type of people whom Thailand attracted. The modernist assessment of missionary work that appeared in the Laymen's Report emphasized the priority of education, medical, and other social works as the proper expression of the mission impulse in the modern world. This emphasis on societal development over evangelism was common to modernist missionaries who saw the Spirit of God working primarily through natural processes and evolving human societies as part of a "this-worldly" advance of the kingdom of God.[36] Given these emphases, it should come as no surprise that in Thailand, APM missionaries with modernist sympathies were more often found in the schools. Given the heavy financial and personnel investment of the Thailand mission into schools, one might think that there would have been more missionaries with modernist views in Thailand. Yet Thailand, as noted previously, had few opportunities for educators at the tertiary level due to its smaller size and comparative slowness to develop universities. In China, an important battleground for fundamentalists was theological seminaries, and Christian colleges and universities, because such institutions were beachheads for modernist

---

35. Ireland, *John Song*, 36–42.
36. Hutchison, *Modernist Impulse*, 2.

views.[37] But theological soldiers were lacking in Thailand, in part because Thailand lacked the proper battlefields to attract them.

Additionally, modernists tended to prefer cities over rural areas because educated people with whom modernist views more often resonated were usually found in cities. However, with the exception of Bangkok and Chiang Mai, Thailand was largely rural and therefore not an attractive field of service for modernist-leaning missionaries. Although the Thailand mission originally had more evangelists than educators, the balance shifted over the course of the early twentieth century and few missionaries designated to evangelistic work remained by the 1930s. Of those that did remain, they were nearly all found in the provinces rather than the two major cities, Bangkok and Chiang Mai.

In considering the six points above and the interactions of the American Presbyterian mission in Thailand with theological matters, especially modernism, it is appropriate to return again to Paul Eakin's statement to Charles Selden referenced in the title of this book. In attempting to avoid controversy in the mission, Eakin provided a fair summary of missionary thinking in Thailand during the late nineteenth and early twentieth centuries, although he diplomatically left out the nuances that have been explored in the preceding pages. The majority of the missionaries were "conservative in theology" and they all wanted to be seen as orthodox and faithful. That notwithstanding, a minority of them held at least some modernist positions or were sympathetic to modernist viewpoints. Various degrees of modernist thinking existed among some missionaries and contributed to their relations with other missionaries and their approaches to their work. While desiring to be seen as conservative, APM Thailand missionaries also desired to be seen as "liberal in spirit," meaning that they did not want to be divisive or mean-spirited in their approach to fellow missionaries. Yet sometimes, strong words were spoken and tensions existed.

Some APM Thailand missionaries were "conservative in theology" and "liberal in spirit." Yet others were "liberal in theology" and "conservative in spirit." And still others fell somewhere in the middle. Paul Eakin's statement may have been accurate as a broad generalization but an examination of the actual situation in Thailand has revealed that reality was more complicated and multifaceted than Eakin was willing to admit.

37. Yao, *Fundamentalist Movement*, 101–2.

Appendix A

List of Thai Names in Romanized and Thai Script

Banchop Bansiddhi	บรรจบ บันสิทธิ์
Banchong Bansiddhi	บันชอง บันสิทธ์
Bentoon "Samuel" Boon-Itt	เบนทูล บุญอิต
Bhanurangsi Savangwongse	ภาณุรังษี สว่างวงศ์
Boon Mark Gittisarn	บุญมาก กิตติสาร
Boon Mee Rungreungwongse	บุญมี รุ่งเรืองวงศ์
Boon Tee	บุ้นตี๋
Boon Tuan Boon-Itt	บุญต่วน บุญอิต
Chamratt Mitrakul	จำรัส มิตรกุล
Chang Mitrakul	แจ้ง มิตรกุล
Charoen Sakulkan	เจริญ สกุลกัน
Charoen Wichai	เจริญ วิชัย
Chomchai Indhabhan	จอมใจ อินทะพันธุ์
Chinda Singhanetra	จินดา สิงหเนตร
Chua Pramuanwongs	เชื้อ ประมูลวงศ์
Civili Singhanetra	ศรีวิไล สิงหเนตร
Damrong Rajanubhab	ดำรง ราชานุภาพ
Esther Pradipasena	เอสเธอร์ ประทีปประเสน
Kawilorot Suriyawong	กาวิโลรส สุริยวงศ์

Lek Taiyong	เล็ก ไทยง
Maitri Chit	ไมตรีจิต
Nai Chune	นายชื่น
Nan Inta	หนานอินต๊ะ
Phrasri-arn	พระศรีอารย์
Pluang Sudhikham	เปลื้อง สุทธิคำ
Prasert Intaphantu	ประเสริฐ อินทะพันธุ์
Pridi Banomyong / Phanomyong	ปรีดี พนมยงค์
Raphi (Rabi) Phatthanasak	รพี พัฒนศักดิ์
Saowapha Phongsi	เสาวภาผ่องศรี
Samray	สำเหร่
Seng Lan Chairatana	เซงลัน ชัยรัตน์
Seng Saa Chairatana	เซงแซ ชัยรัตน์
Sin Saa Qua Kieng	ซินแสก๊วยเซียง
Sing Keo Suriyakham	สิงห์เขียว สุริยะคำ
Sook Pongsanoi (Suk Phongnoi)	สุข พงศ์น้อย
Thianhi (Thian Hee, Thien Hee) Sarasin	เทียนฮี้ สารสิน
Wachirayan (Vajirananavarorasa)	วชิรญาณ วโรรส
Wichit Wathakan	วิจิตร วาทการ

Appendix B

Photograph of American Presbyterian Mission in Siam, 1935

Meeting of the American Presbyterian Mission in Siam, 1935; photographed in front of the chapel at Prince Royal's College, Chiang Mai (Courtesy of Buswell Library Archives & Special Collections, Wheaton College, IL.)

Appendix B: Photograph of American Presbyterian Mission

FIRST ROW (CHILDREN)

Gaylord Knox, Jr.
Robert Knox
John Scott Holladay, Jr.
William Bradley Landon
Doris Bassett
Faye Stewart
Rosemary Hanna
Margaret Seigle
Claralice Hanna
Jean Knox
Jeanette Josephine Seigle
Carol Bassett
Helen Knox
Joan Elder
Alice Kneedler
Carol Landon
Margaret Landon
Eloise Elder
Stewart Elder
Stanley Hanna

SECOND ROW

Leila Knox (Mrs. Gaylord)
Mrs. Ray Bachtell
Margaret Stewart (Mrs. Herbert)
Hazel Hanna (Mrs. Loren Stanley)
Winnie Burr (2nd Mrs. H. Stewart)
Lucy Niblock
Gertrude Eakin
Mrs. Marion Palmer
Josephine Elder (Mrs. Carl)
Mrs. Charles Callender (?)
Mrs. John Holladay (crouched down)
Mabel Cort (Mrs. E.C.)
Margaretta Wells (Mrs. Kenneth E., holding Roberta)
Margaret Cordelia McCord
Marie Park (Mrs. Charles E.)
Mrs. Howard Campbell
Mrs. Alice J. Ellinwood

Christina Harris Kneedler
(Mrs. William Harding)

THIRD ROW

Gaylord Knox
Kru Pluang Sudhikham
Herbert W. Stewart
Loren S. Hanna
Richard W. Post
Asher B. Case
Howard Campbell
Helen Frances McClure
Agnes Barland McDaniel
(2nd Mrs. Edwin B.)
Mollie Macfie McKean
(Mrs. Hugh McKean-Buchanan-Reid)
Miss Mabel Jordan
Johanne Christensen
Faye Kilpatrick (Mrs. Milton Yoder)
Helene Newman
Jeanette Seigle (Mrs. Albert)
Margaret Landon

FOURTH ROW

Prasok (Seng Saa) Chairat
(from Pitsanuloke)
John Lyman Eakin
Paul Anderson Eakin
Alice Bassett (Mrs. Allan)
John Scott Holladay
William Harding Kneedler
Dr. William Beach
Kenneth E. Wells
Charles Callender
Carl Elder
Ray W. Bachtell
Dr. Lucius Constant Bulkley
Kenneth P. Landon
Albert Seigle
Seng Keo (from Chieng Rai)—
Dr. Bachtell's assistant

Bibliography

Almond, Philip C. *The British Discovery of Buddhism.* Cambridge: Cambridge University Press, 1988.

Anderson, Douglas Firth. "Modernization and Theological Conservatism in the Far West: The Controversy Over Thomas F. Day, 1907-1912." *Fides et Historia* 24 (1992) 76-91.

Andrews, James M. *Siam—Second Rural Economic Survey 1934-1935.* Vol. 2. Bangkok: Bangkok Times, 1935.

Aphornsuvan, Thanet. "The West and Siam's Quest for Modernity." *South East Asia Research* 17 (2009) 401-31.

Atherstone, Andrew. "Thomas, (William Henry) Griffith (1861-1924), Anglican Evangelical Theologian and Educator." In *Oxford Dictionary of National Biography.* Oxford: Oxford University Press, 2012.

Baker, Archibald G. "Reactions to The "Laymen's Report."" *The Journal of Religion* 13 (1933) 379-98.

Baker, Chris, and Pasuk Phongpaichit. *A History of Thailand.* 3rd ed. Cambridge: Cambridge University Press, 2014.

Barnhouse, Donald Grey. "Remarks by Dr. D. G. Barnhouse on the Comment of the Foreign Board Executive Council." *The Presbyterian* 105 (1935) 8-9.

———. "The Report of Dr. Donald Grey Barnhouse Concerning His Visit to Presbyterian Foreign Mission Stations in Asia." *The Presbyterian* 105 (1935) 1, 5-10.

———. "Travel Notes." January 2-6, 1935, Barnhouse Papers, RG480, Box 9, Folder 18, PHS, Philadelphia.

———. "Travel Notes." January 3, 1935, Barnhouse Papers, RG480, Box 9, Folder 18, PHS, Philadelphia.

Barnhouse, Margaret N. *That Man Barnhouse.* Wheaton, IL: Tyndale House, 1983.

Barrows, John Henry, ed. *The World's Parliament of Religions.* 2 vols. Chicago: Parliament, 1893.

Bassett, Allen. "Evangelism—Extensive or Intensive?" *MO* (December 1934) 18-19.

Bayly, C. A. *The Birth of the Modern World, 1780-1914.* Oxford: Blackwell, 2004.

Bays, Daniel H. *A New History of Christianity in China*. Chichester, West Sussex: Wiley-Blackwell, 2012.

Bebbington, David, and David Ceri Jones, eds. *Evangelicalism and Fundamentalism in the United Kingdom During the Twentieth Century*. Oxford: Oxford University Press, 2014.

Berg, Johannes van den. *Constrained by Jesus' Love: An Inquiry into the Motives of the Missionary Awakening in Great Britain in the Period between 1698 and 1815*. Kampen: J.H. Kok, 1956.

Bhana, Yusuf. "Saying 'No': How Conflict Avoidance Varies between Cultures." https://www.translatemedia.com/us/blog-us/saying-no-how-conflict-avoidance-varies-between-cultures/.

Blanford, Carl E. *Chinese Churches in Thailand*. Bangkok: Suriyaban, 1974.

Board of Foreign Missions. "The Executive Council of Foreign Board Comments on Dr. Barnhouse's Mission Report." *The Presbyterian* 105 (1935) 1–2, 7.

———. "Is the Board Stalling Foreign Missions?". *Christianity Today* 7 (1936) 4, 14.

Boger, Gretchen E. "American Protestantism in the Asian Crucible, 1919–1939." PhD diss., Princeton University, 2008.

Boon-Itt, Bantoon. "A Study of the Dialogue between Christianity and Buddhism in Thailand as Represented by Buddhist and Christian Writings from Thailand in the Period 1950–2000." PhD thesis, The Open University, St. John's College, 2007.

Bosch, David J. *Transforming Mission: Paradigm Shifts in Theology of Mission*. 20th anniversary ed. Maryknoll, NY: Orbis, 2011.

Bosworth, Edward I. *The Life and Teaching of Jesus According to the First Three Gospels*. New York: Macmillan, 1939.

Bovornsiri, Varaporn, and Gerald Fry. "Higher Education and Thai Development: Past Successes and Future Challenges." *Higher Education Policy* 4 (1991) 30–35.

Braaten, Carl E. *History and Hermeneutics*. London: Lutterworth, 1968.

Bradley, Daniel Beach. *Abstract of the Journal of Rev. Dan Beach Bradley, M.D., Medical Missionary in Siam, 1835–1873*. Cleveland, OH: Dan F. Bradley, 1936.

Brown, Arthur J. "Results of Missions in Siam and Laos." *Missionary Review of the World* 31 (1908) 339–43

Buck, Pearl S. "The Laymen's Mission Report." *Christian Century* 23 (1932) 1434–37.

Carpenter, Joel, ed. *Modernism and Foreign Missions, Two Fundamentalist Protests*. New York: Garland, 1988.

———. *Revive Us Again: The Reawakening of American Fundamentalism*. Oxford: Oxford University Press, 1997.

Cavendish, Richard. "Siam Becomes Thailand." *History Today* 64 (2014). https://www.historytoday.com/archive/months-past/siam-becomes-thailand.

Chaloemtiarana, Thak. "Through Racing Goggles: Modernity, the West, Ambiguous Siamese Alterities and the Construction of Thai Nationalism." *SOJOURN: Journal of Social Issues in Southeast Asia* 31 (2016) 532.

"The Charges All Sustained." *New York Times* (November 30, 1892) 3.

Chisholm, William H. "Hospital Evangelism." *Christianity Today* 3 (1933) 4, 8.

Christensen, Johanne H. "Evangelism—Extensive or Intensive?" *MO* (January–February 1935) 4–35.

"Christianity and Civilization." *New York Evangelist (1830–1902)* 11 (1840) 118.

"Civilization." *Oxford English Dictionary*. http://www.oed.com/view/Entry/33584?redirectedFrom=civilization.

Cort, Edwin. "The Beloved Prince." *Thailand Outlook* 12 (1941) 142–49.
Dahlfred, Karl. "A Bumpy Road to Indigenization: The American Presbyterian Mission and the Church of Christ in Thailand." *Journal of Presbyterian History* 99 (2021) 35–47.
———. *Daniel McGilvary: Pioneer Missionary to Northern Thailand*. CreateSpace, 2013.
———. "Evander McGilvary in Northern Thailand: An Honest 'Heretic' and the 'Conservatives' Who Wanted to Keep Him." *Journal of Presbyterian History* 100 (2022) 4–19.
———. "History of Christianity in Thailand." In *Missions in Southeast Asia: Diversity and Unity in God's Design*, edited by Samuel Ka-Chieng Law and Kiem-Kiok Kwa, 119–38. Carlisle, UK: Langham, 2022.
———. "Missionary Communication When Locals Are Listening." In *Emerging Faith (Seanet 16): Lessons from Mission History in Asia*, edited by Paul H. De Neui, 45–54. Pasadena, CA: William Carey, 2020.
Diskul, M. C. Subhadradis. "Damrong Rajanubhab." Oxford Art Online, 2019.
Dodd, William Clifton. *The Tai Race, Elder Brother of the Chinese: Results of Experience, Exploration and Research of William Clifton Dodd*. Cedar Rapids, IA: The Torch, 1923.
Dorrien, Gary J. *The Making of American Liberal Theology: Idealism, Realism, and Modernity 1900–1950*. 1st ed. Louisville, KY: Westminster John Knox, 2003.
"Dr. C.C. Hansen." *Siam Outlook* 6 (1929) 391.
Eakin, John L. "Siam." In *Interpretative Statistical Survey of the World Mission of the Christian Church*, edited by Joseph I. Parker and International Missionary Council, 286–87. New York: International Missionary Council, 1938,.
Eakin, Paul A. "B. has made Xty." n.d., Eakin Papers, RG017/80, Box 5, Folder 8, PUA, Chiang Mai, Thailand.
———. "Biographical Notes on Dr. and Mrs. Carl Christian Hansen (M.D.)." n.d., Eakin Papers, RG017/80, Box 2, Folder 5, PUA, Chiang Mai, Thailand.
———. "Biographical Notes on Dr. and Mrs. Roderick McLeod Gillies." 1956, Eakin Papers, RG017/80, Box 2, Folder 5, PUA, Chiang Mai, Thailand.
———. "Biographical Notes on Dr. and Mrs. William Harvey Perkins." n.d., Eakin Papers, RG017/80, Box 2, Folder 7, PUA, Chiang Mai, Thailand.
———. "Biographical Notes on Miss Margaret Anna Neuber." 1957, Eakin Papers, RG017/80, Box 2, Folder 7, PUA, Chiang Mai, Thailand.
———. "Biographical Notes on Rev. and Mrs. Samuel Gamble McFarland, 1942." Eakin Papers, RG017/80, Box 2, Folder 10, PUA, Chiang Mai, Thailand.
———. *Buddhism and the Christian Approach to Buddhists in Thailand*. Bangkok: R. Hongladaromp, 1956.
———. "Evangelism—Extensive or Intensive?" *MO* (December 1934) 5–7.
———. "Fundamental Christian Convictions." n.d., Eakin Papers, RG017/80, Box 5, Folder 4, PUA, Chiang Mai, Thailand.
———. "Influence of Foreign Evangelists in Thailand." 1956, Eakin Papers, RG017/80, Box 1, Folder 14, PUA, Chiang Mai, Thailand.
———. "Meeting of Missionaries with Dr. Barnhouse in Bangkok, Jan. 3, 1935." American Presbyterian Mission 1845–1979, RG001/78, Box 3, Folder 14, PUA, Chiang Mai, Thailand.

———. "My Reasonable Faith." n.d., RG017/80, Box 5, Folder 6, Eakin Papers, PUA, Chiang Mai, Thailand.

———. "The New Approach." n.d., Eakin Papers, RG017/80, Box 5, Folder 8, PUA, Chiang Mai, Thailand.

———. "Question: Why is it that Christians today cannot 'speak with tongues' and 'prophecy' as they could in the early Church?" n.d., Eakin Papers, RG017/80, Box 5, Folder 5, PUA, Chiang Mai, Thailand.

———. "The Road of Approach to Non-Christians." Eakin Papers, RG017/80, Box 5, Folder 5, PUA, Chiang Mai, Thailand.

———. *Sermon Outlines*. 1928 to 1931, RG017/80, Eakin Papers, RG017/80, Box 5, Folder 7, PUA, Chiang Mai, Thailand.

———. "What Can We Believe?, n.d., Eakin Papers, RG017/80, Box 5, Folder 5, PUA, Chiang Mai, Thailand.

Eisenstadt, S. N., ed. *Multiple Modernities*. New Brunswick, NJ: Transaction, 2002.

Enns, Peter. "Protestantism and Biblical Criticism: One Perspective on a Difficult Dialogue." In *The Bible and the Believer: How to Read the Bible Critically and Religiously*, 126–73. New York: Oxford University Press, 2013.

Farrington, Anthony, ed. *Early Missionaries in Bangkok: The Journals of Tomlin, Gutzlaff, and Abeel, 1828–1832*. Bangkok: White Lotus, 2001.

Ford, Norm. "History of the CMA Work in Thailand." Thai Missions Digital Library. https://www.thaimissions.info/gsdl/collect/thaimiss/index/assoc/HASH012e.dir/doc.pdf.

Freeman, John H. *Siam: The Need, the Opportunity*. New York: The Board of Foreign Missions of the Presbyterian Church in the U.S.A., 1916.

Fuller, Paul. "The Siamo-Burmese-American Gospel Team in Siam." *Siam Outlook* 8 (1932) 66–68.

Gay, Peter. *Modernism: The Lure of Heresy*. New York: W.W. Norton, 2008.

Gifford, Paul. *Christianity, Development and Modernity in Africa*. Oxford: Oxford University Press, 2016.

Gittisarn, Boon Mark et al. "Excerpts from Letters." *Siam Outlook* 10 (1939) 114–18.

Goodpasture, H. Mckennie. "The World's Parliament of Religions Revisited: The Missionaries and Early Steps in Public Dialogue." *Missiology: An International Review* 21 (1993) 403–11.

Gurock, Jeffrey S., ed. *American Zionism: Mission and Politics*. London: Routledge, 1998.

Hamilton, Michael S. "The Interdenominational Evangelicalism of D. L. Moody and the Problem of Fundamentalism." In *American Evangelicalism: George Marsden and the State of American Religious History*, edited by Darren Dochuk et al., 230–80. Notre Dame, IN: University of Notre Dame Press, 2014.

Hanna, Loren. "Evangelism—Extensive or Intensive?," *MO* (December 1934) 34–36.

Hart, D. G. "When Is a Fundamentalist a Modernist? J. Gresham Machen, Cultural Modernism, and Conservative Protestantism." *Journal of the American Academy of Religion* 65 (1997) 605–33.

Hart, Darryl G. *Defending the Faith: J. Gresham Machen and the Crisis of Conservative Protestantism in Modern America*. Phillipsburg, N.J: P & R, 2003.

Hill, Jonathan. *The History of Christian Thought*. Oxford: Lion, 2003.

Hocking, William Ernest, ed. *Re-Thinking Missions: A Laymen's Inquiry after One Hundred Years*. New York: Harper Brothers, 1932.

Hollinger, David A. *Protestants Abroad How Missionaries Tried to Change the World but Changed America.* Princeton: Princeton University Press, 2017.
Hooper, J. Leon. "An Enlarged Program for the Thailand Mission." *Women and Missions* 16 (1939) 243–46.
Hopkins, Charles Howard. *John R. Mott, 1865-1955: A Biography.* Grand Rapids: Eerdmans, 1979.
House, Austin Lee. "An Ethnohistorical Study of Thai Christians and Their Participation in Cross-Cultural Missions from 1870-1940." DMiss diss., Western Seminary, 2017.
Hudson, Cornelia Kneedler. "Daniel McGilvary in Siam: Foreign Missions, the Civil War, and Presbyterian Unity." *American Presbyterians* 69 (1991) 283–93.
Hutchison, William. "Modernism and Missions: The Liberal Search for an Exportable Christianity, 1875-1935." In *The Missionary Enterprise in China and America*, edited by John King Fairbank, 110–31. Cambridge, MA: Harvard University Press, 1974.
Hutchison, William R. *Errand to the World: American Protestant Thought and Foreign Missions.* Chicago: University of Chicago Press, 1987.
———. *The Modernist Impulse in American Protestantism.* Durham: Duke University Press, 1992.
Indhabhan, Chomchai. "Siamese Students in the Philippines." *Siam Outlook* (October 1934) 126–27.
International Missionary Council. *The Christian Life and Message in Relation to Non-Christian Systems: Report of the Jerusalem Meeting of the International Missionary Council, March 24th—April 8th, 1928.* 8 vols. London: Oxford University Press, 1928.
———. *Report of The Jerusalem meeting of the International Missionary Council, March 24th—April 8th, 1928.* 8 vols. London: Oxford University Press, 1928.
———. *The World Mission of the Church: Findings and Recommendations of the Meeting of the International Missionary Council—Tambaram, Madras, India, Dec. 12–29, 1938.* London; New York: International Missionary Council, 1938.
Ireland, Daryl R. *John Song: Modern Chinese Christianity and the Making of a New Man.* Studies in World Christianity. Waco, TX: Baylor University Press, 2020.
Irvine, William C. "The Inter-Religious Movement in India." *Christianity Today* 3 (1932) 7–8.
Itthipongmaetee, Chayanit. "Kinokuniya Pulls Oxford Researcher's Book on 2010 Bangkok Unrest." *Khaosod* (December 1, 2017). http://www.khaosodenglish.com/featured/2017/12/01/kinokuniya-pulls-oxford-researchers-book-2010-bangkok-unrest/.
"Japanese Christian Leaders Appraise the Appraisal." *Siam Outlook* 9 (1933) 151–52.
Javani, Suda. "Changing Custom." *Siam Outlook* 4 (1925) 140–41.
Jennings, John Nelson. "Theology in Japan: Takakura Tokutaro (1885–1934)." PhD thesis, The University of Edinburgh, 1995.
Jeshurun, Chandran. "The Anglo-French Declaration of January 1896 and the Independence of Siam." *Journal of the Siam Society* 58 (1961) 105–26.
Jong, James A. de. *As the Waters Cover the Sea: Millennial Expectations in the Rise of Anglo-American Missions, 1640–1810.* Kampen: Kok, 1970.
"Justice Minister Supports Vigilantism against Lèse-Majesté." *Prachatai English* (October 18, 2016). https://prachatai.com/english/node/6661.

Kilpatrick, Faye. "Evangelism—Extensive or Intensive?," *MO* (December 1934) 29–30.
———. "Her Future." *Siam Outlook* (October 1932) 113–15.
Kim, Samuel I. *The Unfinished Mission in Thailand: The Uncertain Christian Impact on the Buddhist Heartland*. Seoul: East-West Center for Missions Research and Development, 1980.
"King Asks Aid to Stop Siam's Gambling Evil." *New York Times* (March 16, 1905) 7.
Komin, Suntaree. "Culture and Work-Related Values in Thai Organizations." *International Journal of Psychology* 25 (1990) 681–704.
Landon, Kenneth P. "Nationalization, Whither Bound?" *MO* (November 1934) 17–23, 6–24.
———. *Thailand in Transition: A Brief Survey of Cultural Trends in the Five Years since the Revolution of 1932*. Chicago: The University of Chicago Press, 1939.
Landon, M. "There Were Giants." *MO* (May 1934) 22.
Lauzon, Matthew J. "Modernity." In *The Oxford Handbook of World History*, edited by Jerry H. Bentley, 1–19 (online), 72–88 (print). Oxford: Oxford University Press, 2011.
"The Laymen's Foreign Missions Inquiry." *Christianity Today* 3 (1932) 18–22.
Lee, Leo Ou-fan. *Shanghai Modern: The Flowering of a New Urban Culture in China, 1930–1945*. Cambridge, MA: Harvard University Press, 1999.
Lee, Timothy S. "A Political Factor in the Rise of Protestantism in Korea: Protestantism and the 1919 March First Movement." *Church History: Studies in Christianity and Culture* 69 (2000) 116–42.
Leonowens, Anna Harriette. *The English Governess at the Siamese Court*. London: Trübner, 1870.
Livingston, James C. *Modern Christian Thought*. Edited by Francis Schüssler Fiorenza. 2nd ed. Minneapolis: Fortress, 2006.
Livingstone, David N. *Darwin's Forgotten Defenders: The Encounter between Evangelical Theology and Evolutionary Thought*. Edinburgh: Scottish Academic, 1987.
Loetscher, Lefferts A. *The Broadening Church: Theological Issues in the Presbyterian Church since 1869*. Philadelphia: University of Pennsylvania Press, 1954.
Longfield, Bradley. "William P. Merrill, the Brick Church, and the Fundamentalist-Modernist Conflict." *Journal of Presbyterian History* 97 (2019) 61–72.
Longfield, Bradley J. *The Presbyterian Controversy: Fundamentalists, Modernists, and Moderates*. Religion in America Series. Oxford: Oxford University Press, 1991.
Loos, Tamara. *Subject Siam: Family, Law, and Colonial Modernity in Thailand*. Chiang Mai: Silkworm, 2006.
Lord, Donald. "In His Steps: A Biography of Dan Beach Bradley, Medical Missionary to Thailand, 1835–1873." PhD diss., Western Reserve University, 1964.
Lorgunpai, Seree. "World Lover, World Leaver: The Book of Ecclesiastes and Thai Buddhism." PhD thesis, University of Edinburgh, 1995.
Lutz, Jessie Gregory. *Opening China: Karl F.A. Gützlaff and Sino-Western Relations, 1827–1852*. Grand Rapids: Eerdmans, 2008.
Lyall, Leslie T. *John Sung*. Edited by John R. W. Stott. London: China Inland Mission, 1954.
Machen, J. Gresham. *Christianity and Liberalism*. Grand Rapids: Eerdmans, 1946.
———. "Modernism and the Board of Foreign Missions of the Presbyterian Church in the U.S.A." In *Modernism and Foreign Missions, Two Fundamentalist Protests*, edited by Joel Carpenter, 1–111. New York: Garland, 1988.

Mahidol University. "History." https://www2.si.mahidol.ac.th/en/history/.
The Maitrichit Chinese Baptist Church. "History of the Church." http://www.maitrichit church.org/about-us/.
Marsden, George M. *Fundamentalism and American Culture: The Shaping of Twentieth Century Evangelicalism, 1870–1925*. Oxford: Oxford University Press, 2016.
Marshall, Andrew MacGregor. *A Kingdom in Crisis*. London: Zed, 2014.
Marty, Martin E. *The Noise of Conflict, 1914–1941, Modern American Religion*. Vol. 2. Chicago: Chicago University Press, 1991.
Mathews, Shailer. *The Faith of Modernism*. New York: AMS, 1969.
McAfee, Cleland Boyd. *Changing Foreign Missions: A Revaluation of the Church's Greatest Enterprise*. New York: Fleming H. Revell, 1927.
———. *The Uncut Nerve of Missions: An Inquiry and an Answer*. New York: Fleming H. Revell, 1932.
McDaniel, Justin. *Gathering Leaves and Lifting Words: Histories of Buddhist Monastic Education in Laos and Thailand*. Seattle: University of Washington Press, 2008.
McFarland, Bertha Blount. "Evangelism—Extensive or Intensive?" *Mission Opinion* (January-February 1935) 8–9.
———. *McFarland of Siam*. New York: Vantage, 1958.
———. *Our Garden Was So Fair: The Story of a Mission in Thailand*. Philadelphia: Blakiston, 1943.
McFarland, George Bradley, ed. *Historical Sketch of Protestant Missions in Siam, 1828–1928*. Bangkok: White Lotus, 1999.
McGiffert, Arthur Cushman. *The Rise of Modern Religious Ideas*. New York: Macmillan, 1915.
McGilvary, Daniel. *A Half Century among the Siamese and the Lao: An Autobiography*. Edited by Cornelius Beach Bradley New York: Revell, 1912.
McIntire, Carl, and Boon Mark Gittisarn. *Modernism Takes Its Toll of Mission Work*. Collingswood, NJ: Christian Beacon, n.d.
McLean, Patricia. "Thai Protestant Christianity: A Study of Cultural and Theological Interactions between Western Missionaries (the American Presbyterian Mission and the Overseas Missionary Fellowship) and Indigenous Thai Churches (the Church of Christ in Thailand and the Associated Churches of Thailand-Central)." PhD thesis, University of Edinburgh, 2002.
McLeish, Alexander. *To-Day in Thailand*. War-Time Survey Series. New York: World Dominion, 1942.
Mejuhon, Nanthachai, ed. *175 Years Protestantism in Thailand (1828–2003)* [๑๗๕ ปี พันธกิจคริสต์ศาสนาโปรเตสแตนต์ในประเทศไทย (คศ. ๑๘๒๘-๒๐๐๓)]. Bangkok: Thailand Protestant Churches Co-ordinating Committee, 2004.
Moffett, Samuel Hugh. "The Relation of the Board of Foreign Missions of the Presbyterian Church in the United States of America to the Missions and Church Connected with It in China." PhD diss., Yale University, 1945.
Mostert, Christiaan. *God and the Future: Wolfhart Pannenberg's Eschatological Doctrine of God*. London: T. & T. Clark, 2002.
"Mrs. Buck Resigns; Board Accepts 'with Deep Regret.'" *Christianity Today* 4 (1933) 34–36.
Murray, Iain H. *The Puritan Hope: A Study in Revival and the Interpretation of Prophecy*. Edinburgh: Banner of Truth, 1971.

Nevius, John. *The Planting and Development of Missionary Churches*. Hancock, NH: Monadnock, 2003.

Niblock, Lucy. "Evangelism—Extensive or Intensive?" *Mission Opinion* (January–February, 1935) 17–18.

"Northern Thai Literary Tradition." Digital Library of Northern Thai Manuscripts. http://lannamanuscripts.net/en/about.

Numbers, Ronald L. *The Creationists: From Scientific Creationism to Intelligent Design*. Expanded ed. Cambridge, MA: Harvard University Press, 2006.

Paas, Stefan. "'Notoriously Religious' or Secularising? Revival and Secularisation in Sub-Saharan Africa." *Exchange* 48 (2019) 26–50.

Pascal, Eva. "Buddhist Monks and Christian Friars: Religious and Cultural Exchange in the Making of Buddhism." *Studies in World Christianity* 22 (2016) 5–21.

Paton, William, and M. M. Underhill. "A Survey of the Year 1937—Southeast Asia." *International Review of Missions* 27 (1938) 26.

———. "A World Survey." *International Review of Mission* 17 (January 1928) 11–73.

Patterson, James Alan. "The Loss of a Protestant Missionary Consensus: Foreign Missions and the Fundamentalist-Modernist Conflict." In *Earthen Vessels: American Evangelicals and Foreign Missions, 1880–1980*, edited by Joel Carpenter and Wilbert Shenk, 73–91. Grand Rapids: Eerdmans, 1990.

Peleggi, Maurizio. *Lords of Things: The Fashioning of the Siamese Monarchy's Modern Image*. Honolulu: University of Hawai'i Press, 2002.

Perkins, William. "Personal Report: Dr. and Mrs. William H. Perkins." October 31, 1920, RG84, Box 9, Folder 8a, UPCUSA COEMAR Secretaries Files: Thailand Mission, PHS, Philadelphia.

Perlez, Jane. "A Banned Book Challenges Saintly Image of Thai King." *New York Times* (September 25, 2006). https://www.nytimes.com/2006/09/25/world/asia/25thailand.html.

Persons, Larry S. *The Way Thais Lead: Face as Social Capital*. Chiang Mai: Silkworm, 2016.

Piper, John F. *Robert E. Speer: Prophet of the American Church*. Louisville, KY: Geneva, 2000.

Pongudom, Maen. "Apologetic and Missionary Proclamation: Exemplified by American Presbyterian Missionaries to Thailand (1828–1978), Early Church Apologists: Justin Martyr, Clement of Alexandria and Origen, and the Venerable Buddhadasa Bhikkhu, a Thai Buddhist Monk-Apologist." PhD thesis, University of Otago, 1979.

Pongudom, Prasit. *History of the Church of Christ in Thailand* [ประวัติศาสตร์สภาคริสตจักรในประเทศไทย]. Chiang Mai: Archives Unit, Church of Christ in Thailand, 1984.

Prateepchaikul, Veera. "Sulak Lese Majeste Case So Absurd It Hurts." *Bangkok Post* (October 16, 2017). https://www.bangkokpost.com/opinion/opinion/1343059/sulak-lese-majeste-case-so-absurd-it-hurts.

Presbyterian Board of Publication. *Siam and Laos as Seen by Our American Missionaries*. Philadelphia: Presbyterian Board of Publication, 1884.

Presbyterian Church in the U.S.A. *Manual of the Board of Foreign Missions of the Presbyterian Church in the U.S.A.* Rev. ed. New York: Presbyterian Church in the U.S.A., 1922.

———. *Manual for the Foreign Missions Committee of Synods and Presbyteries*. New York: Board of Foreign Missions of the Presbyterian Church in the U.S.A., 1939.
"Prof. Smith's Heresy Trial." *New York Times* (November 22, 1892) 3.
"Prof. Smith's Trial." *New York Times* (November 29, 1892) 4.
"Protestant Missions Centenary. His Majesty's Heartening Address." *Bangkok Times* (December 7, 1928).
Quirk, Charles. "The 'Auburn' Affirmation: A Critical Narrative of the Document Designed to Safeguard the Unity and Liberty of the Presbyterian Church in the United States of America in 1924." PhD diss., The University of Iowa, 1967.
Rabe, Valentin H. *The Home Base of American China Missions, 1880-1920*. Cambridge, MA: Harvard University Press, 1978.
Race, Alan. *Christians and Religious Pluralism: Patterns in the Christian Theology of Religions*. London: SCM, 1983.
Rajanubhab, Damrong. "Introductory Chapter." In *Historical Sketch of Protestant Missions in Siam, 1828-1928*, edited by George Bradley McFarland, 1-15. Bangkok: White Lotus, 1999.
Rall, Harris Franklin. "Some Modern Interpretations of Christianity: The Faith of Modernism—Shailer Mathews; the Modern Use of the Bible—Harry Emerson Fosdick; Present Tendencies in Religious Thought—Albert C. Knudson; the Supremacy of the Spiritual—Herbert Alden Youtx; Principles of Christian Living—Gerald B. Smith; Religion in the Thought of Today—Carl S. Patton; Dying Lights and Dawning—Edmond Holmes." *The Journal of Religion* 2 (1925) 196-202.
Reichel, Katherine L. "Quarterly Letter—Chiang Mai Station." June 1920, Box 1, RG84, UPCUSA. COEMAR Secretaries' Files: Thailand Mission, PHS, Philadelphia.
"Report of Bangkok Station Meeting." November 18, 1931, American Presbyterian Mission 1845-1979, RG001/78, Box 14, Folder 11, PUA, Chiang Mai, Thailand.
"Rev. E.B. McGilvary: Acceptance of His Resignation Withdrawn by our Foreign Board." *The Evangelist* 65 (March 22, 1894) 27.
Reynolds, Bruce. "Phibun Songkhram and Thai Nationalism in the Fascist Era." *European Journal of East Asian Studies* 3 (2004) 99-134.
Rian, Edwin H. *The Presbyterian Conflict*. Grand Rapids: Eerdmans, 1940.
Rockwell, William Walter. "Arthur Cushman McGiffert." *Church History* 2 (1933) 105-6.
Rostam-Kolayi, Jasamin. "From Evangelizing to Modernizing Iranians: The American Presbyterian Mission and Its Iranian Students." *Iranian Studies* 41 (2008) 213-40.
Roy, Andrew T. "Overseas Mission Policies—an Historical Overview." *Journal of Presbyterian History* 57 (1979) 186-228.
Russell, C. Allyn. "Donald Grey Barnhouse: Fundamentalist Who Changed." *Journal of Presbyterian History* 59 (1981) 33-57.
Rycroft, W. Stanley. *The Ecumenical Witness of the United Presbyterian Church in the U.S.A.* Philadelphia: United Presbyterian Church in the USA, 1968.
Saler, Michael. "Modernity and Enchantment: A Historiographic Review." *The American Historical Review* 111 (2006) 692-716.
Sandeen, Ernest Robert. *The Roots of Fundamentalism: British and American Millenarianism, 1800-1930*. Chicago: University of Chicago Press, 1970.
Schlect, Christopher. "Onward Christian Administrators." PhD diss., Washington State University, 2015.
"Secretary McAfee's Book Hailed by Modernism." *Christianity Today* 3 (1933) 22-23.
Seigle, Albert. "A Life Laid Down." *Siam Outlook* 6 (1929) 312-23.

Selden, Charles. *Are Missions a Failure?: A Correspondent's Survey of Foreign Missions*. New York: Revell, 1927.

———. "Christianity in Asia Today." *Ladies' Home Journal* 44 (1927) 170, 189–90, 193.

Shapiro, M. C., R. A. Shapiro, and Siwaporn Ubolcholket. "Medical Education in Thailand." *Medical Education* 26 (1992) 251–58.

Sharkey, Heather J. *American Evangelicals in Egypt: Missionary Encounters in an Age of Empire*. Princeton: Princeton University Press, 2008.

Sharpe, Eric J. *Not to Destroy but to Fulfil: The Contribution of J.N. Farquhar to Protestant Missionary Thought in India before 1914*. Lund: Gleerup, 1965.

"Siam." *The Straits Times* (September 12, 1854) 5.

"Siam Is Progressive: Dr. Dunlap, a Pioneer Missionary, Talks of Changes of Twenty-Five Years." *The Washington Post* (January 14, 1901) 12.

Sibree, James. *London Missionary Society: A Register of Missionaries and Deputations, Etc. From 1796 to 1923*. 4th ed. London: London Missionary Society, 1923.

Singhanetra, Civili. "Public Health." *Thailand Outlook* 11 (1940) 201–4.

Skinner, Conrad A. *Concerning the Bible: A Brief Sketch of Its Origin, Growth and Contents*. London: S. Low, Marston, 1928.

Smith, Alex G. *Siamese Gold, a History of Church Growth in Thailand, 1816–1982*. Bangkok: OMF Thailand, 1982.

Son, Seung Ho. "Christian Revival in the Presbyterian Church of Thailand between 1900 and 1941: An Ecclesiological Analysis and Evaluation." ThD diss., University of Stellenbosch, 2003.

Song, Shangjie. *The Diary of John Sung: Extracts from His Journals and Notes*. Translated by Pheng Soon Thng. Singapore: Genesis, 2012.

———. *Wode Jianzheng (My Testimony)*. Repr. Hong Kong: Bellman House, 1995.

Speer, Robert E. "The Civilizing Influence in Missions." In *Missionary Principles and Practice: A Discussion of Christian Missions and of Some Criticisms Upon Them*, 412–42. New York: Fleming H. Revell, 1902.

———. *Re-Thinking Missions Examined: An Attempt at a Just Review of the Report of the Appraisal Commission of the Laymen's Foreign Mission Inquiry*. New York: Fleming H. Revell, 1933.

———. *The Unfinished Task of Foreign Missions*. New York: Revell, 1926.

Speer, Robert, et al. *Report of Deputation of the Presbyterian Board of Foreign Missions to Siam, the Philippines, Japan Chosen and China, April-November, 1915*. New York: The Board of Foreign Missions of the Presbyterian Church in the USA, 1915.

Stanley, Brian, ed. *Christian Missions and the Enlightenment*. Cambridge: Curzon, 2001.

———. *Christianity in the Twentieth Century: A World History*. Princeton: Princeton University Press, 2018.

———. "Christianity, Modernism and Modernization: The Chinese Experience in the Context of Global Trends in the Twentieth Century." In *Western Tides Coming Ashore in a Changing World: Christianity and China's Passage into Modernity*, edited by Timothy M. Wong et al., 19–39. Hong Kong: Alliance Bible Seminary, 2015.

———. "From 'The Poor Heathen' To 'The Glory and Honour of All Nations': Vocabularies of Race and Custom in Protestant Missions, 1844–1928. *International Bulletin of Missionary Research* 34 (2010) 3.

———. *The World Missionary Conference, Edinburgh 1910*. Grand Rapids: Eerdmans, 2009.

Starling, Lucy. "Re-Thinking Missions and Siam—a Condensed Report of the Executive Committee's Discussion." *Siam Outlook* 9 (1933) 120–27.
Stated Clerk, ed. *Minutes of the General Assembly of the Presbyterian Church in the United States of America*. Vol. 16. Philadelphia: PCUSA, 1893.
Stewart, Herbert W. "Recommendations Made by Joint Committee, 1927." RG017/80, Box 2, Folder 10, Eakin Papers, PUA, Chiang Mai, Thailand.
Strate, Shane. *The Lost Territories: Thailand's History of National Humiliation*. Honolulu: Univeristy of Hawai'i Press, 2015.
———. "The Sukhothai Incident: Buddhist Heritage, Mormon Missionaries, and Religious Desecration in Thailand." *Journal of Religion and Violence* 4 (2016) 183–203.
———. "An Uncivil State of Affairs: Fascism and Anti-Catholicism in Thailand, 1940–1944." *Journal of Southeast Asian Studies* 42 (2011) 59–87.
Strong, Sarah L. "Nan, Siam Station Report, October 1, 1919 to October 31, 1920." RG84, Box 9, Folder 8a, UPCUSA COEMAR Secretaries Files: Thailand Mission, PHS, Philadelphia.
Suksod-Barger, Runchana. *Religious Influences in Thai Female Education (1889–1931)*. Cambridge: James Clarke, 2014.
Suriyakham, Sing Keo. "Siamo-Burmese Gospel Team." *Siam Outlook* 8 (1932) 64–66.
Swanson, Herbert. "Conservative in Theology, Liberal in Spirit." *HeRB: Herb's Research Bulletin* no. 3 (September 2002). https://www.herbswanson.com/herb-s-research-bulliten.
———. *Krischak Muang Nua: A Study in Northern Thai Church History*. Bangkok: Chuan Printing, 1984.
———. "The Pastors' Revolt of 1895." In *Pastoral Care and the Church of Christ in Thailand: A Report on the State of Pastoral Care in the CCT Today*. Chiang Mai: Office of History, Church of Christ in Thailand, 1994.
———. "Paul A. Eakin." In *Dictionary of Asian Christianity*, edited by Scott Sunquist, 257. Grand Rapids: Eerdmans, 2001.
———. *Towards a Clean Church: A Case Study in Nineteenth-Century Thai Church History*. Chiang Mai: Office of History, Church of Christ in Thailand, 1991.
Tanphaichitr, Sirirat. "Modernization and Tradition: The Case of Thai Education." PhD diss., St. Louis University, 1977.
Tate, Mowbray. "Educational Progress in Thailand." *Thailand Outlook* 12 (1941) 160–68.
Taylor, Hugh. "A Missionary in Siam." Unpublished manuscript, PUA, 1947.
Telecom of Thailand (TOT). "Birth of the Telephone [กำเนิดโทรศัพท์]." https://www.tot.co.th/เกี่ยวกับองค์กร/กำเนิดโทรศัพท์.
Terwiel, B. J. *Thailand's Political History: From the 13th Century to Recent Times*. Rev. ed. Bangkok: ACC Distribution, 2011.
"Thai Police Ban Scot's Book for 'Insulting' Royal Family." *BBC News* (November 13, 2014). https://www.bbc.co.uk/news/uk-scotland-30035282.
"Thailand." In *World Christian Encyclopedia*, edited by Todd M. Johnson and Gina A. Zurlo, 789–93. Edinburgh: Edinburgh University Press, 2019.
Thailand by Train. "Thai Railway History." https://www.thailandbytrain.com/RailHistory.html.

Thomas, W. H. Griffith. "Modernism in China." In *Modernism and Foreign Missions, Two Fundamentalist Protests*, edited by Joel Carpenter, 630–71. New York: Garland, 1988.

Tomlin, Jacob. *Journal of a Nine Months' Residence in Siam*. London: F. Westley and A.H. Davis, 1831.

Trakulhun, Sven. "Among a People of Unclean Lips: Eliza and John Taylor Jones in Siam (1833–1851)." *Asiatische Studien / Études Asiatiques* 67 (2013) 1205–35.

Treloar, Geoffrey R. *The Disruption of Evangelicalism: The Age of Torrey, Mott, McPherson and Hammond*. A History of Evangelicalism. Downers Grove, IL: IVP Academic, 2017.

"Twenty Years Ago." *The Bangkok Times*, September 16, 1933, SC–38, Box 227, Folder 13, Landon Papers, Wheaton College Special Collections.

Vajiravudh. *Wild Tiger Sermons* [หนังสือเทศนาเสือป่า]. Bangkok: Bannakit Printing, 1927.

Van Beek, Steve. *Royal Automobile Stables of Siam*. Translated by Chusak Chomjinda. Thailand: Castrol (Thailand), 1994.

Van Der Veer, Peter. "The Global History Of 'Modernity'." *Journal of the Economic and Social History of the Orient* 41 (1998) 285–94.

Wallace, Irving, and Amy Wallace. *The Two: The Story of the Original Siamese Twins*. New York: Simon and Schuster, 1978.

Walls, Andrew. "Eschatology and the Western Missionary Movement." *Studies in World Christianity* 22 (2016) 182–200.

Warfield, Benjamin B. *The Inspiration and Authority of the Bible*. Edited by Samuel G. Craig and Benjamin Breckinridge Warfield. Philadelphia: Presbyterian and Reformed, 1948.

Watson, J. K. P. "Missionary Influence on Education in Thailand C. 1660–1970." *Paedagogica Historica* 23 (1983) 145–62.

Wells, Kenneth. *History of Protestant Work in Thailand*. Bangkok, Thailand: Church of Christ in Thailand, 1958.

———. *Theravada Buddhism and Protestant Christianity*. Bangkok: Charoen Tham, 1963.

Winichakul, Thongchai. "Buddhist Apologetics and a Genealogy of Comparative Religion in Siam." *Numen* 62 (2015) 76–99.

———. *Siam Mapped: A History of the Geo-Body of a Nation*. Honolulu: University of Hawaii Press, 1994.

———. "The Quest for 'Siwilai': A Geographical Discourse of Civilizational Thinking in the Late Nineteenth and Early Twentieth-Century Siam." *The Journal of Asian Studies* 59 (2000) 528–49.

Winship, Win. "Oren Root, Darwinism and Biblical Criticism." *Journal of Presbyterian History* 62 (1984) 111–23.

Woodward, Walter C. "Too Many Labels." *The American Friend* (March 27, 1924) 243–44.

World Missionary Conference. *Report Of Commission IV—the Missionary Message in Relation to Non-Christian Religions*. Edinburgh: Oliphant, Anderson & Ferrier, 1910.

Wu, Albert Monshan. *From Christ to Confucius*. New Haven, CT: Yale University Press, 2017.

Wyatt, David K. *Thailand: A Short History*. New Haven, CT: Yale University Press, 1984.

Xi, Lian. *The Conversion of Missionaries: Liberalism in American Protestant Missions in China, 1907–1932*. University Park, PA: Pennsylvania State University Press, 1997.

Yao, Kevin Xiyi. *The Fundamentalist Movement among Protestant Missionaries in China, 1920–1937*. Lanham, MD: University Press of America, 2003.

Yim, Hee-Mo. *Unity Lost—Unity to Be Regained in Korean Presbyterianism: A History of Divisions in Korean Presbyterianism and the Role of the Means of Grace*. Frankfurt am Main: Peter Lang, 1996.

Yim, Sung Bihn. "Korea." In *The Cambridge Companion to Reformed Theology*, edited by David A. S. Fergusson and Paul T. Nimmo, 296–306. Cambridge: Cambridge University Press, 2016.

Zehner, Edwin. "Church Growth and Culturally Appropriate Leadership: Three Examples from the Thai Church." Unpublished manuscript, Fuller Theological Seminary, November 5, 1987.

———. "Thai Protestants and Local Supernaturalism: Changing Configurations." *Journal of Southeast Asian Studies* 27 (1996) 293–319.

Subject Index

American Board of Commissioners for Foreign Missions (ABCFM), 20, 34, 76–81, 127, 195, 244
American Presbyterian Church. *See* Presbyterian Church in the USA (PCUSA)
anti-supernaturalism. *See* supernaturalism
apologetics, 84–85, 126–27
astrology. *See* astronomy
astronomy, 52–53, 84–85
attrition, 124, 127, 131

Bachtell, Ray, 140, 144, 149–50, 157, 169–71, 254
Banchop Bansiddhi, 112, 123, 178–80, 239
Bangkok Christian College, 88, 140, 144, 151, 162–64, 167, 220, 223–24, 226, 231, 242
Barnhouse, Donald Grey, 43–44, 130, 140, 157–72, 184, 230, 236, 240, 246–47
Barrows, John Henry, 193
Bassett, Allen, 164–67, 220–21
Beach, William, 168–71
BFM. See *Board of Foreign Missions*
Bhanurangsi Savangwongse, 61
bible, authority of, 16–17
Bible Institute Controversy, 179–83

Bible Institute of Los Angeles. *See* Biola University
biblical criticism, 10–11, 17, 103–13, 149n, 237
Biola University, 139, 151
Board of Foreign Missions, 33–44
  origin, 34–35
  organization, 35–36
  purpose and works, 36–37
  role in Fundamentalist-Modernist Controversy, 37–44
Boon Mark Gittisarn, 174–75, 179–80, 206, 208–10
Boon Mee Rungreungwongse, 182–83
Boon Tee, 76
Buck, Pearl S, 11n15, 41–42, 131, 141–42, 195
Bradley, Daniel Beach, 53, 58, 78–80
Bradley, Sophia. *See* McGilvary, Sophia
Briggs, Charles Augustus, 20, 104–5
Briggs, William A., 126–27, 193–94
Brown, Arthur J., 35, 38, 39, 116–19, 122, 127–29, 149–57, 242, 246–47
Buddhism
  education, 56, 88, 226
  folk beliefs, 87, 122
  missionary attitudes, 124–27, 129–30, 138–39, 192–94, 198, 203–9
  modernization, 52–53, 62–64, 151, 238

Buddhism *(continued)*
  nationalism, 68–69, 71, 127, 170
  religious tolerance, 64–65
  sacred texts, 125–26
Bulkley, Edna, 139n121, 182, 184, 241
Bulkley, Lucius Constant, 241–42

Campbell, Howard, 171
Caswell, Jesse, 53, 77, 79
Catholicism. *See* Roman Catholicism
CCT. *See* Church of Christ in Thailand
Chiang Mai
Charoen Sakulkan, 111, 123, 181–82
China, 34, 48–49, 51, 76, 77–78, 97, 147, 158, 173, 243–48
  education, 167, 225
  modernism, 27–28, 34, 37–38, 40, 42, 99, 114–16, 124–26, 195, 235–39
  Chinese in Thailand, 62, 71, 75–77, 81–82, 88, 96, 127, 137, 166, 175
China Inland Mission (CIM), 23
Chinda Singhanetra, 180–81
Chulalongkorn, King, 47–48, 53–61, 64, 67–68, 123, 238
Church of Christ in Thailand (CCT), 96–98, 166, 174–75, 182, 220, 239
Coffin, Henry Sloane, 32–33, 119. 132n106, 150, 171
Cort, Edwin, 170, 177–78, 183, 202n38, 242

Damrong Rajanubhab, 54, 56, 61, 84, 151, 201, 204–9, 214
damnation, 18, 24–25, 62–64, 127–28, 131–33, 188, 191–98, 204, 227
division, xi, 28, 32, 99, 101, 148, 172, 176–83
Dodd, William Clifton, 127
Dunlap, Eugene Pressley, 83, 164

Eakin, John Lyman, 94, 214
Eakin, John A., 83, 88, 183, 94, 164, 206
Eakin, Paul Anderson, xxi, 13, 94, 109–113, 121, 123, 129, 132–41, 145, 149, 151–66, 178–85, 195–98, 201, 207–10, 216–17, 227–32, 234, 236, 240–41, 246, 249
  theological beliefs, 109–111, 121, 132–34, 227–29
education. *See* schools
Elder, Carl, 112–13, 123. 131, 134–36, 139, 149, 155–57, 162, 171, 177–84, 236, 239
England, 45–46, 48, 54, 61, 68–69, 77, 187
Erdman, Charles R., 33, 38, 42, 200
Esther Pradipasena, 82, 151
eternal destiny. *See* damnation
evangelism, xxii–xxiv, 23, 25, 27, 28, 37–39, 40, 75, 80, 82, 86, 89–90, 93–95, 100, 104, 120–22, 127–30, 133–34, 136–46, 147, 149, 151–52, 154, 167–73, 175–81, 183–87, 191, 198–99, 201, 203, 206, 209–36, 240, 245, 248–49
evolution, 6–19, 32, 114, 116, 163, 186, 223, 237

fatherhood of God, 16, 18–19
First Church, Chiang Mai, 87, 182
First Church, Samray, 81
Fosdick, Harry Emerson, 14, 30, 32, 132n106
France, 45–46, 48–50, 54, 61, 67–71, 74
Fuller, Graham, 130–31, 162
Fuller, Paul, 139–40, 151–53, 155–57, 206–9, 216, 223–24, 230, 232, 236, 240, 242
fundamentalism and fundamentalists, xxi, 12, 19, 25, 30, 40–42, 111–15, 135–39, 148–96, 209, 229
  definition, xv, 30–32
Fundamentalist-Modernist Controversy
  in China, x, 27, 99
  in India, 43–44
  in Korea, 19, 27
  in Thailand, xi, xiv, 101, 147, 234–49
  in United States, xiii, 21, 28, 32–33, 99
  in Board of Foreign Missions, 37–44
Fundamentals, The (books), 17, 30

Gillies, Cornelia, 114, 119–22, 191, 195
Gillies, Roderick, 28–29
gospel teams (Burmese), 139–41, 167, 224
Gützlaff, Karl F. A., 58, 75–76, 192

Hanna, Loren, 135, 139–40, 167–69, 171, 177, 179, 181–84, 224, 229–32, 236, 240
Hansen, Carl C., 128–30
Harris, William, 139–41, 144, 162, 167, 171, 194, 224
hell. *See* damnation
higher criticism. *See* biblical criticism
Holladay, John Scott, 183
Horst, John, 131, 199–200

idols, 126, 128–29, 193, 209
immanence, 16, 18–19, 189
incarnation, 110, 189, 228
Independent Board for Presbyterian Foreign Missions, 43, 158–60
inerrancy. *See* Bible, authority of
International Missionary Council (IMC), 15, 23, 96, 182

Japan, xxii, 37, 40, 56, 70–72, 89, 97–98, 114, 141, 143, 158, 171, 183, 231, 237–38, 259

Kawilorot Suriyawong, 83, 85–86
Kilpatrick, Faye, 149–50, 157, 162, 172, 222–24, 230, 232
Korea, 19, 27, 92, 114, 135, 158, 237–38
Kneedler, Christina Harris, 197
Kneedler, William Harding, 197
Knox, Harry, 171
kingdom of God, 16–18, 23, 25, 27, 227

Lampang (province), 128, 130, 158, 166–67, 171, 175, 219
Landon, Kenneth P., 111, 123n77, 136–39, 138n121, 139, 155, 181–82, 196–97, 216, 232, 240–41
Landon, Margaret, 182, 196, 230, 232
Laymen's Inquiry, 11–15, 18, 21, 24–26, 28, 39–42, 100, 102, 140–45, 158–59, 189, 199, 212, 225n34, 228–29, 248

Leonowens, Anna, 80–81
Lowrie, James Walter, 12
Lowrie, Walter, 36

Machen, J. Gresham, 9, 12, 19, 31, 33, 37, 39, 42–44, 159, 161, 242
Macartney, Clarence, 31, 33, 41, 44, 240
Maitri Chit Church, 77
McAfee, Cleland Boyd, 42, 119–22, 139–40, 142, 144, 159, 190–92, 200–3, 206, 208, 241n17, 247
McClure, Mary Jane, 166, 201–3,
McClure, William, 116n49, 164, 224
McDaniel, Agnes Barland, 182
McDaniel, Edwin B., 58, 116n49, 182
McCord, Margaret Cordelia, 174, 179, 182, 224
McFarland, Bertha Blount, 182, 217,
McFarland, Edwin, 53–54, 61,
McFarland, George Bradley, xiii, 54, 59, 207
McFarland, Jane, 82
McFarland, Samuel Gamble, 53, 56, 82–83, 193–94,
McFarland, William, 54
McGilvary, Daniel, 82–87, 104, 106, 164, 169, 193–94, 197, 219
McGilvary, Evander, 103–9, 112–13, 127–29, 150, 157, 194–95, 236, 246,
McGilvary, Sophia, 82, 88, 89
McGilvary Theological Seminary, 93, 112, 123, 129, 131, 134–35, 175–83, 209, 236, 239
methodology, 14–15, 22, 27, 37, 39, 92–94, 104–5, 133–34, 146–47, 159, 161, 165–66, 169, 178–81, 183–84, 205–9, 211–12, 222, 227–29, 236
miracles, 10, 13, 17, 29, 109–11, 185, 235
medical Work, 36, 37, 40, 58, 78–79, 87, 94–95, 102, 114–16, 130, 144, 166–72, 199, 201, 205, 223, 240, 248
  hospitals, 19n52, 28, 58–59, 62, 65, 87, 95, 118, 128, 158, 166–71, 178, 208, 242

medical Work *(continued)*
  missionary doctors, 19, 58–60, 78, 114–17, 128–31, 168–70, 177–78, 197, 199–200, 241–42
  Thai doctors, 58–60, 95, 180, 202
  medical training, 54, 57–60
Messianic Buddhism, 64, 127
modernism (religious), xiii, xxi, xxiii, 17–19, 23–26
  and Buddhism, 63
  definition, xv, 19–23,102
  and evangelism, 124, 135, 190–91, 154
  and liberalism, 20–22
  on mission fields, 14–15, 27–28, 37–44, 110, 114, 122, 127–34, 158–72
  in PCUSA, 29–33, 37–44, 118
modernization
  characteristics, 3–4
  and civilization, 6–7
  definition, 1–7, 102
  global modernization, 5–6
  multiple modernities, 4–5
  origins, 2–3
  and science, 17–18
Mongkut, King, x, 47, 52–54, 62–64, 74, 77, 79–80, 85, 123, 204
motives, 25, 51, 57 94, 106, 122, 131–32, 180, 186, 188, 190–91, 194–99, 203, 210, 227, 241
Mott, John R., 96

Nai Chune, 82
Nan Inta, 84–85
naturalism, 17–18, 24, 40
Neuber, Margaret, 122, 130–31, 163, 171, 194
Nevius Method, 92
Niblock, Lucy, 222, 224, 230

Palmer, Marion, 139–41, 162, 167, 223–24
Palmer, May, 142n135, 144,
Presbyterian Church in the USA (PCUSA), xxi–xxiii, 16n38, 29, 33, 34, 37, 38–41, 99, 104–6, 119, 141, 145, 150, 155, 190, 195, 200
Perkins, William, 114–19, 122, 150, 239
Petchaburi (province), 58, 61, 82–83, 193
Phrasri-arn. *See* Messianic Buddhism
Pitsanuloke (province), 47, 155, 178
Pluang Sudhikham, 97, 182
polygamy, 55, 60, 68, 80
Post, Richard W., 162, 216–17
postmillennialism, 18, 27, 196–97, 233
Prasert Intaphantu, 112, 178, 180
premillennialism, 24, 27, 162, 178, 187, 197
Prince Royal's College, 88, 93, 140, 162, 167, 219, 224, 253
Princeton Theological Seminary, 33, 38, 105, 136, 151

Rama IV. *See* Mongkut
Rama V. *See* Chulalongkorn
Rama VI. *See* Vajiravudh
Re-Thinking Missions. *See* Laymen's Inquiry
relativism, 11, 40, 124, 129, 145, 171, 189, 194, 203
resurrection (of Christ), 13, 16–17, 29, 110, 116, 163, 191–92, 235
revival, 147, 162, 172–77, 240
Roman Catholicism, 21, 49n16, 66n101, 71, 73–75, 78n25, 95, 192

salvation, 14, 18, 23–28, 102, 109, 116, 118, 124, 127, 132, 133–34, 175, 186, 189, 194, 196, 198, 203, 206–7, 227, 233
Samray Church (Bankgok). *See* First Church, Samray
San Francisco Theological Seminary, 139, 149, 157
Saowapha Phongsi, 57
schools, xxiv, 28, 32, 53, 56–59, 65, 82–83, 88, 93–95, 113, 119, 121, 123, 130, 133–34, 140–41, 146, 148–49, 151–52,164–67, 170–71, 178–80, 182–85, 199, 204–5, 208–9, 211–33, 236–37, 245, 248

Subject Index   273

science, x, 2–3, 7–10, 14–15, 17–18, 22, 32, 40, 52–53, 55–57, 62–63, 73, 80, 84–85, 98, 102, 106, 113, 118, 124–25, 135, 148, 164, 179, 184, 235–39
Second Church (Bangkok), 174, 182
second coming (of Christ), 27, 162
Seigle, Albert, 163, 166–67, 171, 177, 183, 198–99, 236, 254
Selden, Charles, xxi, xxiv, 123, 136, 147–57, 173, 184, 242, 246, 249
Siam. *See* Thailand
Sin Saa Qua Kieng, 81–82
Sing Keo Suriyakham, 179
slavery, 48, 60, 83, 87
Sook Pongsanoi, 137
Speer, Robert, 9, 12, 19, 35, 38, 39–43, 54n32, 65, 108, 116, 126, 143, 247
Stewart, Herbert W., 36n29, 183
Suk Phongnoi. *See* Sook Pongsanoi
Sung, John, xi, xxiv, 101, 112, 135, 147, 161–62, 172–85, 240, 242, 247–48
Song, John. *See* Sung, John
Song, Shangjie. *See* Sung, John
Starling, Lucy, 130–31, 142–44, 167–69, 172, 199n33, 212
strategy, xxii, 63, 84–85, 89, 140, 142, 161
supernaturalism, 17, 64

Taylor, Hugh, 88, 89, 95n77, 220
Thailand
    administration, 66–68
    borders, 45–46, 49–51
    colonialism, 48–51
    education, 56–58, 88, 225–33, 237–39
    historiography, 51–52
    laws, 51, 60–61
    medical care, 58–60
    modernization, 45–72
    name, 45–47
    national integration, 66–68
    nationalism, 51, 66, 68–72, 125
    political history, 47–48, 69–72
    religion. *See* Buddhism
    transportation, 61–62
Thianhi (Thian Hee, Thien Hee) Sarasin, 58
Thomas, W. H. Griffith, 37
tolerance (religious), ix, 31, 33, 145, 149, 184, 190
Tomlin, Jacob, 75–76
tongues (gift of), 110
Trang (province), 136–38, 175–76, 224, 242
Travaille, Forrest, 179

Union Theological Seminary, 9, 13, 15, 20, 22, 104, 147, 173
unity, 28, 32, 39, 48, 71, 100–101, 104, 107–8, 125, 143, 146–47, 150, 157, 161–65, 172, 198, 246–48

Vajiravudh, King, 48, 51, 64–65, 68–69, 71, 88
virgin birth, 13, 16–17, 29, 33, 116, 185, 235

Wachirayan (Vajirananavarorasa), Prince, 56, 64–66
Wells, Kenneth E., xiv, 93, 129, 171n44, 183, 209, 218–19, 225, 227–33
Wheaton College, xiv, xx, 136, 138–39, 253
Wichit Wathakan, 71
World Missionary Conference (Edinburgh, 1910), 37, 100, 189, 194, 219, 225n34
World War One, 25n85, 31, 109,
World War Two, xxi, xxii, 48, 93, 99, 101, 123, 128, 145, 183, 235, 239, 247